W9-BCV-664

THE AWAKENED EYE

The

Awakened

Eye

By ROSS PARMENTER

Wesleyan University Press

MIDDLETOWN, CONNECTICUT

Copyright © 1968 by Wesleyan University

Library of Congress Catalog Card Number: 68-16011
Manufactured in the United States of America
FIRST EDITION

TO

The people of Mexico and their country,
where I discovered my eyes

Contents

Plates

(*following page 212*)

Acknowledgments

Dɪʀᴇᴄᴛ observation, that of my friends and my own, has been the chief source of this work. But books have always been part of my life, so naturally I have been helped by books too. Those that have been cited, either directly or by implication, are listed in the Bibliographical Index.

The twenty-three friends to whom I am most indebted, either because they lent me their eyes, provided objects to observe, or said telling things, all appear as characters in the book. Their names are given as they assume their roles in the story. Most of them have seen what I have written about them and have strengthened my affection by consenting to the use of their names. Other friends I have exploited, though not by name, are Carol Denison, Therese McCaffery, Harold C. Schonberg, Chad Walsh, Jacqueline Jackson, Ronald Dougan, Lewis Funke, Luis Treviño Borton, Enrique Treviño, John Flagg, David Alexander, and Margarita O'Gorman. My hope is that they will chuckle as they recognize themselves and not mind the uses to which their visual experiences have been put.

Two of my characters, Leonard Elliott and Selma Jeanne Cohen, helped in undisclosed ways, too. Besides giving me wonderfully welcome typing help in preparing the manuscript, they also gave me the benefit of their searching intelligences as readers. Nona Balakian, Anna Nalbantian, Marjorie Lipsyte, Fanny Hillberg, Roberta Edel, Charlotte Isler, and Polly Packard (who was especially eagle-eyed) are the other friends who read every word carefully and who caught flaws that, fortunately, I was able to eliminate. I would also like to thank Robert Rooney and Rosalie L. Colie, readers in key positions, who helped with enthusiasm at crucial times. Coming down to chapters, I gratefully acknowledge helpful comment from five partial readers who were experts in their fields: Harold March, formerly of Swarthmore, who read "Transfigured Vision," Milton Bracker, Stanley Levey, and Emanuel Perlmutter, newspaper colleagues who read "The Reporter's Eye," and Monroe Landon, who checked the botany in "Plants and Drawing."

If Aldous Huxley were still alive, I would express especial gratitude to him for the initial stimulus of his *The Art of Seeing*. Meanwhile, I thank Harper & Row, Publishers, for permission to use the passage from Huxley's *Eyeless in Gaza* that appears in chapter 3.

I would like to thank Mr. and Mrs. William A. M. Burden of New York and Felix Valdes of Bilbao, Spain, for permission to reproduce their respective treasures: Seurat's "The Channel at Gravelines, Evening" and Zurbaran's "The Immaculate Conception with Thirteen Angels." And thanks are due for reproduction permission to the following museums: The Frick Collection (La Tour's "Education of the Virgin" and El Greco's "Christ Driving the Money Changers from the Temple"); the Louvre (Fra Angelico's "Coronation of the Virgin"); the National Gallery in Prague (Dürer's "The Festival of the Rose-Garlands"), and the Koninklijk Museum in Antwerp (Massys' "The Entombment of Christ").

The occasional pen-and-ink drawings are my own.

THE AWAKENED EYE

Foreword

THIS book is about vision, but may I make plain it is not intended for the visually handicapped? It assumes your eyes, either naturally or with the aid of glasses, operate normally. And it makes no pretense at being able to make your eyes, as organs, any better than they are. Its aim is not to improve your sight — that is beyond my power and outside my province — but to improve your seeing.

May I also explain something else? Since more alert seeing does not require much knowledge of the processes that bring it about, there will be little physiology in the book and no attempt to account for the miracle of ocular sensing. If it seems I have skimped the structure of the eye and the laws of optics, my reply is that I am dealing not so much with perception as a process, as with observation as an art.

And please try to have a deck of cards handy before you start reading.

Part I

THE POTENTIALITIES OF VISION

CHAPTER I

The Face Cards

I T began with one of Dr. Cottard's riddles. Readers of Proust's *Cities of the Plain* will remember the unforgettable scene at Mme. Verdurin's summer place where the doctor is playing cards with the violinist Morel. After shouting at his dozing wife to wake up, the doctor asks the violinist, "Do you know why the king of diamonds was turned out of the army?" Morel does not, and the doctor explains, "It's because he has only one eye."

Being at home on a day off the morning I read that scene, I had the leisure to act on the impulse the riddle prompted: to get out a deck of cards and see if it was true that the king of diamonds was one-eyed. Laying out the four kings started one of the most exciting experiences of my life.

The first thrill was the way the images reformulated themselves. My common sense assures me the pictures could not possibly have moved. But because my concept of them changed as I looked at them, I got the distinct impression that the stable images behaved like the breaking-up signs common in railroad stations. Their parts seemed to rotate on unseen axes, and when the fragments had regathered into fixed patterns, the pictures were more sharply visible than they had ever been before.

And now, to make what follows easily intelligible, will you open your deck of cards so that you can see for yourself what I saw when the four kings had reformulated? Now you know what prompted the childish riddle: not evidence that the king of diamonds has lost an eye, but the fact that, being in profile, he only shows one.

Because the eye can move more rapidly in scanning than in

reading, you are probably already a jump ahead of me. That is, you have made the observation I made next — that the king of diamonds is the *only* king in profile. And I wouldn't be surprised if you are as thunderstruck as I was. To think I had handled cards so many years and noticed them so little!

Here was shocking proof that concern with the pips had so engrossed my mind that I had never consciously noted what the kings looked like. Certainly I had never observed them comparatively before. And never before had I given them a disinterested look. If I had noticed even so elementary a characteristic as the orientation of their heads, I would not have had to get them out to see the logic of the riddle.

If you knew the king of diamonds was the only monarch in profile, you are, perhaps, feeling my superior. But before you get too proud, and before you get out the queens, let me ask you two questions about them: Which queen has the sceptre? And does every queen hold a flower?

If you are like the friends I tested, you were not able to answer. But now you know. The queen of spades is the one with the sceptre. And every queen has her flower. Perhaps, too, you noticed the flowers are all different.

I had been as unaware of the differences between the queens as of those between the kings. This led to the next step: setting out the jacks. At first sight they, too, seemed to move. For again I unwittingly transferred to the fixed images the sense of movement I experienced in my brain as old concepts broke up and parts shifted into a new alignment. After this, the jacks, too, were more clearly visible, and with my new sharpness of vision I noticed the jack of hearts was the only one carrying a leaf, the jack of clubs was the only one with a leaf in his cap, and the jack of spades was holding up the oddest object. It was shaped like an airplane propeller but twisted like a pretzel.

From then on observations of the court cards came so fast they tumbled over themselves. Each king, I saw, had a weapon. The king of diamonds had an axe, while the other three had swords. The monarchs of spades and clubs held theirs vertically, points up, but the king of hearts had his sword behind his head, as if about to wield it. The king of clubs was the only one with an orb.

The coifs of the queens made them all look like nuns. But they were odd nuns, for each wore a gorgeous Japanese kimono. The Kabuki effect was increased when I noticed two seemed to have fans. And once my attention focused on what they were wearing, I noticed the sleeves, the belts, the dickeys, and the collars of the queens were all different. I was particularly taken with the black and yellow checked collar of the queen of diamonds.

The more I looked, the more I saw. And the more I saw, the more interesting their royal highnesses became. Just the motifs decorating the costumes were a fascinating study. And as I recognized the interest of the face cards, I realized that never in my life had I received such striking evidence of how much there is in the world we don't see. The impact was all the more stunning because I could not claim that cards were something I hadn't looked at. Perhaps, I said to myself, these cards are symbolic. Perhaps everything our eyes light on has the same degree of added interest — the same amount of fascination over and above what is generally conceded.

The cards also brought home how we can be blinded by limited interests and mean concerns. Perhaps we are not playing for money. We may be only playing solitaire. No matter, we always want to win. This desire keeps our attention riveted on only one aspect of the cards: their value in the game. We think only of what they are worth, not what they look like.

These realizations, piled on top of the intriguing details, so excited me that I could not keep my thoughts to myself. As I was still in my pajamas I could not dash out, so I did the next best thing. I picked up the phone and called a friend. Did she know which king had only one eye? She didn't. Did she know which king had his sword raised, as if about to strike? She didn't. She didn't know if any of the queens had a sceptre. Nor did she know if they all had flowers.

I breathed a sigh of relief. I was not unique in my blindness. And I was doubly reassured because Leah Nolan, the friend I called, was one of the most observant people I knew. Meanwhile,

Leah spread out the court cards of a deck in her home and, as she found the answers, she expressed her amazement over the phone. Though she was an artist, she had never looked at the cards as pictures either. She, too, had always been so concerned with them as counters that she had never considered them worth examining for intrinsic visual interest. As she looked, she posed a new question: "Do you suppose they are meant to be portraits of real people?"

Her query made me feel obtuse, for I had never wondered about the matter, and I felt my omission all the more keenly because as a boy I had loved the kings and queens of storybook history. But as I knocked my head for having been so lacking in imagination and curiosity that I had not dreamed of a possible link between pasteboard and historic rulers, I felt joyous at the possibilities of this new line of investigation.

That evening, Leonard Elliott, an actor friend, dropped in. By this time I had made out six testing questions, so I handed him the card questionnaire. Leonard, too, had played cards all his life, but he could not even guess the answers. So I got out the court cards and he saw for himself which king wielded the sword, which queen had the sceptre, and so on.

"The queen of hearts and the queen of diamonds," he said, "look like sisters." I was delighted at the observation, for it had never struck me. But I was even more surprised at another line his seeing took, for he found himself especially interested in something I had not noticed: the characters' hair.

"No queen has any hair showing below the ears," he said. Then he moved on to their husbands. "See," he said, "every king has a beard. They are all forked beards too." Turning to the jacks, he pointed out that, in contrast to the kings, the knaves were all beardless. "But," he added, "all but the jack of clubs have little curled moustaches."

As he spoke, the jacks, which had already moved earlier in the day, seemed to move again. And as those moustaches became visible, the reconsolidated jacks were no longer the early Renaissance princes I used to know. They were nineteenth-century tailors' dummies.

Relentlessly, my friend continued. "The kings and the jacks all wear their hair in long bobs. But see how they vary. Some curl in at the bottom, some curl out. The jack of spades is the only one with two rows of curls."

"Are they the same on all the cards?" Leonard asked. This was another question that had not occurred to me, so I extracted the face cards from two other decks.

The hair styles, we found, were remarkably consistent, but there was considerable variety in the orientation of the heads. The kings of spades and clubs looked now left, now right. And only the queen of hearts looked always to her right; the other queens varied from side to side, though they always remained in three-quarter view. The jacks of spades and hearts were always in profile, but the jack of hearts seemed free to show either his right or left side. The king of diamonds always wore ermine, but costume details varied considerably. And although each queen held a flower, they did not hold similar flowers in each deck. In other words, some aspects appeared fixed, whereas certain details suggested there were elements that could be handled as the designer wished, provided he remained within proscribed limits.

Being especially interested in what the characters were carrying, I looked at the other two jacks of spades to see if they would help identify the propeller-pretzel. Instead, they merely intrigued me further, for in one the object was more like a twisted loop of rope, whereas in the other there was still the suggestion of a propeller but the twist was gone. Could the object be a Moorish knot, I wondered, a wand of office, or something like the ankh — the T-shaped cross with the loop the Egyptians considered the symbol of life?

Contrasting the three sets deepened my conviction that the

cards had an historical richness I had not dreamed of. That the two additional decks we turned to should be particularly stimulating was partly chance. One came from England and was basically the same as the American deck. But there were differences. Clearly the English deck was based on designs older than my two American decks. The English kings were more individually characterized, and their queens did not have the uniform, plump complacency of the American queens. The English queen of clubs, for instance, was delicate, for her cheeks curved in and she had lines under her eyes. The British queen of spades, on the other hand, was a woman of strong character with round cheeks and a determined chin. And the English queen of hearts suggested an ash blonde with very pale, dreamy eyes and a rather sensual mouth. The English jack of hearts was especially interesting. With his prominent nose and his long straight hair caught in a knot at his shoulder, he suggested hunting prints of the young Frederick the Great.

"What do your reference books say about the cards?" asked Leonard. With two sources we drew blanks, but *The Columbia Encyclopedia* had some basic facts. It confirmed the historical richness. Playing cards, it said, came into use in the fourteenth century.

The entry also showed that the slight variations we had observed were as nothing compared with earlier differences. The present Anglo-American deck took two hundred years to stabilize. It was France that evolved the symbols of spades, hearts, diamonds, and clubs. Other countries, we learned to our surprise, had different suits altogether. Those of Italy and Spain were swords, cups, money, and cudgels; those of Germany leaves, hearts, hawk bells, and acorns. There had also been twenty-two tarots, which were symbolic cards without numbers. And in some Italian decks each suit had a fourth face card — a mounted cavalier, who stood in rank between the queen and the knave.

The next evening I had dinner with Kathleen Tappen, a friend in advertising. I went to her apartment armed with my six questions and three sets of court cards. Kathleen was not much of a card player so it did not surprise her that she could not identify the characters from their attributes. But she was willing to lend her eyes for a parallel study. To her, the queens did not suggest nuns. They suggested the coiffed girls and burghers' wives painted by such Flemish painters as Memling and Lucas van Leyden. After noticing generally the ornateness and multiplicity of details in the costumes, and the lack of characterization in the faces, Kathleen's interest settled on a feature that Leah, Leonard, and I had taken too much for granted to consider: the cards' two-headedness.

I had always thought this part of the traditional design, but Kathleen figured out that it was dictated by utility. It made the face cards more manageable for they were never upside down, no matter which way you picked them up. This observation led us to study the skill shown in devising a similar top and bottom whose lines had to flow into each other to make a total design that was balanced and pleasing. For the first time I realized the face cards were busts resting on their own reversed reflections.

The next morning as I looked at the cards again, I suddenly exclaimed, All the kings look like Henry the Eighth! And the resemblance seemed so obvious I kicked myself for not having seen it sooner. And I wondered about the delay. Why had the image of Henry taken almost forty-eight hours to emerge, especially when he was such a familiar figure and I had pored over the cards so much, both alone and in company? Perhaps a tendency to be interested in abstractions led me to suppress visual images more than most people. But once Henry was with me, I recalled the encyclopedia date of the stabilizing of the English pack. It was perfectly logical that the kings should suggest Henry, as it was in his time that the basic models were consolidated. There was the same logic behind Kathleen's vision of the Memlings and Lucas van Leydens — roughly of the same period as Henry. And, reflecting on the costumes of the court cards, I saw how clearly they were pre-Elizabethan.

In the next two days I tried my questions on eleven of my colleagues at *The New York Times*. One chap, who said he had a photographic memory, could answer three of the questions, and a girl identified the king of diamonds as the monarch with one eye, but all the others flubbed every question. "I can't even remember what's been played," said another girl helplessly. I consoled her with the knowledge my testing had brought me. "Don't worry," I said, "there probably isn't one in a hundred who has studied the cards well enough to know their details."

The Times has a good library, and in a spare moment I was able to visit it. To my joy, I found Catherine Perry Hargrave's *History of Playing Cards,* which the encyclopedia had cited as the chief reference book. Because it reproduced many cards, it was wonderfully exciting. It confirmed my first friend's hunch. The cards *were* historical personages. The kings were the four great rulers of the ancient world: David, Charlemagne, Julius Caesar, and Alexander. That the king of clubs was Alexander explained a distinction that had caught my eye. He was the only one with an orb because of Alexander's famous lament that his complete overrunning of the world had left him no new worlds to conquer.

Miss Hargrave pointed out that different identities have been ascribed to the face cards and that during the French Revolution all the nobles were eradicated. However, certain identities have persisted through the ages. To keep them straight, I made the following chart:

	♠	♡	◇	♣
King	David	Charlemagne	Julius Caesar	Alexander
Queen	Pallas	Judith	Rachel	Argine, an anagram for Regina
Jack	Hogier, a Danish hero who was one of Charlemagne's ensigns	La Hire, a Gascon who fought alongside Joan of Arc	Hector	Lancelot

These personages, I realized, had sunk into anonymity by stages. First their pictures had lost their status as portraits. Then their pictured faces had lost individuality. When their names were left off, their identities began to be forgotten. Finally came the ultimate oblivion: the forgetting that they had ever been associated with the cards.

The earliest cards, however, showed the portraiture had never been exact, for the personages always wore costumes of the era in which they were drawn. But there were some attempts to link the people and their identities. David, for instance, was generally shown with a harp. And the early cards depicted the figures full length. Thus one saw the queens' skirts, the kings' robes, and the jacks' hose-encased legs. The invention of two-headed, reversible cards did not come till early in the nineteenth century.

Two variants delighted me especially: the George Washington of hearts, a card of the royalty-hating American Revolutionaries, and an English variant for the queen of hearts. The heart queen was sometimes thought to be Henry VIII's mother, Elizabeth of York, the princess whose marriage to Henry VII ended the Wars of the Roses. Though I have since learned there were card queens who carried flowers before Elizabeth was born, I still like to think of the flower of the queen of hearts as the white rose of York.

Miss Hargrave revealed a fact even my historically-minded friend had not thought of: the suits, too, have historical — or perhaps one should say socio-economic — meaning, for they symbolized the four classes of society. They reflected the social stratification of the late Middle Ages when cards were invented. The spades were the military nobles, the hearts the ecclesiastics, the diamonds the prosperous burghers, and the clubs the peasants.

The same stratification was represented in the Italian deck, and as I found the foreign names for the suits interesting, I made another chart.

CLASS	FRENCH NAMES	ITALIAN NAMES
Nobles	*Piques* (pikes)	*Spade* (plural of *spada*, meaning sword)
Ecclesiastics	*Coeurs* (hearts)	*Cope* (plural of *copa*, meaning cups)
Burghers	*Carreaux* (paving tiles)	*Denari* (money)
Peasants	*Trefles* (clovers)	*Bastoni* (batons or cudgels)

Playing cards, Miss Hargrave said, came from the East. They might have been brought to Europe by mariners, crusaders, or gypsies. The tarots, the non-numbered symbolic cards that have vanished from the playing deck, bore such figures as the Juggler, the Hanged Man, Temperance, the Sun, and the Moon. Gypsies still use them in telling fortunes.

All this was interesting, but I was beginning to feel frustrated. My time was running out and the book did not have the specific information I wanted, such as why the king of hearts is depicted in action, or what the jack of spades is carrying? I decided to look in Miss Hargrave's list of acknowledgments. Perhaps it would name some experts I could consult personally. Two people she thanked were clearly from New York: Stewart Culin, director of the Brooklyn Museum, and Frank Weitenkampf, curator of prints of the New York Public Library.

As the book was published in 1930, it occurred to me these men might no longer be reachable. But a day or two later I telephoned their institutions. My fears were confirmed at the Brooklyn Museum, which said Mr. Culin had been dead almost twenty years. The Library told me Mr. Weitenkampf had retired.

Meanwhile, I showed my charts to Selma Jeanne Cohen and John Briggs, the two colleagues who had proved the most interested in the cards. The fact that the king of diamonds was Caesar gave John the eyes to note something since confirmed: that his axe was derived from the Roman fasces. Selma Jeanne figured out that if the queen of spades was Pallas Athena, she was the goddess who had sprung full-armored from the head of Zeus and the sceptre might be the remains of her spear.

The three of us agreed that the French names for the suits were more logical than the English. The spade emblem did look like the head of a pike, not a shovel. The red rhombus we call a diamond clearly resembled a red paving tile. And certainly the black trefoil looked more like a clover than a club. In fact, we all felt sheepish that none of us had ever thought "club" an incongruous word for that clover leaf.

Then we looked in the Italian column. Quickly John saw that a cudgel was a club. When he pointed it out, Selma Jeanne made the next leap. "How interesting," she said. "We must have borrowed our emblem from the French and our name for it from the Italians."

John picked up the clue, and said, "You can see the same thing with the first suit. We accepted the French pikehead as our symbol, but we took the name spade from the Italian deck. In this case we did not even translate it into English."

Both colleagues have subsequently been proved right, and I am happy to say that, following their clues, I had equal success in working out a further solution.

"See," I said, "the third suit represents the prosperous middle class. The Italians identified the merchants and industrialists with money. Perhaps we decided diamonds would be an even better symbol for them. Maybe that's why we call that rhombus a diamond, rather than a tile."

By this time I thought I had noticed everything to be seen in the cards. But I reckoned without the further scrutiny of Leah Nolan, the artist I had first consulted by phone. When I went to her apartment for dinner, she set out the face cards of one of her decks alongside those I had brought, and began jocularly:

"The kings look happier than either the queens or the jacks. This one" — and here she pointed to a jaundiced jack of clubs — "looks positively ill."

"The blue ink outlining the faces in my deck," she continued, "is stronger than in yours." I had scarcely had time to note the relative refinement of the lines when, with her experience in printmaking, she went on to explain the likely cause. "Probably," she said, "my cards were printed from older dies. As the dies that print cards wear out the lines they make get coarser."

From the royal moods and the mechanics of printing, Leah turned to something else I had not considered. She began assessing the cards as works of art. It almost brought us to blows. All the delight and interest the cards had brought since the start of my investigations had made me increasingly fond of them. I resented hearing a word against them on any grounds. But as a modern artist, loving subtle colors and clean, functional designs, Leah was ruthless. The cards, she said, with their flat reds and yellows, were wretchedly colored. Their lines were rigid and mechanical. And from a point of view of design, they were an incongruous jumble of meaningless disjointed elements, very poorly organized.

In vain did I plead their historical interest. She was not to be swayed. Disliking to hear my new friends slandered, I was relieved when she passed from aesthetic considerations to a feature that especially caught her interest.

It was an element I had hardly noticed myself and one none of my friends had dwelt on — the hands. Some were deformed, Leah said, and, in proportion to the heads, the hands were all too small. Further, the designs left no room for any of the characters, except the king of hearts, to have what you must have to support hands — namely, arms. And the king of hearts, she noticed, was left-handed. He couldn't have been much of a swordsman, she observed scornfully, to swing his sword when a forward thrust would be the best way to wield it.

Next she noticed that it does not seem to matter whether the queens hold their flowers in their right or left hands. It was peculiar, she said, that the orb of the king of clubs could stay put with no hand to support it. And when she examined the king of diamonds closely, she pointed out another flaw.

"His costume is drawn as if that were his chest we are looking at. But it must be his back. Hold your hand as he's doing. See, the knuckles can only be seen that way from the back."

As Leah made me see this, I felt the cumulative effect of the other jogs to vision. Now the hands — as well as the objects held the costume motifs, the facial expression, the hairdos, the two-headedness, and the historical significance — were all part of my total awareness of the pasteboard court. And the cards seemed richer for being more richly seen.

My friends' observations also crystallized a realization: that because I began playing with cards as a child I had learned their names and appearances in the period when I accepted whatever I was told. By the time I began thinking for myself, incongruous names like clubs and spades, reversible figures with two heads, figures with hands but no arms — all the conventions, in fact — were so familiar that they were already too taken for granted to ap-

pear odd. Seeming normal, they had lost their power to stir speculation spontaneously.

Realizing how long ago I had lost the power to see the cards
with innocent eyes led me to wonder what on earth a savage would
make of a face card if he came upon it on a jungle path. Perhaps
not knowing what it was, he would be able to see it and all its incongruities with an accuracy that up to that moment had not
been possible to me. On the other hand, in looking at it one way
and then another, the poor savage might find himself terribly confused, unable to decide which side should be up. Not knowing
it was supposed to be a counter in a game, he might assume it was
one of the mysterious gods he had heard white men worshipped.

The next day was Thanksgiving. The idea hit me that even if
Mr. Weitenkampf was retired he might still be living in New
York. So I consulted that great index of leads to sources of information, the Manhattan telephone book. Only one Weitenkampf
was listed and his initial was F. That was clue enough for me. I
decided to take the plunge. To my delight, I got the right man.

Being interested in music, the eighty-four-year-old Mr. Weitenkampf recognized my name. We had the friendliest chat, but alas,
he was not a card expert. He could not remember Miss Hargrave
and he felt he did not deserve her thanks. Perhaps he had just
made the facilities of the Library's print room available to her
without knowing who she was. He suggested I would find quite a
lot about cards if I went to the Library.

Unfortunately, he was overly optimistic. I leafed through the
card catalogue and found the Library was poor in material on cards
in English. *The Romance of Playing Cards* proved nothing but a
superficial essay published in the 1930's. *The Origin and History
of Playing Cards* was a small book brought out in 1916 that had
only what I had found in Hargrave. "Playing Cards: Their History and Their Symbolism" was a fanciful article in an archaeological magazine, and "A Pack of Cards" was an article from *The
Strand*, vintage 1911, that told which cards had been famous in
history. Because the Library was terribly crowded that day, waiting
for such hard-to-find items took more than four hours. I came away

discouraged and frustrated. But I had learned there was an Association of American Playing Card Manufacturers, and it was in New York. The marvelous phone book yielded its number, and a girl who answered the telephone said that if I came in I could browse in its library.

As it turned out, I did not have to wait for that opportunity. When I got to the office the next day I found the message: "Please call Mr. Weitenkampf." I did. He asked if I had seen the full-page book advertisement in that morning's Sunday *Times*. At the bottom of an enormous list was a book he thought might have what I wanted: W. Gurney Benham's *Playing Cards: The History and Secrets of the Pack*. As I hung up, I realized that even in retirement he was the proverbially helpful librarian.

I managed to buy the Benham book that evening. Oh, what a wonderful book! It was just exactly what I wanted, for it devoted a whole chapter to each of the twelve face cards. Best of all, it reproduced a deck of French cards issued in Rouen about 1567. This was vital because the Anglo-American deck is based on Rouen cards of that era. By studying those Rouen cards and reading the text, I was able to answer all my original questions, as well as clear up subsequent incongruities I discovered.

Most of the trouble came from poor copying of models that were not fully understood. Take the case of the jack of hearts: Benham showed that early in their careers the heart knaves carried torches with small flames at their tips. A later copyist overlooked the bottom of the jack's torch and left it out. Thereafter, what the jack held was almost unintelligible. A still later copyist assumed the flame on the almost vanished torch was a leaf.

The king of hearts was not such an inept fighter after all. What he held originally was an axe. His raised arm is meaningful then, for to get a good blow with a battle axe you would have to swing it from behind your head.

In the 1567 deck the king of diamonds is indeed standing with his back to the viewer. And the fingers of the 1567 king of clubs are clearly shown under the orb he holds. But later cards showed how those fingers, thought to be part of the orb, gradually disappeared.

The 1567 jack of clubs holds a large arrow with a turned shaft, which accounts for the odd sort of striped lath held by our jack of clubs. All these explanations delighted me, but one proved an anticlimax: the secret that had puzzled me most — the object held by the jack of spades.

Originally he had a halberd. As he grew larger in subsequent copies, his weapon got half-crowded off the page. By 1675, one could no longer be sure the half-shown object was a fancy sort of pike. By 1750, the long shaft of the pike, like the lower part of the jack of hearts' torch, had disappeared. By 1830, the propeller-pretzel was the copyist's interpretation of what he thought his predecessors had drawn. So the object was not a mysterious symbol dating back to ancient Egypt, but only a confused corruption of the old pikehead.

As I neared the end of the Benham book I felt sure I had observed everything about the face cards. This was largely because I had tracked down the meanings of their features. But meanings and appearances, though they influence each other, are not the same thing. More eye openers lay ahead, many caused by the page showing modern Italian face cards. That those Italian figures were full-length hardly surprised me, but I was struck by the fact that they were placed so far back as to give the illusion of standing in a three-dimensional world; and, being almost in the middle distance, they were small — so small, in fact, that they came nowhere near filling their whole frames.

Instantly, four new facts about the Anglo-American face cards became apparent: Our kings and queens are at the very front of the picture plane. There is no sense of space behind them. They themselves are as flat as if they had been run over by a steam roller. And they are so big their frames cut them off on all four sides.

When I came to the modern French face cards, my eyes again benefited from the fact that my mind was released from the search for meanings. With eyes open to perceive instead of squinting to interpret, the French cards were vividly set apart from ours, enabling me to note still more aspects of our deck.

Initially, though, I noticed a similarity. Because Dr. Cottard and Morel must have been using a French deck, the characters of the French court that interested me most were the kings. Sure enough, the king of diamonds was one-eyed. For in the French deck, as in ours, he is the only king in profile.

The first stimulus of contrast came after I had compared the French kings and jacks. They showed why I had the notion that our jacks were princes, when actually they are servants or even lower — as knaves, their alternate name, suggests. It is because their caps in our decks are almost indistinguishable from the kings' crowns. But in the French deck the headgear of the social ranks differs noticeably. The jacks wear squarish tams; whereas the kings have open crowns with freestanding ornamental gold leaves.

The almost unruly locks of the French kings also made me aware that their English counterparts, with never a hair out of place, would make good advertisements for Brylcream.

Everything about the French figures was freer, more naturalistic, less stylized. They were drawn fully in the round, and the natural curves of their shoulders made me aware that, for all my hard looking, I had not consciously noticed that our card courtiers' shoulders are straight lines that slope away from their chins. And I say chins rather than necks, because when I examined our kings and jacks I became aware of still another unnoticed feature: They have no necks; the block-like heads rest directly on their shoulders.

Wondering if this was true of the queens, too, I looked to check, and saw our queens did seem to have necks. But I noticed how completely they were covered. And I realized a factor making our queens suggest nuns is being chucked to the chins in wimples. All the French queens, in contrast, had bare necks. The queens of hearts and clubs, in fact, had dresses cut quite low. And the rounded fullness below gave me an awareness that amused me more than any previous discovery. You look at the queens in the Anglo-American deck and see if it isn't true. Not one of them has a bosom!

When I finished Benham, I bought another copy for the Public Library. In presenting it, I gave it in Mr. Weitenkampf's name. And now, should any reader go to the Library on a quest like mine, he will not be frustrated. Thanks to the alertness of that kindly old gentleman, the book with all the answers is there.

CHAPTER 2

The Fire in the Courtyard

Mexico City is in the tropics, but, at over 7,000 feet above sea level, a little extra warmth is needed if one is to sit outdoors there on September evenings. The Hotel Cortés, a former rest home for Augustinian prelates, has an inner court which is charming for such sitting, and the hotel provides the needed warmth at night by placing wood fires on portable grates near the tables.

At the start of a vacation the body is often so tired it imposes immobility, even though the spirit is restless. Thus, one evening after dinner, despite vague plans for doing something energetic, I found myself glued to a chair beside a fire at the Cortés. Perhaps my body's reluctance to stir prompted the idea. Perhaps I had already absorbed some of Mexico's casual feeling about time. Perhaps it was merely that the fire was warm, its smoke like a relaxing drug. This could be, for woodsmoke has one of the pleasantest of all scents. Or perhaps I felt at loose ends and a little depressed. At all events, suddenly and unexpectedly, I said to myself, I know what I'll do. I'll spend the whole evening watching the fire.

The portable grate suggested an iron coffee table, with a top of transverse bars. Below, in place of stretchers, it had a tray to catch the ashes. The logs burning on it were stacked in a pyramid that had flattened down as the flames had taken their toll of the wood's strength and rigidity. The outer butts of the split logs were blackened, but I noticed they were still undiminished in size and no flames curled round them. In contrast, the inner ends of the logs — the tips that touched or crossed each other at the heart of the fire — were much reduced in size, and were all a fierce orange-gold with flames crackling from them.

This led to a question that had never occurred to me before any previous fire. Curious about a well-known phenomenon, I wondered why logs burn best at the point where they cross each other.

The first answer that suggested itself was fanciful. Perhaps, I said to myself, logs are like human beings, achieving their best work and being most warm and glowing, when they have the loving companionship of close contact with each other.

I liked the metaphor, and perhaps it reflected a good deal of truth about humans. But I knew it was unsatisfactory. Wanting a more scientific explanation, I cast around in my mind for what I knew about fire.

My schooling had been hopelessly unscientific, so recalling schooldays was no help. But the Army had provided a lecture on fire. As I tried to remember it, my impressions were hazy. There was a lot, for instance, about oxygen's role in combustion. I recalled that you could end a fire by cutting off its oxygen supply. Why smothering a fire was so effective was not clear to me — that is, in chemical terms. But bringing back this much of the lecture made me aware that the officer had used a striking phrase. But what was it? What was the unexpected yet eye-opening term he had used to define the dancing part of a fire? Suddenly, I had it.

"Burning vapor. . . ." To prove its aptness the officer had staged a demonstration with a lighted candle. First he blew it out to show how the candle's vapor was made apparent by the smoke particles that arose in a wisp of grayness. Then, after relighting the candle, he asked us to watch carefully. He blew the candle out once more and quickly applied a lighted match to the ascending thread of smoke. Instantly the vapor caught fire and the flame raced downward to the wick to relight the candle.

Subsequent investigations have made me aware that the lecturer simplified matters for our limited soldier minds. What follows, therefore, is not to be taken too literally as an account of the combustion process. But it gives my thought process in the courtyard as I built on the explanation that seemed so convincingly proved by the downrushing flame.

The first stage took the form of a question: Could the hypothesis that fire was flaming vapor provide the clue as to why logs burn best at their point of contact?

In my schoolboy notion it was the solid part of fuel that burned. The officer's phrase led me to invert this idea: to come to the theory that the solid part of fuel never burned; that, instead, it distintegrated as it released its inflammable vapors.

As I studied this particular fire with the phrase "burning vapor" in mind, I noticed something I had never seen before with such clarity: The flames had an almost separate existence from the solid fuel. I noticed this because the logs, though some were glowing with intensity, were not themselves flaming. The flames I saw all seemed to shoot out from cracks or curl up from the logs' undersides.

This apparent separateness of the flames made me feel surer than ever that only vapors burned. Thus the next question that arose in my mind was: What is the agent that enables fuel to release its vapors. Almost immediately I lit on a tentative answer: Heat. Perhaps, I said to myself, those outer butts are flameless because they are cold.

Clearly, the fire had greatest heat at its center. So I could test my theory if I reversed the logs by lifting them up and setting them back on the fire with their colder butts at the center. Tentatively, I touched a blackened butt with my forefinger. It was cool enough to be lifted with bare hands. And when I had reversed all the logs, I sat on the edge of my seat to wait for what would happen.

Almost immediately, gray smoke began to lick up from one of the black butts. As more of the butts began smoking, some of the emerging vapor turned bright blue. Suddenly among the blue flames there was a tongue of bright gold. Then came another, and another. Soon the black butts were almost lost in a thicket of golden flames. I think if there hadn't been other diners in the patio I would have shouted for joy. My theory was proved. It was heat that released the vapors. And as those butts heated further they crackled more and more merrily. Meanwhile, the glow had died out at the other ends of the logs where the tips, once flame-enfolded, turned ashy at the cold outer edges of the fire.

My excitement was heightened because I felt I had also figured out something that had often puzzled me: why coal is harder to ignite than wood. Coal requires more heat to release its vapors. This, in turn, suggested that fuels could be classified according to their capacity to yield vapors. Some yielded vapors at the mere touch of flame, others had to be thoroughly warmed. This explained why you have to set down a bed of paper and sticks if you are to get coal to ignite. The burning paper warms the small bits of wood and then transfers its flames to the vapors that begin rising from the heated sticks. The flaming kindling, in turn, warms the coal, and then, like runners in a relay race, the bits of kindling pass on their torches to the released vapors of the coal.

At least, this was the picture as I saw it then. Subsequently I learned I was right about the need for different degrees of heat. Different fuels have different kindling temperatures. But I am not sure that vaporizing is necessary for ignition. It may be that the vapors are not the *cause* of combustion, but the *result*, once the volatilization temperature has been reached.

Meanwhile, my particular fire had begun to die down. When I caught the eye of a waiter, I asked if he could bring a little more wood. He was busy, however, and it was some time before the fresh logs were forthcoming. The delay was instructive.

With no new fuel, the flames diminished. Less dazzled, I became increasingly aware of how many colors a fire offered. There were intense blacks, ashy whites, several blues and a great range of yellow reds, from the white-gold of the sun to the near red of a ripe pumpkin. As some embers ceased flaming, I noticed they were much redder than those surrounded by flames. Was this a true color difference, I wondered, or an illusion? Did the flaming embers only seem less red because their flames swallowed up their redness as the sun in the daytime seems to rob luminosity from lesser lights? It was certainly true that the flames shed more illumination on the embers they enveloped than on the redder embers that were farther away. But those flameless red embers were still smoking and giving off lots of heat. Clearly they must be burning. This undeniable evidence showed I had gone too far when, at the stimulus of the officer's words, I had leaped to the notion that only vapors burned. In a lively fire, you always have two elements burning: vapors *and* solids.

When the mind has started moving along a given track, it tends to persist in the direction of its stimulus. My own, having taken up the properties of different fuels, began thinking of the wood's obvious capacity to retain heat, even if it lost light. Coal, I knew, has this capacity in an even more remarkable degree. But paper and sticks never go on radiating heat as these embers were doing.

Why don't they? Again I cast around for a scrap of scientific information that might help. I recalled that in electric heaters, coils are used that offer great resistance to the current, generating heat by this resistance. Could it be that wood and coal go on radiating heat for so long because they, as substances, resist the fire? The idea seemed plausible, and two things seemed to support it: the way their solidity at the start did not respond to the first, unwarming, superficial licking of the flames; and the ashes and cinders they left behind, showing that, ultimately, they were too resistant to be consumed totally.

But flaws in the parallel presented themselves. Coils do not burn up; and electricity is not fire. Seeking an alternative explanation, a phrase swam into my consciousness: "division of the particles." This brought the rest back. Someone once told me — or perhaps I read it — that the rate of burning depended on the density of a substance. It burned slowly if it was closely compacted; it burned more rapidly if it was porous; and it disappeared, almost in a flash, if it was powdered.

It was the density of this wood, then, that enabled it to go on radiating heat, making its burning slow and protracted. Conversely, paper, with scarcely any density at all, and kindling with hardly much more, burn so rapidly that soon there is little of them left to give off anything.

At this point the waiter dumped an armful of fresh logs on the grate. My first fear that so much wood might smother the smouldering embers was soon ended. Wisps of smoke quickly showed the new logs were warming up. Then came tiny leaves of gas-blue flame, and before long the whole fire was raging fiercely again.

Theory and observation have an operating inter-relationship. This had been demonstrated by the way the theory that flames were burning vapor had sharply stepped up my ability to observe this particular fire. Filled with excitement and delight at the result of that interaction, I was eager for more. Was there, I wondered, some other useful scientific scrap in the recesses of my mind, another intermediate hypothesis that, in the course of being tested by this fire, could further heighten my power to observe all fire?

The new guide that came was the old law: Hot air ascends.

Again I had the impulse to shout in gladness, for this law explained so much. Flames did not just leap upwards in sheer joy; they were carried upwards by heated air, and the hotter the air the higher and more irresistibly they were carried. The basic law explained, too, why this particular fire looked and acted as it did at that moment. Its lower flames were shooting up vertically, with remarkable directness and force, but at a certain level they lost their unwavering direction and the golden tongues were ragged and wild, sometimes darting in one direction, sometimes in another. Having no protecting side walls, the fire on the open grid was at the mercy of the patio's crosswinds. The heat was so great at the heart of the fire that the uprush of hot air lifted the flames with such force that the crosswinds had no power to divert the fiercely hot updraft. In the space above, though, the hot air passed into cooler night air, and, in being chilled, lost some of its force. It was here, where the updraft was feebler, that the crosswinds had a chance to alter the course of the mounting flames. Needless to say, those crosswinds did what they could, and this accounted for the darting wildness of the distracted golden tongues.

As I watched, I could hardly tell which I enjoyed the more: the physical beauty of the fire, or the pleasure I felt in the heightened vision that came from being able to understand its vagaries. Certainly, it had proved far more stimulating and interesting than I had suspected when I made the unpremeditated resolve to watch it.

My depression had vanished and I felt I had had a full evening's entertainment. In fact the experience seemed so well-rounded and satisfying that, even though I no longer felt tired, I resolved to go to bed. Anything else would be an anticlimax that would interfere with my contented savoring of the fire. But then I turned and saw what was behind me.

Never will I forget the seraphic beauty of that candle.

Serene, luminous, and marvelously golden, its spear of flame hovered above its white shaft of wax with hardly a trace of movement, for the candle was sheltered in a glass chimney, whose chaste curves might have been the cupped hands of an unseen spirit. And the beauty of the vision was heightened by the tiny highlights on the beaded opening of the chimney and by the soft yellow glow that spread downward on the red and pink checks of the table cloth.

The candle, too, was irradiated by significance. This, perhaps even more than its visual beauty, accounted for its impact, for the significance in question had never hit me before. Perhaps knowing candles all my life had been a blinding factor. For as I gazed on this one, it was as if I had never before seen a candle so stripped of familiarity. Freed from the veils of visual custom, its wonder was dazzlingly apparent. And what the lovely apparition so effortlessly proclaimed was that the candle is one of man's greatest achievements.

With it he learned to domesticate a single flame. This achievement seemed all the more remarkable as the fierce, thickly congregated flames of the patio fire tumbled over each other as they leaped upwards in my mind's eye. With the candle, besides learning to isolate and tame its single flame, man had also found the way to minimize its heat so that it could be exploited for its light alone. Surely this was an achievement on a par with the wheel.

That I had never recognized this drove home how blinding habitual attitudes can be. Always, I had taken candles for granted. And because I had grown up in the era of electricity, from the technical point of view I had looked down on the candle as a primitive lighting device so ineffectual that, for all workaday purposes, it had rightly been superseded. Now I saw I had assessed the candle from the wrong end of its history. To really appreciate it, one had to look at it from the standpoint of its primitive beginning — probably a smoky torch.

That string running down the center of a wax cylinder was not so simple after all — or rather it had the simplicity of an invention that had been brought to the apex of refinement. I recalled those burning logs glowing so long with red-orange heat, giving off so much smoke, untouchable when properly burning, black and misshapen as they burned, yielding only part of their substance to the fire, and finally dropping their charred, unconsumed parts into such dirty heaps on the tray below. The recollection gave me a totally new appreciation of wax. In finding it, man had found a suitable fuel for his new invention.

It was clean and cool. It gave beautiful light, with a minimum of heat and practically no smoke. It yielded all of its substance in the service for which it was employed. It retained its shape as it fed its wick. And, wonder of wonders, unlike a liquid fuel, it could be carried in the hand without a containing vessel.

There was wonder in the wick, too. Besides being an efficient medium between the fuel and the flame, it was flammable enough to burn easily, durable enough not to be totally consumed, and rigid enough to hold the flame sufficiently far from the wax to prevent wasteful melting.

These lyrical thoughts, however, bumped up against the prosaic consideration that, basically, a wick is only a piece of string. The true wonder, then, lies not in the wick itself, but in its interfunctioning with the wax — an interfunctioning, really, of two forms.

A candle is only a string embedded in a tube, but the way the combination is arranged is marvelously ingenious. Considering the puddle of oil at the heart of most lamps, one would think a candle might have taken the form of a short stem rising from the center of a wax disk. But no, the fuel is solidified in a cylindrical mold, and, by running lengthwise through its fuel, the wick does its duties in the most efficient way. By emerging at the top in an area of small circumference, it holds the flame where the updraft of heated air will carry it still higher from the wax whose melting surface is so economically concentrated.

Once man had the candle, he learned that steadiness of burning led to still greater conservation of wax. And I realized the crystal chimney was a refinement of the basic invention. Or rather it was the exploitation of still another of man's great inventions — glass — to improve the candle's performance.

As I gathered my thoughts, I was better able to understand why that candle, burning so serenely in its crystal sheath, seemed so extraordinarily beautiful. One factor was seeing it as a picture, for on my first glimpse the candle's own radiance had set it apart, framing it as it were, so that it hung like a glowing oval against the dark walls of the gallery of night. And not content with absorbing it as a lovely impression, I went on to take in its details, noting them carefully and exactly.

Then, as I thought about its significance as an invention, as a human achievement, I realized that the candle was also a symbol. Its tranquil luminosity, so startling after the wildly ragged fire, showed not just what man had achieved, but also symbolized how the best part of him works towards comparable achievements.

I am sure that candle had also stirred associations of home, childhood and peaceful summer evenings in places without electricity; perhaps even of birthdays, Christmas and church. Then, too, there was another factor.

During the war years when I felt so much helplessness and despair, so deep a sense of outrage at the cruelties being perpetrated, I came upon a saying that steadied me then and has guided me since: the Chinese proverb attributed to Confucius — "It is better to light a candle than to curse darkness." It distills, I feel, so much of a good attitude towards life. And I think the emotional reverberations of this saying also influenced my feeling for that candle.

Observing the candle, then, was not a simple visual act. The experience included many elements that, because they did not come directly from what the eye took in, might be called extra-visual. I saw the candle as a symbol of a wise attitude, as well as a symbol of man's idealistic spirit. It had philosophical overtones in addition to emotional associations. Besides providing the aesthetic pleasure of pictorial beauty, it stirred the excitement of a truth apprehended for the first time. And there was the sense of discovery in all the additional apprehensions of the candle's various features as a series of inventions. And I am sure all these extra-visual considerations — few of which had been present when I had looked at other candles — were important elements in heightening my vision of this particular one.

I had a feeling of calm joy, and as it was getting late, my body, as well as my mind, was ready to retire. Getting up from my chair, I was certain my visual adventures had ended for the night. After all, the candle had outdone the fire and nothing could top the candle. And not in a dog's age of office work had my brain reached out so far in so many directions in one evening. Surely it had passed the point where it could respond to any more visual stimulus. But I had reckoned without the lantern that caught my eye on the way to my room.

It was an antique lantern, much like those one sees outside Dickensian inns on Christmas cards. What made it so stimulating at that particular moment was that, incongruously, it housed an electric bulb. Naturally, my mind leaped from the flame in the glass chimney to the incandescent filament in the bulb. With the bulb, man learned to get light without fire. And no sooner had I realized this extension of man's chain of invention, than I became aware of the sequence of the links. Obviously, the crystal chimney in the courtyard stood midway between the lantern and the bulb.

The lantern had partially solved the problem of achieving a transparent flame shelter, but it still had iron elements that obscured some of the light. Glass had solved the problem completely. Then the bulb adapted the molded glass casing of the chimney, closing it over the top because it had to shelter a delicate filament rather than a flame that needed oxygen.

And still the adventures weren't over. When I passed into the open gallery of the patio I was staggered by a great electric sign a block away, visible because it was higher than the two-story hotel. At that moment the sign was indulging in the more spectacular of its two great performances: simulating the bursting of a rocket.

No sooner had the last descending circle of light expired than the sign went into its second big act in which a blue knight on a blue horse paused a moment and then rode charging at a red windmill which, at the moment of impact, turned into a huge yellow bottle. Then, ten great white letters appeared, spelling out the brand name of the mildly alcoholic beverage contained in the bottle — Don Quijote.

The letters lasted long enough to be read comfortably. Then there was a whoosh of red light up the side as the rocket act started again. The effect of the explosion was created by the flashing on of hundreds of circles and stars of neon. Not only did the yellow, blue, red and green balls of light curve out as such lights in rockets do, but they immediately started raining down, the descending illusion being achieved by the coming on of lower lights as upper ones went out.

As quickly as the great chrysanthemum of light expired in

the last falling spark, my mind leaped from the incandescent tungsten in the bulb to the neon gases in those hundreds of tubes. Here was still another means of gaining illumination and still a new way of moulding glass to hold it. And the invention of neon in tubing had proved so flexible that man, utilizing principles discovered in making animated cartoons, was able to create such a marvelous thing as this sign. What a poor way station the candle seemed in comparison. Yet ironically, the great sign had a way of bringing me down to earth. In the courtyard the candle had given me a mystical feeling about the idealistic spirit of man. The sign showed man was not always so purely noble, or so lofty in his aims. From the smoky torch to the animated neon sign — what a long chain of invention to advertise beer!

Further thoughts crowded to my mind, especially about the way in which one visual experience had been the stepping stone to another. But I do not want to go into them here. My specific purpose has been served by the story of how observation of the fire led to the type of vision with which I saw the candle. I would like to add, however, that I have now sounded nearly all the major themes of the book. The influence of the extra-visual was touched on directly, but, by and large, in this chapter, as in the first, I relied on implication. The next will hold a third narrative, but before the story opens I will start being more explicit.

CHAPTER 3

Transfigured Vision

ONE motive for not bringing a pointer to themes implicit in the first two chapters was novelistic. Wishing to convey some of the reality of visual adventure, I did not want to kill the narratives by smothering them with excessive analysis. But before I can pass on to the next step, I must pause to indicate what was inherent in the first two.

When not reading, many people use their eyes only for recognition and orientation. Psychophysically, such uses are wonderful and mysterious, but I want to take them for granted. Ordinary day-to-day vision, which merely enables us to get about and do things, is not my primary interest. What I'm concerned with is vision that is better than ordinary. And I have found that above-common vision can be classified by the degree it exceeds our seeing when we are using our eyes merely as guides to action.

The first degree above ordinary vision I call *sharpened vision*. The purpose of the story of the face cards was to give an example of this kind of vision. In it, the general picture before the eyes is seen much more clearly and accurately. Details, too, are noticed and enjoyed with new exactitude. And knowledge is brought to bear so that both the whole picture and the details are understood more perfectly, at the same time as they are seen more precisely.

The stage above sharpened vision I call *heightened vision*. How it differs from sharpened vision should be plain from contrasting the candle story with that of the face cards. Heightened vision has what sharpened vision has — greater exactness, more grasp of detail, and fuller intellectual understanding. But it has additional elements. One is a greater sense of wonder; so that what has been seen with heightened vision is revealed as being much more significant than it seemed. The emotional element is stronger in heightened vision too. One responds not merely by finding the object more interesting, but by finding it more beautiful, or, if the object is a sad one, more pitiful. And in heightened vision there is an apprehension of a wider context. One does not have merely a sharp vision of a candle lighting a red-checked cloth; one sees it as a symbol of a wise attitude and of man's idealistic spirit, and one sees it in its rightful place in the long history of humanity's inventive progress.

I come now to the stage that is still higher, which I call *transfigured vision*. Again I would like to introduce it with a clear-cut example. First, though, let me make plain that by "vision" I mean ocular perception, and I use the word as an optometrist does in speaking of a patient's 20-20 vision. I state this so it will not be thought that in referring to transfigured vision I am speaking of hallucinations or visitations from angelic personages. Nor am I speaking of things seen only in the mind's eye — products, that is, of escapist fantasies, Dionysian raptures, or world-denying religious meditations. I am speaking of things observed by the physical eye; things springing from concrete objects, which, far from ignoring reality, are rooted in it. I refer to a type of vision that carries with it . . . but let me tell the story first.

Inscription Rock is one of the most interesting monuments in the Southwest. With its startling rise from the desert floor to an enormous height, its deeply riven cliffs of buff-colored sandstone, and its frontal edges like prows of congregated ocean liners, the great mesa is outstanding, even in a region of towering and marvelous erosional forms. Small wonder the Spaniards called it *El Morro*, meaning the headland. And then, of course, it has all those inscriptions, supporting its claim as the world's largest autograph book. For it lay on the old Acoma-Zuñi trail and, beginning with Oñate in 1605, those who camped at the deep pool at its foot took to carving on its sheer walls their names and the record of their passage.

I visited Inscription Rock in June of 1949. That summer, Thyrza Cohen, a retired schoolteacher, who had been very hospitable to me while I was in the Army, wanted to be driven from her home in California to her sister's in Denver. I had given up my usual vacation to act as her chauffeur. But neither of us wanted the drive to be a headlong race to cover the territory in the shortest possible time. We wanted to see what was interesting en route. Thus we made side trips to the Grand Canyon, the Petrified Forest, and the Painted Desert. We were traveling on Route 66, and when I looked at the stretch between Gallup and Albuquerque I saw there was a road that looped down from Gallup, ran parallel with the highway, and then rejoined it at Grants, a trading center for ranchers with 1,541 inhabitants. Because the Indian pueblo of Zuñi and Inscription Rock were both on the side road, we decided to take it. The loop would lengthen the trip, but surely the interest of those two sights would be worth it.

We were both too inexperienced in New Mexican road conditions to be concerned by the fact that the looping road was not paved. Lots of unsurfaced roads in the East were pretty good. So at Gallup, lightheartedly we turned south. My companion was seventy-nine, and her four-cylinder car, being a 1932 Plymouth sedan, was perhaps older than she, for, in human terms, a seventeen-year-old car is incredibly ancient.

The road to Zuñi was fair and we got over the forty miles in an hour and three-quarters. From Zuñi to Inscription Rock was another forty miles and because this road was only a little poorer we made it in about the same time, with a stop for a picnic lunch making the going easier. Once at the Rock, its interest seemed well worth the effort of reaching it. We studied it so long that it was a quarter of four before we started on the last leg to Grants.

What that road from Inscription Rock to Grants is like now I can not say, but in 1949 it was appalling. Half the time, in fact, I could not tell it was a road at all. As there were no signs to point which branch went to Grants when we came to a fork, we just took the road that seemed the more likely. When one became a couple of ruts through a ploughed field, I was sure we had taken a wrong turn. But it seemed sensible to continue until someone could set us right. The trouble was that in this upland terrain there were hardly any settlers. With two elderly responsibilities — my friend and her car — I dreaded the thought of being lost so late in the afternoon in such an uninhabited area. Finally, however, we saw a woman ahead. To our enormous relief, she assured us that, although what we were following seemed like two furrows, it was nevertheless the road to Grants.

For some time the dusty ruts paralleled a mountain ridge on our left, and at a certain point the ruts veered towards those great hills. Though I did not realize it then, what we had to cross was the Continental Divide.

As we began to climb, a new fear was added: that the old car would not be able to make the steep ascent. We had to go most of the way in low, but there were times when even that gear did not seem to have power enough. Whenever the engine seemed on the point of stalling, my heart was in my mouth. Always, however, the old car managed and I blessed its mechanical heart whenever it got over a seemingly impossible rise.

Each time it did, Miss Cohen and I would look at each other and smile; and secretly I blessed her for being such a good sport. Having a lively imagination, she must have been as worried as I, yet she pretended to feel confident and even managed to be cheerful. Her calmness was definitely helpful. For anxiety's usual vicious cycle had begun, and the keener my responses to the threatening aspects of the environment became, the more the environment seemed to threaten.

If Miss Cohen had begun to grow querulous or fearful — and her age justified such reactions — my tension would have stepped up. But instead, her bravery made things easier. While I had been in the Army I had often felt depressed and cut off from life, so these moments of smiling exchange were not the first time she had cheered me when I was in low spirits.

At the height of our pass we were confronted with a marvelous panorama. A great wide valley lay athwart our path and, rising beyond its far ridge, was the blue tip of Mount Taylor. It stood as a distant and isolated cone, for the opposite ridge was so high that it obscured all the lesser peaks of the San Mateo Mountains. Normally, I would have rejoiced in the presence of such wild grandeur. But I saw the ridge primarily as a new threat, something hateful we had to climb. Thus I had little appreciation for the view, which we quickly lost as we began descending among the scrubby pines.

On the way up, fear that we would have a puncture had increased my anxiety. After all, the road was barely scraped from the bedrock of the hill and it was full of sharp stones. On the way down, this fear increased, for there were boulders as well as stones. There were tree stumps, too. Indeed, it no longer could be called a road. It was a track. At every jolt, I expected the car to settle with a list at the corner where a tire had been smashed.

And fear of a blowout was now augmented by the old fear of getting lost. The track had such little definition that at one stretch I was sure we were off it. I had the impression of descending a rocky hill, dodging trees where I could, and hoping for the best. The idea of being lost on that wooded hilltop was worse than any thought of being lost in *El Morro*'s arid valley. The valley at least was flat and occasional fields showed we might find shelter. But here we were truly in the wilds. (And I was not just imagining this, for several years later, when Mike Todd's plane crashed among these same desolate mountains, I read that the regional Indians called this wilderness "Malpai" or badlands.)

As we bumped downard, I kept my foot on the brake and my right hand ready to grab at the emergency. And as I felt the steady cushioning of the tires, despite the punishment they were taking, I was swept by a fresh wave of affection. I blessed their air-filled hearts.

At the end of the descent, I was relieved to find we had not lost the trail. The road, although still poor, was recognizable as a road. And the climb up the far side of the valley was not as hard as I had anticipated, although my hope that at its highest point we would see Grants was blasted.

We were still in the wilds, though now we were entering canyon country. Down and down and down curved the road, and, correspondingly, the canyon walls on either side grew higher and higher. Soon they were so high that the slant of the afternoon sun could not penetrate the gorge; and as we drove in the shadow it seemed later than it actually was.

How much further, how much further? I began asking myself. From the map we had calculated the distance from Inscription Rock to Grants as forty miles. Surely we had driven that much already? Was the territory so little known that the mapmaker had just sketched in the road approximately? Was it really much longer than forty miles? As this idea dawned I looked at the gas indicator. We had less than an eighth of a tankful left.

By this time the road was wider and, for a dirt road, reasonably smooth. I no longer feared a blowout and we knew we were not lost. But now a new and harrowing question arose: Would we run out of gas before we reached the Promised Land?

The day before, Miss Cohen had almost fainted when overcome by the heat at the Petrified Forest, and she was terribly tired when we stopped for the night at a wayside motel in Arizona. Since we had left that motel at seven o'clock in the morning, we had been on the road more than ten hours. I was naturally anxious about her with-standing this grueling ride, my concern being complicated by feeling guilty for having let my historical curiosity subject her to such an ordeal.

"I'm all right," she said cheerfully. Knowing my own fatigue, I was grateful for such gameness.

Under happier circumstances I think I would have considered that winding canyon a scenic wonder. At the time, however, it only seemed a darkening and interminable labyrinth. Doggedly I drove on. And suddenly . . .

Suddenly, the canyon walls fell away and we were in open country. We curved up over a slight rise, and there, beyond rolling green fields, built partway up the slopes of a great hill, was Grants. With its low, flat white buildings, it had a romantic, faraway beauty, like something one might see from the Mediterranean in approaching the coast of North Africa. And this Tunisian scene was bathed in a magical light. The sun, shining from the left over the pass, was not as low as the gorge had led me to expect. Its slanting rays seemed to gather on the village with an almost platinum radiance; and the surrounding buttes and foothills were flooded with a golden light that gave further emphasis to contours already inked by long, dark eastward shadows. Not only was the scene visually lovely, but it seemed to glow with inner significance. As I feasted my eyes on it, my whole being felt at one with the landscape. Simultaneously I felt liberated into a state of timeless bliss.

I broke into song, and what came spontaneously was the hymn

John Mason Neale created in translating the description of
Heaven that Bernard of Cluny wrote in the twelfth century. As I
sang, I was amazed at how closely the words described what was
before my eyes. Grants was undoubtedly a place that had milk, and
probably honey, too. And as I looked on that sweet and blessed
country, "all jubilant with song," I had a sense of the goodness of
its people. Maybe there were no martyrs among them, but the
town at that moment, nestling so peacefully among its green fields,
seemed "bright with many an angel."

That hymn, "Jerusalem the Golden," has a wonderful old
tune. Its melody pours out exultantly, lifting the heart at the same
time as it raises the voice. Though I'm not much of a singer, my
happiness and relief poured out as I sang:

> *I know not, O I know not*
> *What joys await us there,*
> *What radiancy of glory,*
> *What bliss beyond compare,*

When I came to the second verse about the halls of Zion, the
goose pimples stood on my arm. Perhaps my deepest perception
was expressed in the hymn as the descriptive words grew even
more exact:

> *The Prince is ever in them,*
> *The daylight is serene,*
> *The pastures of the blessed*
> *Are decked in glorious sheen.*

Surely that monk must have seen some medieval town in the
late afternoon with the same sort of insight that I was seeing
Grants. The capitalized spelling of Prince was proof that he, too,
felt . . . But I do not want to wear my soul on my sleeve. Let
those religious emotions, as well as other thoughts and feelings,
emerge between the lines a few pages hence when I try to analyze
the experience.

Meanwhile, there is a little more to the story. The last miles
went easily, but, once we got to Grants, I needed to look after my
two responsibilities. Luckily, we found an acceptable motor court

and, as soon as I saw that Thyrza was stretched out comfortably to rest, I went to get gas and to see what damage, if any, the old car had suffered on that awful ride.

Perhaps the owner of the run-down service station was not exactly a bright-eyed, winged being, and by no stretch of the imagination could his overalls be considered a white robe, but he was extraordinarily good-humored and obliging. With his reassuring kindness, his fund of local lore, and his mechanical skill, he seemed a symbol of man. Beneath his grease-stained exterior, I saw one who was conquering in the fight — that is, a father who worked hard for his family, a good neighbor, a settler who put up cheerfully with hard conditions, and a householder who had enough goodness left over to befriend a passing stranger. And he was just one of the good people who managed to survive in Grants. For that matter, he was only one of millions of such humans who, by pertinacity, mutual kindness, and inventive skill, manage to survive throughout the world, transforming the places where they live into oases where a lost traveler can find security and shelter. Perhaps my vision of the angels had not been so misleading after all.

I felt sure of it after I had encountered his cheerful wife. She filled our thermoses with hot coffee and willingly sold us some bread, butter, and a little cold meat. Then she refused to accept money for the ice she chipped for the tin-lined box in which we kept our perishables.

Even though it meant working after dark, the man agreed to give the car a careful overhauling. "I'll do the whole jigger," he said, when I mentioned air, greasing, water for the battery, etc. Then, knowing the car was in good hands, I went to the court and helped prepare our picnic meal. Thyrza ate with good appetite, but she did not want to stir from her room. So after supper I went for a stroll.

As I walked down the road, I thought of the afternoon's vision. The shriek of a train whistle reminded me that Grants was a coaling station on the Santa Fe Railroad. And I wondered which was the correct aspect of the town: the dingy row of houses and filling stations strung along the highway, or the gleaming white Tunisian village I had seen from far off? The unglamorous aspect certainly could not be dismissed. But after that vision it could not be accepted as the total reality either. To those with eyes to see, Grants probably looked as beautiful every afternoon in the setting sun as it had looked to me. And didn't it only seem drab in contrast with more prosperous places? Compared with that water hole where seventeenth-century Spaniards camped at the foot of Inscription Rock, Grants was a miracle of modern comfort and hospitality.

The illumined aspect of Grants, then, was a true one — certainly truer than any I might have perceived had I been a rich motorist passing through in a faultless limousine. And my realization that I had pierced through a drab exterior to a deeper reality strengthened my conviction that what I had seen was no illusion. This, in turn, heightened my sense of wonder about what had happened as we emerged from the canyon. Clearly my relieved imagination had played a role in the experience. Perhaps it had superimposed too beautiful an image on the physical aspect of Grants. But curiously enough, this had led not to delusion, but to apprehension of deeper truth. For it was the heightened outward beauty that had revealed the normally invisible inner beauty — the essential value of the town and its people.

In other words, my questioning intellect could accept what my heart already knew: that the experience had been an authentic instance of transfigured vision.

That instance enables me to define what I mean by the term: It is an experience in which the everyday aspect of a person or a scene is so altered that one feels it looks markedly different than it does under normal circumstances. Yet, paradoxically, as one sees it differently, one gets the impression that one sees it more accurately; it seems not itself, and yet more itself. By this I mean that, at the same time as it seems transformed by added elements, it is also seen momentarily with the exactitude of sharpened vision.

Insight is one of the elements added. And I do not mean just a small insight, but insight into things beyond measuring and, ultimately, beyond proof; insight, in fact, into the nature of existence. And this gigantic glimpse is not so much a single insight as a cluster so thick as to suggest total revelation. Just to catalogue the elements grasped *consciously* takes time enough; and often it is years before one becomes aware of the major lessons absorbed *unconsciously*.

The basic insight, however, tends to be of such force that forever after it stills one's questioning whether existence has meaning. One is sure it has. And this gives rise to another of the elements added: the conviction of significance. For whether all the insights are grasped or not, one has a feeling of understanding something of profound importance. So complete is one's confidence in this understanding that it does not seem to matter if it is rationally explicable or not.

If this seems an abdication of intelligence in favor of self-delusion, let me point to the fact that I analyzed carefully as I weighed the Grants experience in the drab twilight. The impression of truth is one of the strongest sensations one carries away from the illuminated experience. The sense of veracity is so strong, in fact, that fundamentally it accounts for the conviction of significance. For the mind, far from feeling it has been subject to illusion, feels it has reached the heart of reality. This belief is one of the features that distinguishes transfigured vision from heightened vision. Heightened vision, too, brings with it a rush of insights; but it does not bring with it this sense of having penetrated to a reality that transcends at the same time as it underlies appearances.

The next element I find difficult to phrase succinctly. In defining the difference between heightened and sharpened vision I said that, in the former, there is an apprehension of a wider context. This third element I am talking about in transfigured vision widens the apprehension of context by as much again. Actually it is a combination of two types of extended awareness: awareness of context and awareness of relationship. Thus, one sees Grants not merely as the place where one is staying for the night, not merely as a town on Route 66 where gas is available, but as a New Mexican village among the foothills of Mount Taylor on the North American continent. One even sees it as a point on the earth which is orbiting around the sun in an enormous universe. As one sees it thus, one also sees the far-reaching relationships of its people. Besides seeing how they are related to the land they live off, one sees their relationships with all the other inhabitants of New Mexico, with other Americans, with their own ancestors.

And as one sees their place in space and in time, one sees them as symbols of human beings on earth, existing independent of their particular lifespan. One sees, too, one's own relationship to them and to that same earth. Perhaps one might call this particular addition a sense of the universe.

A sense of eternity is another addition. And it is one of the curious consequences of transfigured vision that one's sense of time and of timelessness are heightened simultaneously. What one seems to capture is both a moment of eternity in the midst of time and a moment of time in the midst of eternity.

Another major addition is, in part, a result of the others. It is not just the stronger emotion that distinguishes heightened from sharpened vision, but an intensity of emotion that thrills the entire being. For the emotion of heightened vision tends to be that of keener aesthetic response or deeper sympathy; but in transfigured vision one does not merely see a scene as a beautiful picture or something put on the stage by a compassionate playwright. Instead, one has a sense of doors opening, of light breaking, of canyon walls falling away. One is thrilled, transported, or overwhelmed. Bernard of Cluny gave a clue to the intensity of feeling. The New Jerusalem, he wrote, was so marvelous that beneath its contemplation the heart and soul sank "oppressed." Others have used exactly opposite terms, speaking of happiness and exaltation and of coming into tranquility and peace through comprehension of transcendent reality. No matter what the feeling, one is left with a sense of awe and wonder.

Curiously, however, in the long run the pictorial residue is not as sharply detailed as that left by heightened vision. You remember having seen, but you do not recall precisely what you saw. The essence and the over-all impression remain with you, and they remain with you always. You know that what was revealed and the moment of revelation itself were high points of existence, yet you cannot find a metaphor much more exact than a village seen across the Mediterranean to describe to others what was so abundantly clear to you during the time of the illumination.

My hope is that my words have stirred you to recall comparable instances in your own life. If you have read some of the writings of the great mystics, particularly those who believe in illumination in and through the world, perhaps you have been struck by a similarity between what I have been saying and their descriptions of mystical experiences. The Christian mystics have always claimed that a major element in their experiences of transfigured vision is the presence of God — a belief I happen to share. But I do not want to insist on the point. To some, the introduction of God would make the subject seem irrational, and I want to make clear that it is not necessary to believe in God to accept the reality of transfigured vision. Non-mystics might not have experienced it so often or so consciously, but it is common enough to be considered a human phenomenon, not necessarily a divine one.

The reason I spent so much time building up to the description of Grants was to make the experience more intelligible. Besides wanting the reader to feel *how* such a thing could happen, I wanted to provide grounds for analysis.

Experiences of transfigured vision, I used to think, were wholly gratuitous. Because they generally come suddenly and unexpectedly, I also thought they were like miracles from the blue; that they were gifts we did nothing to earn and happenings over which we had no control. But Saint-Exupery freed me of this notion when, in *Flight to Arras*, he wrote that "illumination is vision suddenly granted to the spirit, at the end of a long and gradual preparation."

If our illuminations are the result of long preparation, they are not accidental. And I began seeking what factors might be preparatory. This is a matter I want to discuss at greater length in the chapter on the electrodes of vision, but the Grants story involves a few of those factors that elucidate the experience.

In Aldous Huxley's most compassionate book, *Eyeless in Gaza*, there is an account of transfigured vision. Though given as the recollection of a character in a novel, I would like to quote it as evidence of the experience from another source (a writer with marvelous powers of verbal communication).

"He thought of the day when they had gone walking in Winchelsea marshes. The hawthorn was in bloom; dotted here and there on the wide, flat expanse of grass, the sheep and their lambs were like white constellations; overhead, the sky was alive with white clouds gliding in the wind. Unspeakably beautiful! And suddenly it seemed to him that they were walking through the image of their love. The world was their love, and their love the world; and the world was significant, charged with depth beyond depth of mysterious meaning. The proof of God's goodness floated in those clouds, crept in those grazing sheep, shone from every burning bush of incandescent blossom — and, in himself and Joan, walked hand in hand across the grass and was manifest in their happiness. His love, it seemed to him, in that apocalyptic moment, was more than merely *his;* it was in some mysterious way the equivalent of this wind and sunshine, these white gleams against the green and blue of spring."

The elements already isolated are all there: the insight, the impression of truth transcending appearances, the sense of the universe, the intense emotion and the feeling of God's presence. And note the factor that was the chief inducer of the experience — love.

In this case it was the love of a young man for a young woman. But romantic love is only one kind of love. There was love in my story, too: love for the pioneering old schoolteacher who was with me, love for the old car that, despite our fears, had the strength to get us over the Continental Divide, love for the tires that bounded back from the sharp stones. And if these loves seem shallow and transitory, let me point out that they were welling ever more fully as the ordeal grew more protracted, and I am sure this fullness of love was a major preparation for the vision. When I saw Grants, that longed-for haven of safety, looking so beautiful in the afternoon sun, my cup ran over.

Perhaps if you will remember your own moments of illumined vision you will see that they, too, were moments of over-brimming love.

That ride to Grants was humbling. Its danger in a car so decrepit and its hardship for a woman so old showed me I had been stupid to undertake it without proper investigation. My growing awareness of my dependence on that engine and those tires heightened my sense of helplessness in such rugged country. Removed from such rudimentary things as drinking water and shelter — and fearing being removed from them much longer — I was aware that, for all the education poured into me, I was like the lowliest serf in my need of them. Increasing fatigue made me realize how grateful I would be for just a bench where I could sit down without having to drive any further. I am sure this humility was a preparing factor, too. All my intellectual pride, my propensity to sit in judgment, had been jolted out of me. Like a man handed a cup of cocoa after a bombardment, I was ready to see with fresh eyes because I had been reduced to being grateful for small mercies.

Our eyes are bodily organs and seeing is a physical act. I am sure the drive's effects on my body — and I include my nervous system in this — were part of the preparation, too. As we emerged from that canyon I was very tired, yet so keyed up that my senses were alert. Fatigue was not having its customary effect of slowing or deadening the faculties, but instead was operating in the region of ideas. For I was too tired to formulate mental concepts or preconceived notions through which to filter my impressions of the world. The screen of perpetual rationalizing that, for most of us, stands between our eyes and reality had been battered down. The scene before me was extraordinarily beautiful and it spelled "home." And part of the strength of its impact was that it struck through to my feelings when all my intellectual defenses were down.

Again, if you will remember moments when the world seemed to shine for you with an especially radiant loveliness, I think you will find they were moments when, because of great exertions, either physical or mental, you had a special kind of receptive tiredness; when you were not a bit sleepy, yet too tired to think, too tired to be active, too tired, in fact, to do anything but gratefully perceive beauty as a beneficence needed by the soul.

I did not come to understand the final element in my spirit's preparation till six or seven years later. By then I knew moments of illumination were not entirely mysterious, and indeed could even be induced. I knew, however, that, since normal living conditions militate against them, one has to be in an exceptional state to have them.

Once, I had an "opening" of vision immediately after an enormous load had been lifted from my mind. The vision coming so instantaneously after the feeling of relief made me realize the two must have been interconnected. What was the cause of the alleviation? I asked myself. In general terms, it was being released from a tension I had been under for some time. Understanding this was a key that fitted many doors. Many of my previous experiences of illumination, I saw, had also occurred at moments of release from tension, the experience at Grants being a prime example. After hours of fear, anxiety and suspense, the tension was suddenly ended by the sight of the Promised Land. No wonder it looked so dazzlingly golden.

I now think this state of mind — that following sudden liberation from prolonged tension — is one of the states most propitious for transfigured vision. Somehow great relief — and the greater the tension or the anxiety, the greater the relief — has a way of stripping away our normal visual veils. Then we have the power to recognize things, especially those spelling peace, safety, and health, in their full goodness. I think this element of relief is what makes the first day of spring so ravishing; or accounts for the scientist's feeling that the world is marvellously beautiful after he has finally solved a problem on which he has been working for years. And again I ask you to consult your experience: Hasn't it happened with you, too, that joy in being released from tension has enabled you to see a transfigured world with new eyes?

Part II

OBSERVATION OBSERVED

CHAPTER 4

Single- and Double-Level Perception

In the summer of 1944 the U.S. Air Force decided to start assembling the history of its medical installations. So the decree went out that by the middle of September each installation should submit its history to Washington in triplicate. I was stuck with the job of compiling ours. Having been on the desert airfield in California for almost a year, I could remember a good deal from personal experience. But I had to rely on others for information about the year prior to my arrival.

The first soldiers to reach the field came in trucks, and since no buildings had been erected, they had to live in tents. It was the tent era I needed most help on, and fortunately there were three or four men still at the field who had been there from the start. But when I sought them out I was frustrated. They had all been on sick call, and while they remembered some humorous anecdotes, they could not furnish me with the precise details an official history needed — exact dates, complete names, and so on. Even when I took them to the part of the field the tents had occupied, I found they could not remember just where they had lived or where the dispensary tent had been.

By this time all trace of the tents had gone and the area was studded with single-story barracks of brown sheetrock. Since I did not know one of vision's cardinal facts, I was inwardly exasperated at those G.I.'s. They seemed so dimwitted. To be in the actual area where they had spent so much time and not be able to locate their tent sites — I just didn't think it possible for anyone to be that unobservant.

Now, however, I look back on them more tolerantly. The first experience that shocked my own self-esteem came several years later, when I found myself unable to figure out just where the old stairs had been in the days before our office lobby was remodeled. The second shock came when a row of houses was torn down across the street from the apartment building in which I found a home after the war. Looking from my window at the park that had replaced the houses, I realized that, had anyone asked me, I would not have been able to describe the vanished houses.

The cardinal fact about vision is involved in all three of those instances. It is a condition that governs most of our ordinary seeing. And having dwelt so much on better-than-average vision, I must now give average vision some attention. For if any improvement is to be brought about, we must seek the factors, conditions, and habits that keep day-to-day observation the limited thing it is.

However, before trying to explain what made those tents, stairs, and houses disappear, I need to establish what I will temporarily call "the opposite factor." This involves exploring further instances of seeing with uncanny sharpness. Some are so common they do not need detailing: such as coming to a strange place for the first time, or the heightened vision we have when we return to a once-familiar place from which we have long been absent. Heightened vision is also common in a well-known place we are leaving, especially if we are going for good.

Often we see with great sharpness, too, if we are confronted with two worlds side by side that are generally miles apart: a bearded beatnik, say, entering the flashy new Metropolitan Opera House, or a Moslem delegate to the United Nations, his sheik's robes billowing as he is lifted in a Ferris wheel at Coney Island.

Sometimes the experience of seeing with new eyes happens when a friend we have known only as a young person, reappears unexpectedly in middle age. Sometimes we have the experience as we step out of a museum and suddenly see the trees more vividly against a Ruysdael sky. Or sometimes it will happen when music touches us in a particular way.

Some instances, however, are more complex, as I can illustrate with three of my own. The first occurred at the induction center a week or so after I had entered the army. Along with other draftees I was in a work detail being marched to a warehouse. On our way we passed a group of fellows in civilian clothes marching from the train. We knew they were about to go through the same processing we had undergone a few days earlier. What surprised me was how this insight into what faced those men heightened my vision of the physical setting through which they marched. Suddenly I saw the snowy flatness of the scene, and the intense, clean blue of the sky, with its few streaks of white clouds. I noticed, too, the frost of the men's breath, as, in their dark city clothes, they were ordered along by a few sergeants in khaki. Meanwhile the grey warehouses we approached took on the vividness of something painted by Charles Sheeler.

The second instance was on December 26, 1944. I can name the day because it was my parents' wedding anniversary, which from childhood had been easily remembered as the day after Christmas. I can place the year because while I was a soldier I got East for only one visit. On the evening in question I was sitting in the dining room of my mother's apartment where we were having dinner before I had to take the train back to California.

The fact that it was her wedding anniversary led me to conjure up a picture of her standing at the steps leading to the choir as the minister asked her if she took my father to be her husband. Then I suddenly imagined her incredulity, and perhaps horror, if the Genie of the Future had whispered into her ear:

"Thirty-seven years from now this man you are marrying will have been dead for five years. You will have lived through one World War and you will be in the midst of the second. You will be sitting in a dining room in the apartment you took after you were widowed, having dinner with the son you will bear from this man, and that son will be a soldier about to return to that second World War."

As I imagined that impossible visitation, making that improbable prediction — all of which had proved true — I saw that dining room with a new vividness: the mahogany table, the silver entree dishes, the sheen of the dusty rose drapes, the maroon carpet, and especially the pleasant-looking, white-haired woman with the blue eyes, who was rather too stout, sitting with her back to the cream-colored swinging door that led into the pantry. I saw myself, too, sitting at right angles to her in an Air Force battle jacket. And that scene, which a moment before had hardly existed, has remained imperishably with me ever since.

The third instance was to lead not only to understanding the other two, but almost all moments of better-than-average vision.

It happened in Mexico. I knew I was about to visit Monte Alban, the hill rising above Oaxaca that is surmounted with ancient Zapotec ruins. The Oaxaca stores had many post-cards of the ruins and, because in those days there were no guidebooks of the site, I decided to arm myself with post-cards instead. The cards, I reasoned, showed the principal features and would help me in my viewing by leading me to look at what was pictured. Their captions would give me the names of the leading monuments.

I allotted a whole day to the ruins, and because I had walked up I was in no hurry because no driver was waiting. After looking casually at the pyramids and temples shown in the cards, I got the further idea of trying to find the exact points from which the cards were taken.

I selected one, obviously taken from the northeast corner. When I made my way there I was not content to take in the scene generally. I moved about until several of the landmarks were in the same relative positions before my eyes as they were in the card. A single shade tree proved especially useful here; for in trying to make that tree occupy the same position in my vision that it had in the card, I had to keep looking first at the small card and then at the large view. I had to retreat farther than I expected, and mount still another pyramid I had hardly observed. This shifting of vision from the small card to the large scene was wonderfully stimulating. The reality made details on the card intelligible which at first were not, because in the photograph they were too small in scale. The card, on the other hand, by making me focus my attention on the view it contained led me to concentrate on a single area. Because the card was old I could discern what reconstruction of the ruins had been done since the photograph was taken. The stumps of twelve huge pillars at the head of a nearby flight of steps, for instance, were clearly reconstructions, for in the card you could see only the circular patches where the pillars had been. And the majestic stairway at the far end of the great plaza was now almost fully revealed. In the card, it was still a huge mound.

I was swept by many thoughts, most of which will emerge when I come to the chapter on Times Square. Here the pertinent one was a realization felt at the time, though not crystallized until some years afterwards, that the remarkable feature of the day was that I had looked at something with two visions of it simultaneously. Could it be, I asked, that there are always two images in the mind's eye in moments of heightened seeing?

The way to test the theory was to bring the question to specific instances. Did it apply, for example, to the sharp vision of a place seen for the first time? Put in another way, was it a factor behind the well-known phenomenon of the vividness of first impressions? It seemed to be, for doesn't one always approach a strange place full of one's familiar mental impressions? Thus, to a New Yorker visiting a prairie town, the lowness of the buildings is striking, his mind still being dominated by visions of buildings towering around him. And the instance pursued further seemed to prove the theory doubly. It is another well-known phenomenon that after a few days in a new place the sharpness of first vision dies away. Isn't this because, in getting accustomed to the new, memories of the old place fade, and one no longer has two visions simultaneously?

The heightened vision on coming back to a well-known place after a long absence also has an inherent element of doubleness. What come rushing back are memories. For instance, besides seeing the country station, you recall the time you saw a friend off there after a wild dash to make the train. Besides seeing the cabs there waiting to pick up passengers, you recall a winter night when there was no one to meet you and you had to wait in the cold, hoping against hope that such a cab would turn up. Then as you drive through a leafy lane you recall how beautiful it seemed in June of 1940 just after the Fall of France, when its trees reassured you that nature goes on putting forth new leaves no matter what disasters occur in man's world.

Always the secondary element showed up. But what gave me pause in these eye-opening juxtapositions was that the secondary element was not always pictorial. Sometimes it was merely a re-membered feeling or a recollection of an incident — even of a train of thought — while other memories were part pictorial and part non-pictorial.

In one's parting vision of a place one may not see again for a long time I also discerned the secondary element; and again I found the rush of memories the great source of such elements. Things the eyes fall on in farewell glances stimulate many memo-ries, and the recalled significance of what happened in relation to those objects or scenes gives you the desire to memorize them visu-ally. The impulse makes them vivid. But with memories of this kind, too, I realized that some were visual while some were not — and some were so inextricably part visual and part extra-visual that it was impossible to classify them as one or the other.

In the case of the separated worlds incongruously brought to-gether, the doubleness was apparent and classifying the secondary element was easy. No matter which was considered subsidiary, both juxtaposed elements were definitely visual: the red and gold of the Met, full of people in evening dress, and the tieless beatnik with his shabby coat and sneakers; the mechanical steel framework of the twentieth-century Ferris wheel and the sheik, a figure from remote antiquity, being borne on high.

By this time I was excited, for obviously there was something to my theory. The instance of the once-young person suddenly seen in middle age supports it. Clearly, the lingering image of how friends used to look is the secondary image behind the older person whose aging is so vividly and, in some cases, so appallingly appar-ent. In the museum example there is further support. Here the second image is not something remembered from an old environ-ment, but the recently imprinted image of the Ruysdael one has just studied. Because that image is so recent, the mind holds it with an accuracy that causes one to recognize — and, more important, to be struck by — the identical blue of the sky over the museum.

But does the theory apply to the heightening of vision under the influence of music? Halted by music, which is clearly aural rather than a visual, I felt my case weakening. But wait a moment. Is music, in this situation, really the secondary element? Or is it the agent inducing the secondary element? I thought of a New

Year's Eve party at the home of total strangers, a party ever since memorable because of my sudden intensification of vision when all the strangers joined hands and sang "Auld Lang Syne." As I recalled the scene, I realized it wasn't the old song that really accounted for the eye-opening, but the memories summoned by the song. They were memories of singing the same tune on other New Year's Eves when I had been among my loved ones. And I realized that what set these strangers in such high relief — what enabled me to see them so vividly, as well as sense their affectionate camaraderie — was feeling again (and seeing again in my mind's eye) what I had felt singing the song at the year's end in similar circumstances while I was still a boy living at home with my sociable and friend-gathering parents.

This analysis, however, did force me to yield some ground. Those parental New Year's Eve parties weren't all visually distinct; chiefly I remembered what they felt like, rather than what they looked like. I thus came to the conclusion that the secondary element that touches off new vision can be extra-visual, as well as visual. I was also ready to concede that the second element is not the only factor inducing sharper vision, but certainly it is a key one.

Being more practiced in detecting the secondary image, I had no difficulty probing two of the visions I described more fully. And I was fascinated to see how they differed in character. Behind the stout, kindly woman who sat at that table was a vision of her as a young girl of twenty-two as she stood at the altar being married to my father. Here, the secondary vision was one of the past, whereas with the new draftees the secondary image was one of the future. Knowing just what they faced — the herding into the long mess hall for the first briefing, the passage through the assembly line as their uniforms were issued to them piece by piece, the innoculations, the distribution of bedding, the first night between Army blankets, the shrill waking in the darkness the next morning, the days of uncertainty about shipment, the work in the kitchen and the latrines — knowing these things, I was able to see those draftees as they could not see themselves. And this knowledge of their next few days framed them indelibly on the snowy road under the Sheeler sky.

In both instances, then, not only was there a secondary element to highlight the primary one, but also the rarer element of doubleness: the experience of visualizing in two different time planes simultaneously. Notice the word "visualizing" — the facts make me rule out "seeing" — for obviously I could have no memory of having seen a wedding that took place before my birth. In this case imagination was the source of the secondary image, imagination supplemented by knowledge as to where and when the marriage occurred and remembering old photographs of how my parents looked at the time. Imagination and knowledge also played roles in my vision of the men arriving at the induction center. I knew from my own experience just what was going to happen to them, and my imagination was able to project this knowledge to their days ahead.

By this time, as well as having come to recognize the normal presence of the secondary element in moments of stepped-up vision, I had also come to recognize the usual sources of such elements. What remained was to test my theory against the incidents related in the first three chapters. Though I had not thought of it when I was examining the face cards with such excitement, secondary images were obviously at play. Here the contrasting images were not just remembered pictures, but the kings, queens and jacks of the other suits. With a rush, I realized there had been concrete secondary images at every stage of that investigation: The kings who were not in profile show that the king of diamonds was; the queens who held only flowers made me aware that the queen of spades held a sceptre as well; and the intelligibility of what the other jacks were carrying made the object in the hand of the jack of spades puzzlingly apparent. Comparing the face cards of one Anglo-American deck to another stimulated secondary images of a new kind, as did, still later, examining the Italian and French decks.

Then I remembered the words of my friends: the actor who saw the red queens as sisters, the copy writer who saw the queens as the wives of Flemish burghers, the artist who realized the absence of arms, etc. And I recognized a new source of secondary elements — the spoken impressions of other minds. Remembering

Hargrave and Benham, I realized you can also get the impressions of other minds from what they publish, for their books had provided many secondary elements by supplying eye-opening information.

The fire in the courtyard, I realized, held a succession of double images: Behind the tranquil, single flame of the sheltered candle was the raging, many-tongued fire on the wind-swept grate; behind the incandescent filament in the bulb was the flame in the glass chimney; and behind the rocket of neon tubing was the electric bulb.

Behind the vision of Grants in the late afternoon sun had been the image of the dark canyon. And with the Grants experience I uncovered a new facet of my theory. Not only were visual images contrasted — a place of milk and honey against desolate mountains — but there was also a contrast that was not visual at all: two emotional states arising from opposite situations — safety and danger.

Our emotions and their projections, then, are also rich sources of secondary elements.

When I had got this far, I wanted a descriptive phrase applicable to all instances of vision in which what is before the eyes is made more visible by the simultaneous apprehension of a related secondary element. Double-level perception is the term I formulated, and this is what I earlier referred to as "the opposite factor." For once I had grasped that moments of double-level perception were the exception rather than the rule, I asked a fruitful question: Is single-level perception the prevailing condition of our seeing?

To test this, I again decided on specific instances as touchstones: the soldiers who could not remember where the tents had been, and my own inability to describe the razed houses or to relocate the vanished stairs.

The old office stairs, I found, could be conjured up fairly readily in my mind's eye when I sat at home and closed my eyes; so could the row of brownstone houses. It was when I went to their former sites that I had difficulty in visualizing them. This gave me the clue that tangible objects before our eyes claim the attention of the mind so totally — I almost said hoggishly — that when we are confronted with them the mind, in most cases, is robbed of its power to visualize anything else.

I remembered the old saying, "out of sight, out of mind," which I had always interpreted as merely a commentary on human fickleness. But now I saw it as a folklore recognition of what I was analyzing. Why should something not before the eye be out of the mind? Is it just because humans are naturally forgetful? Or is it because new objects before the eyes are so absorbing that the mind, gripped by the new, cannot think of the old — except at rare moments?

Then I remembered the red magic lantern with the gold trim that was one of my cherished Christmas presents as a child. In playing with it, I had often wanted to be able to dissolve one picture into another, but no matter how I slid in the cards I was always frustrated. The lantern could throw only one picture on the screen at a time, and was so constructed that I had to lift out each card before I could insert another. Because of this one-picture-at-a-time characteristic, I thought of the magic lantern as a metaphor for the comparably limited seeing apparatus.

When a picture is in the slot — if I may use that parallel to describe a scene before the eyes — it does seem that there is some limitation in our perceiving, so that as a general rule the slotted image is the only one that can flash on the retina.

Much as I liked to operate the magic lantern myself, I loved it more when Old Mary, our cook, gave us showings in the library. Not only did she provide running commentary, but she made my sister and me feel very sophisticated by serving our milk in wineglasses. As I recalled those showings, I saw that, even if the parallel between the seeing apparatus and the magic lantern might not be perfect, the magic lantern, through the power of its projections, supported my theory.

During those showings, the library, with its heavy oak furniture, was always obliterated. Our attention was claimed so completely by the luminous pictures on the screen that even objects within eye-shot were invisible. So if a brick fireplace and book cases can be blotted out by what we are looking at with absorption, isn't it all the more likely that merely remembered things can be, and generally are, blotted out still more completely?

In the office lobby, then, it had been the grip on my attention of the new stairs, so much more graceful in their curve upwards to the left, that had paralyzed me from recalling the old heavy marble steps with the unimaginative square landings. In the new park, the trees and the toddling children prevented the picture of the vanished houses from getting into the central slot. This same phenomenon had operated with those G.I.'s on the desert. The picture of the barracks before their eyes was in the slot, claiming their minds so totally that they could not get the picture of the tents into place.

This brings me to the cardinal fact of vision first mentioned in connection with those soldiers. While some visual appearances undoubtedly have more power over the attention than others, and people vary in the extent to which they are gripped by the visual, the impact of scenes before the eyes is much greater than is commonly recognized. I believe, in fact, that the impact is so great that the mind is slightly stunned. I believe, too, that the mind's difficulty in picturing anything else simultaneously comes from being held in its immobility by the continuing force of the present scene. It is this combination of the brain's limitation with the image's force that accounts, I think, for our seeing nearly always being single.

Once I had isolated the effect of the present scene — the stunning of the mind into a sort of magic lantern-like rigidity — I was struck by another phenomenon: how easily the mind can shift from scene to scene when one's eyes are closed. If, say, one sits in the corner of a sofa, closing one's eyes, or perhaps merely shielding them with the hand, one can readily summon a host of visual impressions. The magic lantern becomes, as it were, a motion picture projector. Isolated slides, jerked in and out of place, become a roll of film where scenes of childhood dissolve into recollections of a few days back, and vice versa. Double exposures often present a large, animated portrait like a diaphanous veil, with remembered scenes taking place behind the huge close-up. And montages of Canada, Mexico, Europe, the United States follow each other with the same easy elimination of the space barrier as different periods of one's life reel off unimpeded by the time barrier.

The ease of visual recall when the eyes are released from the impact of what is before them deepened my conviction of that impact to stun. Knowing more about secondary elements, too, I could now analyze just why this stalling of the mind could curtail vision at the very moment when one would think it would be most alert — that is, when the eyes are deliberately staring. It is because such mental stalling bars the entrance of secondary elements. Memory, whether of past images, incidents, or feelings, is the great source of secondary elements. Intent single vision by its very nature — being so much in the present — tends to inhibit memory. Similarly, absorption in the actual, in the concrete world of objects, tends to inhibit the imagination, which, with its capacity to summon up projections, fantasies and possibilities, both likely and unlikely, is another great source of secondary elements. Since looking is a form of studying, concentration on comprehending physical forms also tends to block our access to another source of secondary elements — the bits and pieces of knowledge that are often jumbled in our minds. But notice the word "tends." I used it because, as moments of double-level perception prove, deliberate looking does not always cut off the secondary elements. It merely tends to — especially when there is no relaxation in the looking.

The rare instances when the secondary element is not only visual but simultaneously present (the sheik and the Ferris wheel, for example) illuminate the whole subject. When this occurs, the resulting vividness is so much greater than in normal vision that we are generally slightly startled. Generally, too, we have a sense of the preciousness of the experience. We also feel the sudden stepping up of vision has been spontaneous and effortless.

In a sense it is effortless, for in these instances the secondary element has been supplied, not by ourselves, but by circumstances. The feeling of spontaneity comes because the mental effort of correlating the two gratuitous images is so slight as to seem no effort at all. In other words, there has been none of the usual work of summoning the secondary element from either memory, imagination, or knowledge, and then finding the significant relationship between the present image and the things recalled.

That this combined effort is necessary before double-level perception can be deliberately induced, I think, explains why most of us do not have more of it. It is not just that we are lazy — though that plays its part — but because the human brain, wonderful as it is, tends to be like a messenger boy who can do only one thing at a time. And the brain finds it nearly impossible to make this combined effort while also striving to absorb sense impressions from the retinas.

Small wonder, then, that for most of us our only experiences of double-level perception are not induced but accidental. That such experiences are a bit startling reveals their rarity. And the way they surprise us indicates the degree to which singleness of vision is the prevailing mode of visual apprehension.

The sense of preciousness, too, points to the rarity of these moments. Even when they are not recognized as being caused by contrapuntal perception, emotionally we sense that most of the time our seeing does not have such vividness. For with single-level perception, too, the cause need not be recognized to have effect. One can be inhibited by one-track vision without ever being aware of the source of the limitation — or the nature of the loss.

CHAPTER 5

The Rivals: Reading and Seeing

ONE beautiful spring day I took a train ride into the country. Although I was properly appreciative of the sky's soft blueness and the subtle bud colors that haloed the skeletons of the trees, my eyes, exasperatingly, kept snapping to the billboards. Almost invariably, in fact, when given a choice between an effect of nature and a sign, they would choose the sign. Since the city-dweller sees so little of the changing seasons this seemed a particularly trivial choice. Why, I asked, should I waste this precious opportunity of looking at spring trees in favor of reading about Mrs. So and So's Snow-White Laundry?

Perhaps of all present images, printed words have the most power. That is, of course, to eyes that have been broken in to reading. For printed words may not stun or stall the mind — we are too accustomed to them for that — but they do grip it. And again and again, when they compete for the attention with other images, words win. For this reason reading can be a major factor in limiting our seeing.

Later, printed matter will be praised as an aid to vision, but in this chapter I will present it as a dreaded rival. And it was on that morning in the train going into the country that I figured out why the printed word has such power and why it generally wins the battle for our attention.

First, a simple fact dawned on me: The eye goes naturally to what it can comprehend most easily.

I had been taught to read and I had come to know the meaning of most words. Well-defined writing on signs was easier to discern than nature's elusive calligraphy, communicated through the colors and forms of trees, hillsides, clouds and stretches of sky. A big, sharply outlined symmetrical form like a *W,* for instance, was easier to grasp visually than the wavy, irregular outline of a tree's crest, so diaphanous with hints of buds that one could not tell where buds ended and sky began. And the curves of an S were so much more seizable than the curves of the hills descending to meet each other in the distant valley far off to the left.

Not only were letters easy in form, but they presented ready-made words. With trees one had to seek for species' names. Was it an oak, or perhaps a beech? With the sky, one had to search for the word to indicate the hue — cobalt, robin's egg, turquoise, sapphire, or what? No wonder one tends to grasp at *Gum, Beer,* or *Delicious,* where no word seeking is required.

The speed of the train, too, played its part. With everything flashing by so fast, mere scenes — even though momentarily framed — were harder to grasp than usual. And this swiftness of passage accentuated the headstart in ease of comprehension given the signs by our education.

I was beginning to resist the billboards, but, try as I might, I was still reading the damn things. The ease of comprehension theory obviously needed supplementing. Printed words, I realized, have also gained power from our education being so book-centered. For the stress on reading is not fortuitous. It derives from the value placed upon books — an evaluation so high that printed words have gained an authority out of all proportion to their intrinsic worth, an authority strengthened by the everlasting pressure on the student to devour books and more books. Those signs had such tugging power, then, because they benefited from the enormous authority printed words have gained and from the unrelenting pressure to consult them. Since my education has made me addicted to books, the signs also benefited from my addiction.

The tendency to *read* rather than to *see* is wonderfully illustrated by a remark made by G. K. Chesterton one evening, when he was strolling down Broadway. "What a glorious garden of wonders this would be," he exclaimed, "to anyone who was lucky enough to be unable to read."

To get the full irony, one has only to go to Broadway on a

rainy night and look at the reflections of the signs on the gleaming black pavement. Inverted and distorted, the reflected colored words are no longer legible. Not being able to read them, one sees them instead. Thus a staff of letters spelling out FRANKFURTERS will hang downward and, instead of evoking a piece of red tubing in a bun and the smell of mustard, it will be seen as a marvelous column of tremulous pink wavering a bit like a Chinese prayer on the black and splashed silver of the road bed.

Yet in a very real sense reading *is* seeing. Reading the page of a book, in fact, is a very remarkable feat of observation. If this has never struck you before, try the following experiment.

Take down a book from your shelves that you know has full-page illustrations, then time how long it takes you to read one of the printed pages.

For example, reading page 145 of Berenson's *Italian Painters of the Renaissance* just took me two minutes and fifteen seconds.

Now turn to one of the full-page illustrations and see how long you can look at it comfortably.

When I tried, I deliberately kept my eyes on the illustration longer than normal — beyond comfort, that is. Yet what did I find when I lifted my eyes from Boltraffio's "Head of the Madonna" and consulted my watch? Only thirty seconds had elapsed.

In other words, it required an effort for me to give the picture even a quarter of the time I could devote effortlessly to type covering the same number of square inches. In this new contest with looking, then, the printed word won as easily as it did with the billboards, scoring in fact a four-to-one victory. Perhaps you found the attention spans in your reading and viewing experiment had roughly the same ratio. If so, I hope the relative feebleness of your power to look at pictures greatly increased your respect for your ability to look at type.

Reading is indeed a remarkable visual skill, and relatively a new one, for there was no need for it in the centuries when communication was exclusively vocal. Even after man had invented pictographs as a means of sending messages and keeping records, reading, in the sense that we know it, had to wait on the invention of writing: that is, the use of abstract symbols to communicate meanings. And perhaps the most remarkable aspect of reading is the comprehension of these abstract characters, for, after all, groups of letters bear no resemblance to what they are meant to convey.

The deciphering aspect will come up later, but for the moment let us consider only the direct sensing of the characters, which obviously must precede translating them into known letters. And my further hope from the illustrated book experiment is that it made you realize that concentrating one's eyes for more than two minutes on an area as small as a book page is an amazing feat of discipline. Remember, too, the eyes were not merely held on the page haphazardly, but began at the top and traversed line after line to the end.

To fully appreciate this discipline one must recall how eyes are always moving about when one is not reading. In a room, say, they will go from ceiling to wall to window to floor to bookcase to table to ceiling to chair, and so forth. This is perfectly normal, for they need to take in many aspects of an environment to impart its nature to the mind. And the eyes move doubly: when we turn the head to aim the eyes in new directions; and when we shift the eyes within the unmoving head.

There is a good physiological reason for this, and, though I want to limit the discussion of ocular mechanics, I will cheerfully touch on it here, because I can use it as a single stone to kill two birds. For the physiology needed to explain why the eye moves so much will suffice for most of the book.

The man who has had no eye trouble to stir his interest in how his eyes work is apt to have two misconceptions: one, that only the front of the eye has much importance; the other, that the eye is like a spotlight that is flashed on the objects one wishes to see. The former arises, of course, from the fact that only the front of the eye shows. The latter comes from the sensation of seeing: objects the eye sweeps over do seem to come into view in much the same way as objects caught in the rays of a searchlight.

Despite appearances, the eyeball is not an ellipse made up of iris, white, and pupil. It comes by its playing-field name honestly, for, being bulbous, it actually resembles a ball. And at the back of the pitch-black interior is the retina, an area perhaps more important, and certainly more mysterious, than anything at the front.

For it is on the retina that impressions are formed. And the retina does not cast beams; it receives them.

The searchlight simile, because it seems to fit the facts, is hard to give up. Fortunately, however, modern science has provided a simile even more graphic in an invention closer in operation: the radio telescope, a giant parabolic reflector that can be rotated skyward to catch radio signals coming from outer space. Radio waves and light rays, it is true, are not the same, but the direction of the stimulus is: from without, inward. And note the name of those circular reflectors — dishes.

Retinas, being on the concave interiors of the backs of the eyeballs, are shaped like dishes, too. And in each such dish is an area known as the *macula*. Though more receptive than the retina's lateral fields, its responsiveness is sluggish in comparison to the tiny spot at its center known as the *fovea centralis*. Because the fovea is the eye's point of keenest alertness, light rays that hit the fovea form clearer and more detailed images than the rays falling on surrounding areas. Thus, when we want to see anything particularly clearly, we shift our eyes so the rays reflected from the chosen object will shine directly into our foveae.

The optic nerve is the conductor that carries the retinal images to the brain. I do not know how it works, and I have found that opinions differ as to whether retinal images are actual pictures or clusters of signals that get developed into pictures. Happily for our purposes, all we need to know is that the process operates in the manner demonstrated by the act of reading.

Take your vision of this page. At the point you have reached you will notice you can see the words clearly enough to discern their meaning, whereas, although you can see the other words in the page, you can not see them well enough to read them — that is, not unless you shift your foveae to focus on them.

Because our eyes are set with a space between them, each retina absorbs a slightly different image. However, we have a comfortable sense of a single image because the brain fuses the two pictures into one; in the process, merging the impressions that register on the two foveae. As a result, the pooled resources of the foveae suggest a single span, which this page can be used to demonstrate.

The foveae provide a narrow cone of clear sight. It has been calculated that a hundred feet ahead, the cone has a diameter of only five feet, and that at a thousand feet, it is still only fifty-two feet. Naturally, any cone that spreads so slightly is very narrow at the point where one commonly holds reading matter. And you can gauge its narrowness by noting how many times you shift your eyes as you take in a single one of these lines.

Experts who want to equip us to read more than we do call each pause an "eye fixation." More than three fixations a line, they say, is bad. Eye spans, they hold, can be extended, but even the most sanguine feel that the span is never likely to exceed a single line in a book, and they admit that half a line is exceptional. These limited spans, of course, are dictated by the foveae. And whatever the shift count in your case, it probably convinced you that the diameter encompassed by the foveae is small.

This restricted compass helps explain the constant moving of the yoked eyes. Not content with the vague, general impressions taken in by the fringes of the retinas, we supplement them by moving the foveae to focus on the items of greatest interest.

In contrast to all this directed movement, the eyes do a lot of unsystematic moving, most of which is unconscious. Not only does their structure allow it, but the eyes, it seems, always have to be on the move. As the experiment with the picture in the book showed, the foveae, like two pilots in close formation, love to have a large flying area. For it was restriction that made them desert the picture after a mere thirty seconds.

This brings us back to consider that however innately restless the eye, however undisciplined it is in most viewing situations, the control it exercises in reading a page of type is positively astounding. The average page has at least two thousand letters. They are all relatively small, yet the eye observes each one carefully enough to recognize the letter it represents. Furthermore it makes its observations along a predetermined and rigidly followed course, probably endurable only because that course allows the eye to move continuously.

How did such discipline ever become possible? The answer, of course, is training, training, and more training. Yet unfortunately, this drilling to read is about the only eye-training our educational system gives us. That system, which places so much emphasis on what it calls teaching us to think — using that as an excuse for inflicting some of the deadliest material on the youthful brain — ironically enough, pays practically no attention to training one of the organs that does most to feed the mind with the impressions it needs to think about.

For the present, however, our general lack of eye-training is a side issue. What is pertinent here is that our specific eye-training in learning to read provides still another explanation for why the eye snaps to billboards when often the visual field holds matter of so much beauty and interest. It is because the eye, through training, has learned to observe words skillfully. When one considers too, that reading is habit-forming, and that educational pressures have all been on the side of words, it is only natural that the eye should feel more at home with words than with anything else.

Having established that reading is seeing, let me now elucidate how this type of seeing is stripped of some of the chief benefits of normal ocular sensing. The first example was implicit in what one loses in reading the Broadway signs instead of seeing them as beautifully colored Chinese characters. A second instance came about from another contest between the rivals, also unpremeditated. It, too, took place on a train, but on a winter journey, during which I decided on a particular visual diversion: to look only at colors.

Along the roadbed, projecting through the snow, were clumps of tall withered grass. What was its color? I poked and poked at my brain, till finally I had it: lion hair — specifically, the color of the long wild hairs of the male's great mane. Next, what was the color of those winter-bound cedars? Again I poked until I realized that their combination of green, black, and brown suggested the discolored lapels of a dinner jacket left unused in a closet for many years.

My perceptions tend to be form-bound, for I see objects primarily as forms, only seeing their color later, and then generally as coats applied externally. Thus for me to suppress the perception of form in favor of color was hard. Nevertheless, as I made a conscious effort to see colors as distinct entities rather than as the properties of objects, I noticed that very few colors were pure primaries.

Most of them were mixtures. My fountain pen, for example, was blue, but not a pure blue. At first, though, I could neither name its shade nor define its admixture. Finally I arrived at teal blue, and realized I could not separate its elements because they were so completely blended. Some mixtures, however, were not blended at all, as in the particular red of a weathered barn we passed. A compound, it was created in part by the faded paint and in part by the ancient boards whose gray showed where the paint had worn away.

As I continued trying to identify and analyze color effects, I became quicker at it. I also became more acutely aware of colors all around me. Just how acutely, I found when a call from nature took me to a room at the end of the coach. There, to my amazement, I saw that the mundane instruction, "To Flush Use Foot Pedal," was emblazoned in letters of gold.

It was the gold that amazed me. Although my reading addiction had led me to read the sign on an earlier visit, I swear I never saw the gold. This time, besides the gold, I saw the black outlines of the lettering displayed on its field of olive green. On this second reading, then, direct sensing triumphed; I took in the words' appearance, whereas before I had absorbed only their message.

This is quite common, for unless there is something extraordinary about the lettering — like the beauty of an illuminated manuscript — we scrap the visual impression of words as soon as we perceive them. If we read a story with a good deal of description, we see not the words themselves, but what they conjure up. Even with abstract discourse, our mind tends to absorb the thing said and not the type face in which it is set.

That color perception is not needed for reading is amply demonstrated by the fact that the majority of printed matter is in black and white. To the practiced reader, even form perception is minimal; he sees letters not as forms, but as symbols. Even the beginning reader soon ceases to see the capital A like the legs of a sawhorse. Instead, it hits him as the first letter of the alphabet. Actually, he is more apt to think of its sound than its appearance, while more advanced readers lose the appearance of letters still further by absorbing clumps of them as words of known meaning.

Reading and seeing, then, each make a distinct use of the eyes.

Visual perception is concerned with taking in the image; and this means absorbing its colors, textures, forms, placement in space, every thing, in fact, that contributes to its exact appearance. Reading, on the other hand, discards the image in favor of the meaning. One discerns, the other deciphers.

Calling attention to this distinction, however, does not imply making a value judgment. If we didn't suppress type images we would hardly achieve any reading at all. And it is interesting to note that those who advocate faster reading have worked out devices, including mechanical reading pacers, that goad the reader into still fewer eye fixations, still less dwelling on type appearances, as he tries to keep up with the crossbar of the pacer as it sprints down the page at the speed his reading is supposed to equal.

It would be nice if all the efforts to speed up reading were motivated by the desire to reduce the time spent, thus liberating the eyes for more observing. Alas, one has only to glance at the average prospectus for a speed-up course to see that it is after more reading in *as much* time.

Reading being the absorbing thing it is, all this emphasis on more rapid reading — with, as we are assured, "improved retention" — will, I feel, also lead to more hours spent in reading. But already reading seriously interferes with observing. Most obviously it does so by claiming the eyes and the ocular energies for long periods of time. But it also interferes with practice.

In reading, the deciphering eye races past familiar symbols, suppressing each visual impact at the instant of recognition. Consequently, the eye, far from exercising and developing its discerning skill by coping with the subtleties of the unfamiliar, observes as little as possible. Whether its observing faculties are actually weakened by prolonged disuse, I cannot say. But I am sure they are not strengthened. It stands to reason, too, that where one ocular faculty is employed constantly and its opposite hardly at all, the imbalance in favor of the frequently used is sure to increase. Further, because what we do most becomes habitual, the more we fall into the habit of reading the more we fall out of that of observing.

Habit brings up another factor. Since this chapter takes the side unfriendly to books, I will call it their pernicious magic. The interest of books is endless; besides which, they offer romance, adventure, escape, beauty, information, ideas, and the enormous pleasure of good story-telling. That books can become an addiction in themselves — as distinct from greed in gobbling print — is proved by children who fall in love with books even before they can read.

Our education, then, chains our eyes to reading, and books make us hug our chains. An ironical situation develops. The use of our seeing faculties for one purpose — to decipher characters that convey meanings — becomes a deterrent to our using those faculties for observing colors, forms, shapes, etc. We read instead of looking. Often, because we read so much, we have no time for looking. And many get so that they would rather read than look. With far too many people this preference prevails regardless of the worth of what is read. The proof is to be found on our railroads. Again and again, in walking down the aisle of a train, you will find that, heedless of the scenery, the eyes of nearly all the travelers are occupied with their newspapers, their magazines, and their paperback novels. It is sad to think that the only eye-training we get, instead of enabling us to see more, frequently fixes us in habits that insure our seeing less.

CHAPTER 6

The Camera Eye and the Valve Mind

Once, when preparing illustrations for a book on Mexico, I had the problem of indicating the façade of a church. I stroked in some pillars and roughly outlined the saints, doing only ovals for heads, and merely suggesting the shoulders, the robes and a few draped sleeves. I worked quickly and freely. Yet at a certain point, when I lifted my hand from the paper, I was startled by the result. The façade looked so much more lifelike than I expected. It was so like itself, in fact, that I was puzzled.

Why, I asked myself, when I have drawn so little of the detail, is so much of the façade suggested? How can a few scratchy lines give the impression of solid, fully enclosed forms?

I showed the sketch to a few friends, who responded as I did, which showed I had not deluded myself about its effectiveness. Ensuing discussion enabled me to rephrase my question: How could so rough a sketch seem such an adequate representation of reality?

Since the sketch did not correspond with the reality of the façade, I saw the answer must lie in the realm of psychology. Surely there was some psychological consonance between what one felt in front of the façade and what one felt in front of the sketch. This gave me my clue. Perhaps the sketch seemed to represent reality because we see sketchily.

I tested the theory by thinking of other sketches that people obviously have no difficulty in accepting as representations of reality. In fact, a sketch by a great artist like Toulouse-Lautrec seems to catch the reality of a character more sharply than the more developed studies of many lesser artists. And when I remembered Berenson's discussion of how people "visualize" I knew I had an ally. For in classifying people's power of visual recall, Berenson said very few have the ability to visualize perfectly: that is, to conjure up what they have seen with complete clarity. When I reread his words that the recalled image was generally "so vague, so elusive, that it tantalizes rather than satisfies," I felt elated. The phenomenon of the elusive image not only confirmed, but was explained by my theory that our seeing is sketchy. But the theory led to many more questions. Formerly, I had always thought we saw photographically.

I had good reasons, for, in many ways, the eye does operate like a camera. It can certainly observe with remarkable exactitude. Take Roger Fry's shrewd example that the eye can look at margarine and detect the almost indiscernible signs proving it is not butter. Further, the eye can convey to the brain what an object feels like to touch. The eye, then, can take remarkable close-ups — and it can snap them with the ease and speed of a camera's shutter.

The eye, too, can take remarkable long shots, for it can look on a big scene and, in an instant, scan every area. The proof is that in a scene before us every inch of the visual field is filled, unlike an uncompleted painting with blank patches where the canvas still shows. Provided the light is strong, the eye can also see details of a big scene with remarkable clarity.

To "flash-glimpse" is the phrase I developed for this particular capacity, and its resemblance to taking a snapshot strengthened the photographic notion. Only after much thought, recollection and reading, did I resolve the apparent contradiction between the fact that the eye, obviously, does have camera-like faculties and my newer discovery that we see sketchily.

A cross-section of a human profile, glimpsed in a drugstore window, provided the first breakthrough by reminding me that the eye at the front of the head and the brain on top are different organs. This recalled Aldous Huxley's description in *The Art of Seeing* of how the brain and eye act differently in the process of observing. Huxley's differentiation led me to forget the eye for a moment and to think of the brain's role in isolation. And here gleanings from other people came back to me. One was Elizabeth de Treviño's story of how her two sons had reacted when, on different occasions, they had seen the same statue in the Alameda in Mexico City.

The statue was of a nude woman lying with her face down and one knee bent up under her, her hands chained behind her back. The younger son, a lad of tender heart, looked at the statue, turned to his mother and asked: "What did the poor lady do?"

The older son, passing the statue on another day, asked: "Do you mean to say they carved all that out of a single piece of stone?"

Obviously, both boys saw the same thing. Yet the brain of one abstracted from the marble the impression of a living woman being cruelly punished, whereas the other was impressed primarily by the marble itself.

The more I questioned people about what they saw most vividly, the more I became aware that the differing elements selected from the statue by the two boys illustrated a good deal about human vision. Eyes take in similar things, but by the time individual brains, whether consciously or unconsciously, have worked on common visual material the end results differ.

Take, for instance, the following colloquy: Four of us were sitting around on a summer evening, and one friend, Stephan Nalbantian, an electrical engineer, not content with questions about vision in the abstract, proposed that each man say what went through his mind when looking at power lines. The first thing he looked at, he said, was the size of the wires. Then he thought of the currents going through them, wondering what their voltages were. To help with this problem he counted the number of insulators. I laughed out loud. His testimony was so different from my own. I saw patterns against the sky: upright posts threaded together by long, slightly sagging filaments. Equally surprising were the two other answers. The television program director saw only one thing: communication. The writer of advertising copy for Madison Avenue saw "something that should not be there, spoiling the scenery."

Surprised by the variety of our answers, we were struck by how each response was conditioned by individual life experience. The engineer, who had installed power lines in his youth, could not help but think of practical factors. I, on the other hand, who had done a lot of sketching and had never even watched an installation crew, could see only the picture the wires made. The television man, whose life was tied up in communication, saw in the wires a symbol of his great concern. The country-loving ad man, in contrast, saw none of these — only a desecration, something ugly to wipe off his visual slate.

In having our vision shaped by our lives, the four of us, I was to find, were typical human beings, particularly in having what we observe influenced by our interests. People interested in automobiles, for instance, tend to notice the makes of different cars, whereas those with no such interest see only giant metallic beetles. Women interested in clothes notice things in store windows that escape men altogether. And so forth. The tendency is for the mind to admit some visual images and to exclude others. Excitedly, I realized the brain acts as a sort of valve.

Although I have since come to feel the valve metaphor is too mechanistic, the idea of it helped greatly in resolving my sketch-photograph contradiction. What it dramatized and clarified is that if the eye is a mechanism acting in one way, the brain is a mechanism acting in another. Seeing is the combined result. And although the eye has a camera-like ability to take in everything on which it focuses, the mind selects so little from the visual field that, almost invariably, we bring away no more than a sketch.

Paradoxically, the camera-like eye itself contributes to sketchiness of vision. This arises from the three-part nature of the retina: the fovea, which records with extreme sharpness only at its very center, the macular region around the fovea, whose recording is definitely less distinct, and the lateral fields, whose recording is downright vague.

Thus, although every scene before the eye appears to be complete, its parts are recorded with varying degrees of definition. Furthermore, students of the perceptual sciences have discovered that there is a relationship between retention and reception. Objects seen with central, highly focused sight are remembered longest, while objects glimpsed from the corner of the eye fade most rapidly from the memory.

The eye's structure, then, abets the mind's natural tendency to suppress at the same time as it selects. But even when this is recognized the eye's camera faculties remain so remarkable that the photographic concept of the visual system is hard to shake, even harder than the notion that the eye resembles a searchlight.

Once I understood that the eye's power to flash-glimpse is probably what has done most to foster the illusion that we see photographically, I could clear up other misconceptions spawned by its flash-glimpsing ability. I now believe that one of the ironies of this great gift is that awareness of it helps keep vision limited by making us overconfident. Because we can flash-glimpse so well, we tend to think we see everything. And this ocular overconfidence is perhaps an even greater restricter of observation than single level vision and excessive reading.

This can be illustrated by the delusions created by this flash-glimpsing power. The most obvious is that we see a great deal. But in truth, because the valve of the mind is nearly always set at a screening angle, we observe relatively little — certainly, far less than what we have the power to see. Flash-glimpsing also breeds three other misconceptions — all mischievous: that seeing is effortless; that it requires no time, and that, being photographic, it is objective.

Surely the reading illustration disposes of the first two delusions. There we saw that, although the eye can see a whole page of type in a twinkling, such a flash-glimpse is so vague that none of the type registers sharply enought to be legible. Most effortless glances are equally superficial and cursory. If one really wants to see what a page contains, one must patiently direct the foveae to decipher the characters. Besides effort, this takes time. In fact, few readers manage more than 250 words a minute.

But reading is a peculiar kind of seeing, you may retort, quoting my theory that visual images are suppressed in favor of the meanings they convey. But even the more normal type of seeing — that which depends on visual images — also requires time and effort.

This was brought home to me in Mexico when making a detailed drawing of the church façade that I had merely sketched earlier. The façade's three main stories were all elaborately carved. Once I had its skeleton blocked in, I began depicting its details, working from the top down. The work took hours because I was drawing with painstaking accuracy. When I finally got to the lowest story, I became aware of what I had not noticed before: The style of the carving here differed slightly from the carving higher up, and this lower carving had a quality of . . . And here words failed me. I could define neither the carving's distinctive nature nor what it recalled.

Since my immediate task was to depict the façade in lines — not describe it in words — I let the literary frustration pass and went on drawing, for the pedestals of the lowest pillars and their heraldic emblems still had to be done.

Half an hour later a phrase came effortlessly to mind — "embossed leather." And I realized the unusual lower carving resembled the organized welts one sees on old books that have been bound in richly tooled leather.

When my literary problem was solved, I pondered how that simile came to me. Detailing the carving on the upper stories had taken time, and this time had played perhaps as big a role as exact observing in making me familiar with their style. Later, recall of what had grown familiar above had enabled me to realize that the upper style differed from the lower style — as figured brocade differs from embossed leather!

Time, then, had operated on my conscious mind in three main ways. The most obvious was in visual digesting: Taking time to examine the façade had allowed me not only to notice many features but to absorb them. Time's two less obvious roles were no less important. Understanding the way visual impressions can stun the mind enabled me to explain the first, for the size and complexity of that façade had fixed my mind in the sort of magic-lantern rigidity described earlier. The characteristic style of the lower tier carving eluded me because my mind, gripped by the force of the present image, was not free to think effectively. Time, by slowly diminishing the effect of being stunned, allowed me to recover from the impact. The other process — the growing familiarity with the absorbed details — helped dissolve the paralysis, too. When the recovery was complete my mind had its old freedom to operate and I found my simile.

Time had also helped my unconscious mind, for when I abandoned my search for a definition of the carving style I committed the problem to what Henry James has called "the deep well of un-conscious cerebration."

That well always includes a vast reservoir of visual memories. The ease with which we can tap the reservoir varies from person to person, and from period to period in the same individual's life. Obviously the particular effect of embossed leather — could it have been deposited in childhood by our huge Family Bible? — was one of the visual memories buried in my own reservoir. Time allowed forces in my unconscious to stir the reservoir, until the image of the embossed leather was pried free. Once loosened, that secondary image, which simultaneously fixed and defined the resemblance, came to the surface easily.

That I gained so much from this long session with the façade only pointed up how little I had gained in many previous glances. It convinced me that, in direct sensing, the flash-glimpse is as in-adequate as it is in reading. For at a glance, although every detail may register on the retina, few details reach the brain unless the effort is made to grasp them, and this involves, among other things, freeing the brain for their reception.

The need to free the brain to receive exact images brings us to the final misconception — that seeing is objective. And the valve concept was introduced chiefly to demonstrate that seeing is not nearly as photographic — and hence as objective — as it seems.

Once I had evolved the valve idea I turned to experimental psychology to see what it had to say about the matter. I turned in the right direction, for in the field of visual influences that are non-optical — that arise more from the intellect and the psyche than from appearances — experimental psychologists have made remarkable discoveries. The photographic concept of seeing, as I had discovered for myself, did not take into account the mind's role in the seeing process. What the psychologists, particularly Kurt Koffka, showed was that my idea that we saw objectively, but only sketchily, was based on a more complete concept of the visual system. But this idea, including the mind as well as the eye, was still not complete enough. For the psychologists enabled me to under-stand that a third great factor in the system is the ego.

When the mind selects, it is not governed merely by the things logically pertaining to the mind that I have singled out — life experience, specific interests and particular associations. It is also governed by emotional needs, by twists of personality, by values, by expectations, by purposes and by such well-established tricks of the ego as repression, projection, sublimation, and defense mechanisms.

The valve, if it can really be considered as such, is indeed a versatile mechanism. Besides regulating inflow and outflow, it has suction power; it can throw lights of varying intensity on what slips past it; it can color; it can elaborate; and it can distort.

Evidence of these capacities will keep emerging in future chapters, so I do not want to discuss them fully here. Some, however, can be suggested by examples that have already appeared. My seeing threats rather than marvelous scenery in the mountainous badlands of New Mexico is one example of projection. Another is the television director's "seeing" something so invisible as "communication" in power lines. In contrast, the ad man's seeing the same lines as scenic desecration is an example of repression. There is repression, too, in the instant rejection of the appearance of type faces in reading.

By coining such phrases as "selector tendencies" and "reaction sensitivities," psychologists like Robert R. Blake, Glenn V. Ramsey, and Norman Cameron gave me deeper insight into the two reactions of the boys before the statue in Mexico's Alameda. Being young, their vision had not yet been influenced by worldly careers as had those of the electrical engineer and the television director. Instead, the boys responded according to their natures. The younger boy, who wondered what the poor lady was being punished for, and the older boy, who was amazed that such a thing could be carved from one piece of stone, obviously saw the same thing — objectively. But, because they had different sensitivity reactions, what they saw *subjectively* was different.

Their reaction sensitivities — emotional, compassionate, humane, and shrinking from injustice in the case of the one boy; intellectual, detached, and technically calculating on the part of the other — were already determining their selector tendencies. And it is interesting to note that the boy whose greatest interest was in how the statue was carved grew up to be a professional artist.

The world, then, for most of us — because our vision is so

swayed by our natures and backgrounds, our needs and our values, our egos and our minds — is like a great Rorschach ink-blot. We interpret it as we will. And this brings me back to the danger of overconfidence generated by the ability to flash-glimpse. For the tendency to see the world as a magnified Rorschach blot is particularly strong in those who rely chiefly on panoramic glances for their impressions. They are the ones who interpret it most wildly — regardless of visual reality.

Our seeing will probably always be swayed by subjective factors, yet, thanks to the nature of the eye, we need not be at the mercy of those factors. By the nature of the eye, I mean its photographic nature, for even if the camera metaphor also tends to be too mechanistic, it corresponds to physiological facts more exactly than the valve metaphor. The eye in isolation *is* like a camera, and can be remarkably objective. But what needs to be more fully realized about this marvelous instrument is how much of what it does or does not perceive depends on the intelligence of the will directing it. Eliminating the misconceptions of over-confidence can aid the intelligence.

When, for instance, we wipe away the misconception that seeing is objective we are no longer deceived about the ego being absent. And when we recognize it as a strong influence, we are no longer helplessly victimized by that previously unrecognized distorter. We can watch for, and, by constantly checking and rechecking, counteract what prove to be its discolorations. This, of course, involves the two things our flash-glimpsing powers tend to make us feel we don't need — time and effort. But they are vital, not only for what they pick up themselves, but for how they can correct what the ego picks up incorrectly or scrappily.

The eye is quicker and more willing than the brain, and registers an enormous amount of data. Because it takes ocular snapshots that can be studied like photographs in news magazines, the eye itself, if we will let it, can assist the intelligence. But we need patience to examine and think about all it takes in. For, if one is to become truly observant, one must learn to stir the mind to operate on the visual field, and give it time to go about its business. Without time and effort, even though the eye takes marvelous pictures, we neither retain them nor see a tenth part of what is in them.

CHAPTER 7

The Reservoir of Visual Images

A solitary journey can often be made more interesting if you invent a visual game to help pass the time. My looking exclusively at colors on the train is an instance. An even better invention occurred to me one winter morning on the Ottawa airfield as I sat in a plane waiting to start the first stretch of a dogleg flight to New York. The spontaneous finding of three similes set me off.

The upside-down cups shielding the strip lights were like the blue glasses that hold flickering votive candles in many Roman Catholic churches. Next, a stand of unpainted wood resembled the drill instructor's stands in the Army's basic-training centers. Snow was swirling off the paved runway, and the third simile came as I watched it blow over the snow "dunes."

The unsummoned similes gave me so much pleasure that I decided I would spend the rest of the trip deliberately hunting more of them. Actually, what I had hit on was a device for speeding up the process I showed operating slowly in the last chapter. There the embossed leather simile had surfaced because time and relaxation allowed some mental gate to swing open, making possible an interchange between the present image of the façade and the past image of the Family Bible. Stated generally, I had established a two-way connection between present seeing and the reservoir of visual memories. My simile game, then, was a means of opening the turnvalve between past and present visual experience so they could merge with an ease of interflow they do not have normally.

In the plane, however, I was not nearly that analytical — or as comprehending. Instinct, though, told me to set up certain ground rules. To get my mind working on objects my eye might light on, I decided to ask: "What does it recall"? I further resolved that I would insist on an answer different in species: I would not let a small lake, say, remind me of a small lake, or a railway track of a railway track. The lake would have to be something like a jigsaw puzzle piece, or the railway track a ribbon with metallic threads.

The rules set, I found myself stumped by the first thing that caught my eye: a hoarding with white and orange checks that we taxied past. Though I could not place it, I was pretty sure it recalled something. Some vibration of memory insisted that somewhere in my reservoir of visual images was the counterpart of that checkered hoarding. What's it like? I asked myself urgently, for I realized we were leaving the hoarding behind and soon there would be new objects to veil my memory of it. What does it recall? I asked, to renew my efforts, for now I was completely certain it had touched a visual memory.

Suddenly my memory threw up the phrase: A cereal package! I breathed a sigh of relief — I had located the buried image. Immediately, I tried to get the image clearer: What kind of cereal? What's the brand? What's the name?

It was no use. I could not make the final identification. Meanwhile, the plane had made its rush and lifted into the air and I was distracted from my quest by seeing roadtracks looping below in the snow. Easily, I recalled a row of three old-fashioned tortoiseshell hairpins. A stream suggested wormtracks in wood.

Now we were in a world uncomplicated by color, the over-all impression of whiteness being heightened by a white sun shining diffusedly in my eyes from an all-white sky. What did those field boundaries suggest as they converged towards the gleaming mist that obscured the horizon? The answer came fairly readily: the perspective lines in a drawing by Uccello.

Then, an isolated patch of trees caught my attention. What did it recall? An island of crew-cut hair on an otherwise shaved head with the snow at the roots of the trees resembling the skin of the skull.

Because the Ottawa Valley is flat, the terrain between Ottawa and Montreal is not particularly interesting. Despite my game, I wearied of nothing but Uccello sketches. Perhaps looking would be more fun inside the plane. And as I turned my head away from the window, I saw a girl sitting across the aisle, her face framed in sharp profile against a circular window. I am sure it was because I had got into the simile swing that I saw her so instantly as a head on a coin. And I am equally sure this swiftness of response came, in part, from the mental agility developed by my exercise with the landscape outside. The young woman's frizzy hair and earrings gave her a slightly gypsy look. Her nose was prominent and there was a rounded fullness under her chin. Something about her was — and here my mind paused an instant before it formulated the impression — Pompeian. I knew that in thinking of classical antiquity I was on the right track. A moment later I had located even the currency — a Greek coin.

I was amazed. I had never had any interest in coins and in quickly passing over pictures of ancient money I had assumed they had left no visual deposits. I would have sworn I had never observed Greek coins carefully enough to have a definite notion of their character. Yet here, in this recognition of the gypsy look, the projecting nose, and the fullness under the chin, was proof that those pages, so quickly leafed through, had dropped precise visual images into the reservoir of my memory.

Suddenly the rounded jaw began to move. I almost laughed out loud at the incongruity of a Greek goddess chewing gum. As I chuckled, I realized a new advantage of my game. If I hadn't seen that young woman so vividly as a figure on a coin, I would hardly have noticed she was chewing gum. Certainly, I would not have been entertained by any sense of the disparity between her classical appearance and bovine activity. In other words, seeing one aspect of a thing vividly automatically makes you aware of other aspects, too.

Montreal was the hinge of the dogleg and as the plane descended for its stopover, the outside world reclaimed my attention. Montreal is on an island that splits the Ottawa River as it flows into the St. Lawrence. The island is linked to the mainland by several great bridges, and the one that caught my eye had a deck hung beneath a huge girder arch. I put my question and got the answer: It recalled New York's Hell Gate Bridge. But my rules forced me to disqualify this simile for being a description of the object in its own terms. Again I had a sense of urgency, for my brain still had not produced a simile and the banking of the plane showed that the bridge would soon be out of sight. At last the simile came. The bridge suggested two construction cranes curving their necks forward to kiss each other.

Once we were in the air again, the flight route went along the course of the St. Lawrence. The center of the river was not frozen over, but a shelf of ice reached out from the nearest bank. Traced on the snowy shelf were black paths. What did they recall? Again, I knew it was something vaguely familiar, without being able to say just what. Then I got an approximation: primitive rock painting. Was it paleolithic, something from a cave, or something closer to our own era? Suddenly, to my amazement, my mind produced the answer: Bushman art.

Leafing through art books had left another unrealized deposit. I had hardly looked at those thin human figures with small heads and jutting rumps, yet obviously those South African paintings had left a sufficiently clear impression for me to recognize their counterparts on the snowy ice. I realized, too, that the accidental Bushman art below had caused me to notice the ice shelf in my effort to account for the flat snow on which the figures were drawn, another example of how observing one aspect leads to seeing a related one.

The Bushman image had swum up from a remote part of my visual experience. A moment later a very recently acquired image came to my aid when I muttered that the vapor rising from the dark river was like snow blowing in slow motion over an asphalt runway.

We passed an island with a snubby nose. At first it suggested a tear drop, but not exactly, because its tail curved. I fished in my reservoir and soon had what I wanted: The island was like a lozenge in a Paisley shawl.

Another island, with an escarpment at its stubby front, was shaped like the cap of the airline stewardess. With the images of the lozenge and the cap fixed in my mind, I was struck to see how many other islands had stubby fronts. I deduced that the current had given the islands their shape — or rather, they had survived the river's erosion because they were like ships with sheltering stone bows. I further deduced that, because we were headed in the same direction as the rounded bows, we were flying upstream. The stewardess confirmed this, and again I was delighted at how one observation had led effortlessly to others.

But even pleasant mental exercises grow tiring and after a while I relinquished my game. As lunch was served, though, the game gained a new lease on life. We were now over the Adirondacks and dessert happened to be vanilla ice cream with chocolate sauce. Glancing out the window I was surprised to see how closely the snowy hills resembled my sundae, with their ice cream-like contours and their "chocolatey" trees.

Food as a source of visual similes — this was the corner of the reservoir that, once tapped, revitalized the game. Immediately I decided to seek gustatory aid to define the color of the exposed lining of a camel's hair coat that lay over the back of a nearby seat. Caramel came to mind but was rejected; too brown and too dark a shade. Then I got the word butterscotch — which was exactly right, and suggested the lining's glossy lustre as well as its hue.

As we came over a lake district, the bodies of water prompted simile after simile. A fat side of beef, a weasel with no front paws, a footprint, an arrowhead, a lamp on a bicycle's front fender were among the objects effortlessly suggested by the shapes below. And when we neared New York and shot out over the ocean, I rejoiced in this last set of impressions, for I was able to see that the cloud shadows were like lake shapes, only a little more jaggedly edged. And what was the color of the water on which these shadows rested? The dark green of boiled string beans left too long on a plate. Again I had my lunch to thank for an image.

We made a U-turn over the string bean sea and began approaching Kennedy Airport. Near the shore was a church whose color I tried to define. It was not yellow, nor was it brown. What color was it then? Remembering food as a field of reference, I thought of maple walnut ice cream. Not close enough, for it wasn't sufficiently yellow, but at last the right shade came. That church, with the two stubby front towers, was caramel custard.

And what did I see when we were on the ground? Strip lights guarded by inverted cups like the blue glasses that shelter candles before Catholic altars. Their familiarity showed with what memorable clarity that simile had enabled me to see the strip lights in Ottawa. That those in New York had yellow bouffant skirts made me realize that, without registering the impression at the time, I had nevertheless noticed the Ottawa lights had similar tin skirts.

The airport bus takes about an hour to get into the city, which allowed time for thought about the flight. Having given the name, "Look Only at Colors," to the visual game I had developed earlier on a train ride led me to seek a designation for the game I had played on the plane. Perhaps the vaguely remembered childhood game of Hunt the Slipper suggested "Hunt the Simile." At all events, that was my choice, and I began assessing the new game's virtues.

The second experience with the strip lights enabled me to summarize a number of them. Not only did the game make you consciously take in salient aspects, but it also induced you to see additional aspects unconsciously. Also, it fixed objects in the memory in a way that gave pleasure at both the moment of the fixing and later when the retained object showed up again like an old friend. The fact that I was eager to tell my friends at the office about all I had noticed showed, too, that the game makes visual experience so exhilarating you want to talk about it.

Next, I realized the game provided a series of fresh examples of double-level perception. Because each object seen from the plane was compared mentally with the object it suggested, the game underlined how contrapuntal perception makes one see with preternatural sharpness. The game, then, was a method of inducing double-level perception. Not only this; it also provided a means to escape the rut of single-track vision. And the game's influence in the airplane made me aware of how double-level perception could be extended. It did not need to be confined to an incident or a scene. It could also be used to bring isolated objects into unforgettable focus.

The way the similes began coming more quickly and with less effort showed another advantage of the game; you got better at it as you played. Thinking about its acceleration was instructive.

The turnvalve between past and present visual experience often opens of its own accord, but, whether moving spontaneously or being turned deliberately, it tends to act like a water tap with a spring in it: that is, to snap shut the moment the hand is lifted. The swift, easy coming of all the later similes surely was evidence that my game did more than open the valve; it wedged it so it remained open.

That each source of the interflow was stimulated was proved by the fact that at the same time as I had readier access to my visual memories I kept picking up more present sights. And the multiplicity of the new impressions showed the game was worth playing for the sake of the future. It was an excellent way of enriching one's store of visual impressions.

Visual memories are stored in the mind in the form of pictorial images. And such images, I realized, comprise a visual vocabulary — one whose role in seeing is comparable to a verbal vocabulary in thinking. Just as you don't get stuck for a word in thinking if you have a large vocabulary, so you don't get stuck in seeing if you have a large collection of images. Similarly, just as your verbal fluency is increased by having your words easily accessible, your visual fluency is increased by having your images freely on tap. And just as words help you to grasp and hold abstract ideas, parallel images help you to grasp and hold concrete impressions. Witness that caramel custard church that stands out so vividly in my memory amid all the welter of buildings we flew over in coming into New York.

My mind was shifting from the idea of similes to the idea of the images, which were the base of those similes. And the name of another childhood game came to me. Perhaps "Fishpond" would be as good a name as "Hunt the Simile," for actually I had been fishing in my reservoir of visual images to catch those that, through similarity, would help describe the things I had been seeing.

As this clarified, I realized it would be fun to examine some of the images I had caught, to see from what parts of the reservoir they had come. Some, like the snow blowing off the runway, the stewardess's cap, and the chocolate sundae had come from the flight itself — in other words, from the very surface. But others came from greater depths: the drill instructor's stand from my days in the Army; the tortoise-shell hairpins from my grandmother's visits when I was a boy; the dunes from happy summers by the sea; the construction cranes from watching skyscrapers go up in New York; and the blue altar glasses from earlier visits to Catholic churches in French Canada. The cereal package must have come from idle moments waiting for service in grocery stores. Goodness knows where the Paisley lozenges came from — perhaps from a scarf I had been given once for Christmas. The crew cuts probably dated from the late Thirties when they became the rage with college students.

Three of the images clearly came from reading art books. One was the recollection of Uccello's studies in perspective, which had not surprised me, for I was well aware of my interest in Italian Renaissance art. In contrast were the two memories that had been surprising: the Greek coins and the Bushman art.

The images, then, came from many different pockets of experience, and from all periods of my life. Some came from far back in childhood, some from only half an hour before. Some had been fixed in my mind with a recognition of their impact at the time they were received, but others had registered without my knowing it. With some the unrecognized moment of registration had become plain when a similar object had recalled the original. But with others the registration had been so unconscious as to be totally forgotten.

Realizing how the stored images had vivified the things I had seen on the flight, I resolved to stock my mind with still more visual images. Meanwhile, consciousness of my own brain-load of remembered images made me realize that every one else's brain was crammed with mental pictures. I saw that they too, whether consciously or unconsciously, brought their old pictures to things they saw.

This gave me fresh insight into my friends' reactions to the face cards. The actor who saw the queens of diamonds and hearts as sisters, did so, I realized, because of his own two handsome sisters. Kathleen Tappen, who saw them as the wives and daughters of Flemish burghers, did so because she had memories of paintings by Memling and Lucas Van Leyden.

That evening with Kathleen provided another illumination of this new insight. We had looked together at a large baroque form in the shaft of one of her lamps. To me it suggested a plume, which amazed her, as she had always seen it as a leaf. We had seen the same form, then, but had interpreted it diversely because we had brought to it different visual memories. Hers had been a similarly shaped leaf, mine a plume. And a day or two later I tracked the memory down to the erect central plume in the cluster of three in the coat of arms of the Prince of Wales, whose visit to North America in 1927, unaccountably, had made an indelible impression on my boyish mind.

Our stores of visual images, then, are among the associations that tamper with the camera-like recording of the eye. And my game, I further realized, had increased my sense of the subjectivity of seeing, as well as amplifying why such influences as I mentioned in the last chapter — working careers, social backgrounds, specific interests, values, and the like — play such a role in what we select to see. All those sources contribute their own particular images to our specific reservoirs. Stored images tend to pick out their counterparts from new visual fields. They also influence the way the counterparts are seen. When seeking how to describe the huge riven cliffs of *El Morro,* I had had an interesting experience, and this, too, was illuminated by the counterpart phenomenon. What I did was show a postcard of the cliffs to several friends, my twofold hope being that, by means of the similes they might offer, those friends might enable me to do for those cliffs what Proust said a writer should aim to do with all the objects he describes: to make "their essential nature stand out clearly by joining them in metaphor, in order to remove them from the contingencies of time"; and to link cliffs and metaphor "with the indescribable bond of an alliance of words."

My friends were quick and articulate, and images rushed to their minds: "huge, hanging fish," "standing Egyptian mummies," "immense stalagmites," "something phallic," "the ruins of an ancient castle," "a group of Manhattan skyscrapers rubbed down with coarse sandpaper," "a giant, ruined molar." Clearly all their similes for the cliffs were influenced by the images in their respective reservoirs. And it came to me why I finally preferred my own image —

the prows of ocean liners — was because of my year covering the waterfront.

The responses of my friends had delighted me, for I have always relished the conversation of those who are ready with apt similes. Being slow at finding similes myself, I have also envied such facility. But this new understanding of the relationship between images and similes made me realize I could do something about my sluggishness. My game had shown you need not depend only on similes that come spontaneously. Similes can also be induced. And because the reservoir can be deliberately fished in, the time needed to formulate similes can be considerably shortened. I saw that if I read less and played the simile game more, I could acquire many fresh and magnetic visual images, all the while becoming more adept at fishing out old ones. For one gains a degree of control over old visual memories once they have been reactivated by being stirred up and utilized. Such memories, too, are easier to summon than those that remain deeply buried in the reservoir, untouched because of ignorance of their presence.

I understood, too, wherein my friends and I differed. It was in rate of visual recall. They could summon their visual recollections easily and quickly; normally I could not.

So people varied, not only in the images stocked in their reservoirs, but in their ability to recall them. Their vision, in turn, was affected by their rate of recall. And it dawned on me that slow recall was a factor limiting vision. With little capacity for being struck by interesting relationships, those with slow recollection undoubtedly must find the world less stirring to the imagination, less delightful in its incongruities than those with quick recall. And those who instantly recall many images probably see continuously with the liveliness of vision I enjoyed on the plane.

By the time I got to the office I was bubbling with excitement. Because it was Sunday, few people were in, but one colleague was — John Briggs, whose sharp eyes had helped with the face cards. This was a stroke of luck because, being observant himself, he was always interested in visual exploration. Knowing I had a willing listener, I began telling him about my game. Recalling the hoarding with the orange and white checks, I told him how it had stirred a recollection I could not identify, how I had fished in my mind to seek the buried counterpart and how, finally, I had realized it was a cereal package . . .

"Ralston," he broke in, supplying the brand-name even before I had told him my frustration in seeking it.

I seized on it happily, and realized that in the story of identifying that whole wheat cereal I had a first-class example to illustrate a newly revealed aspect of the pictorial reservoir. Besides containing images from different areas of experience — images deposited at all ages, from childhood on — the reservoir contains images deposited at classifiable levels.

The level where the image of the Ralston cereal box had rested was a deep one. It was not so far down, though, that it was totally lost, as was proved by the fact that its forgotten presence set up a vibration of affinity when my eye fell on the checkered hoarding. Perhaps this might be called the level of warning vibration.

Once the vibrations had signalled that the hoarding's visual counterpart was in that murky level, I let down grappling hooks. After a while, they found the counterpart and lifted it to the level above, where I could make out its main shape, realizing it was a cereal package. Perhaps this might be called the level of vague identification.

When John exclaimed the magic word "Ralston!" the image bounded from that level so fast that it cleared the water before falling back to float on the surface of complete consciousness.

All people, I realized, have images in their memories at all three levels and their rates of visual recall are conditioned by the levels. Though occasionally deeply buried visual recollections well up so suddenly they amaze us, the common sequence is that images at the level of clear consciousness come quickly, those at the level of vague identification emerge more slowly and those from the stratum of warning vibration are extremely slow.

One memory revivified by the concept of levels was Helen Irwin's account of an experiment that had been carried on at her son's school. The children had been shown three pictures. A house, a Roman temple with a pillared portico, and a crocodile with open jaws were the subjects. At given periods the students were questioned as to what they remembered of these pictures. The experiment, by testing the retention of images, was meant to see which children learned best by eye and which by ear.

A week later, three weeks later, and six weeks later were the questioning times. And after the final polling, the experimenters found the children divided into four classes: those who could not even remember being shown the pictures; those who remembered the pictures, but could not say what they represented; those who could name the subjects, but could not describe what they were like; and those who could recall the pictures so sharply they could report correctly the number of windows in the house, and even how many teeth the crocodile had.

The experiment, I realized, confirmed my classification of the levels. With those children who remembered they had been shown pictures, without recalling what of, the images had sunk to the level of warning vibration. With those who recalled the objects in the pictures without being able to describe them, the images had sunk to the level of vague identification. With those who could count the teeth, the images hadn't sunk at all.

This experiment introduced a new element: the rate of sinking. Obviously, those with quickest recall were those whose visual images sank most slowly. The children who could not even remember having been shown pictures gave proof of a fourth level, which was below those I had classified: the unconscious. For these children the images had plummeted to the bottom. And clearly, except for accidental upspurts, this is the level from which it is hardest to deliberately release submerged images.

That some students could recall the crocodile and the temple with photographic accuracy points to what the experimenters knew: that some children are more "eye-minded" than others. Obviously adults, too, have different native capacities for grasping and retaining the objects that pass before their eyes. And it occurred to me that those who are most fully eye-minded — that is, who retain almost everything they see — are less in need of similes as visual aids than the rest of us.

With so many new thoughts assembled, I recalled that stewardess with a cap like an island in the St. Lawrence. She had certainly got her wish when, as the door closed, she said on behalf of the crew: "We hope you enjoy your flight." And I was glad I had not cut myself off from all its visual enjoyments by burying my eyes in one of the magazines she offered before we took off.

CHAPTER 8

The Two Electrodes of Vision

As I was writing the six episodes of my first book on Mexico I was relieved to see how much they differed. It meant the book would have enough variety. Yet when the episodes were finished, I was struck to see they all had a major feature in common. The climax of each was an experience of transfigured vision.

How did it happen, I asked, that in three visits to Mexico I had more such experiences than up to that time I had had in my whole life?

Since I also had many experiences of sharpened and heightened vision in Mexico, I realized I was more observant there than I had ever been anywhere else. It occurred to me it might be instructive to find out why. For I got the idea that through analysis of this particular visual acuity I might discover a lot about vision in general.

It worked out as I hoped, and I now want to tell the story of those discoveries. But it means deepening the introspection, for what I am embarking on is more comprehensive than my previous tasks. Earlier chapters have dealt with specific visual experiences, each of limited duration — the length of a train ride, say, or an evening in a hotel courtyard. Here I want to speak of whole periods, and although they contained instances when I saw vividly, I do not want to analyze those instances for specific causes or for any facets of seeing they might illustrate. Rather, I want to deal with the Mexican experience for what it reveals of the visual process in its totality.

How individual visual memories influence seeing was developed in the last chapter. Earlier I hinted at how extra-visual factors — such as needs, emotional responses, associations, interests, etc. — also influence seeing. In fact, I said the whole ego was involved. In accounting for my Mexican seeing, therefore, I must relate much that is personal on a level deeper than recalling the Family Bible or a year covering the waterfront. For that seeing involved my whole being and the chief lesson it taught me was that important seeing is always a deeply personal matter.

Actually, my visual acuteness in Mexico had aroused my curiosity for some time before I resolved to track it down. And this preliminary curiosity stood me in good stead for it had led me to pile up a number of notes.

At first, my heightened vision in Mexico had seemed so mysterious that I had despaired of ever being able to understand it. Attempts to explain it always left me baffled and defeated. But every now and then a particular cause of visual stimulus would come into my mind. That I had used my eyes more carefully than usual in examining objects was one instance. Another was that, in those first visits to Mexico, World War II was just over and I still had a feeling of the precariousness of life. When these specific insights came, I jotted them down. At the back of my mind was the thought that some day the problem I could not solve wholesale might be solved piecemeal.

I made a point of recording each insight on a separate slip of paper. As the slips accumulated, I coined a name for the factors they noted. Each element that made me more observant in Mexico than at home became a "vision sharpener."

Knowing how fruitful it is to use the particular as the basis from which to move to the general, it did not take me long to decide on my first step. Obviously, it would be to assemble all those little slips. The notes, scribbled down over a period of years, were in many different boxes. But I never throw anything out, so ultimately they were all rounded up. Then I typed them in a single list.

The next stage was much harder, for once the list was made my mind was paralyzed by its bewildering length. When I recovered, however, I realized that before I could make any headway in analyzing all those "sharpeners" I had to find some preliminary generalizations about vision that would enable me to classify so much raw material. After several tries that got me nowhere, I decided to begin at the very beginning.

Obviously, if a thing is to be seen it must be looked at. This meant, then, that there are three main elements in vision: the object beheld, the eye of the beholder, and the fact that the beholder's eye is aimed at the object.

Then I remembered the experiment in physics classes at school which showed that electricity would flare between two electrodes if the electrodes were brought close together and were properly charged in relation to each other. Could it be that similar laws operated in vision? Perhaps the object was one terminal, the eye of the beholder the other. And perhaps sparking depended on how they were charged.

At this point I could not tell if the parallel held, but at least I had a formula enabling me to classify the vision sharpeners. Happily, I divided them into three piles: the factors that made me look at everything that passed before my eyes; those that made Mexico highly charged for me, and those that made me particularly charged for Mexico.

Many factors that made me give everything full attention, I found, were not specific to Mexico. They were the ordinary sharpening factors that come with most traveling.

When we see things for the first time, we see them, as it were, in a privileged manner. They hit us as they never have the power to do again, for they induce freshness of vision with no effort on our part. And the first sharpener of travel was that I was seeing hundreds of things for the first time. The second was that everything was unaccustomed. If this seems merely a repetition of the first, let me suggest the distinction. Many things I saw in Mexico, even though I was seeing them for the first time, were basically familiar. After all, houses, streets, churches, crockery, etc., are all recognizable as such no matter where they are found. But the houses I saw in Mexico, the streets I walked in, the churches I visited and the clay vessels I saw in the markets were not the houses, streets, churches and ceramics I was accustomed to. Thus they had not slipped into the realm of objects so familiar that we have lost the power to notice them. My metaphor, I found, helped clinch the distinction. The clarity of vision experienced in seeing something for the first time comes from the other electrode — that is, from the object's own particular charge. The clarity of vision in seeing the unaccustomed comes from within us, and it arises because we are seeing in a new way: that is, with eyes free from the film that normally coats them in the midst of the familiar.

The next sharpener involves a distinction of some subtlety, too. In Mexico, everything was foreign. I separate this from everything being unaccustomed because "foreignness" is not mere novelty or unfamiliarity. An Iowa cornfield may be something a New Yorker has never seen before, and therefore unfamiliar to him, but it will not strike him as being foreign. It will seem merely an extension of his own culture. Foreignness, on the other hand, is something that emanates from a different culture. Our language, with such words as strange, exotic and alien, admits its existence, even if it does not clarify its nature. And foreignness endows an object or a vista with eye-opening power.

The fourth travel element that made me look so hard was awareness that I was passing through. I knew that, if I was going to observe things, it was now or never. I could not move through the country with the complacency of the permanent resident, who hardly bothers to look at things, feeling they will always be there to see.

Since one seldom sets out alone, or remains alone in the midst of travel, I found the eyes of companions were also elements sharpening my observation. Companions provided vision from a different angle, and their mental pictures gave an additional dimension to my own, as in a stereoscope the second picture, taken from a slightly different position, adds the sense of depth. I was especially influenced by two companions: On the first trip was my friend of the ride to Grants, Thyrza Cohen, who, being very old, kept leading me to realize how everything must seem to one who knows there cannot be many years ahead. On the third was Rafael Gutierrez, who, being very young, kept seeing the world in morning light.

My theory that a visual electrode could carry a high voltage charge was strengthened when I examined three factors specific to Mexico. Her beauty was the first. Beauty, especially when of a high degree, has a marvelous power of unsealing the eyes. And again and again Mexico's peopled landscapes unsealed mine just by the sheer force of their visual loveliness.

Mexico also has a visual charge almost entirely lacking in the United States: the presence of the past. Here we live on top of the moment and everything is up to date. We hardly think of the past because nothing stirs us to visualize it. But everywhere in Mexico one is aware of the heritage left behind by the long-departed Spaniards. The ways of the Indians, and the ruins of their ancient places of worship, conjure up eras even more remote. The unchangingness of the still visible past provides a secondary image, which brings the stimulus of double-level perception. For as one sees the past and present coexisting, each contrasting element is seen more sharply, and vision is kept lively by being jerked from one to the other: from the gleaming modern skyscraper, say, to the barefoot Indian in pajamas who walks by it with a load of firewood hung on his back by a tumpline across his brow.

The other Mexican factor I singled out as a vision sharpener is its multiplicity of worlds. For, besides the old and the new, Mexico has enormous contrasts of rich and poor. And there is the contrast between the world of the native and the life of visitors on the tourist circuit.

It was when I turned to the factors making for my personal charge that I gained fullest confidence in my electrode theory. There is no need to list the smaller charging factors for, although I did not use the term then, I have already illustrated how charging influences vision in showing how I was electrically ready to see Grants as a New Jerusalem. If that is recalled, the role of inner charges will be self-evident. Besides, some of the charges in Mexico will emerge of themselves. But I do need to cite the most important: being humbled and tired after prolonged tension. For I set off on my first trip to Mexico just a few days after I was discharged from the U. S. Army. For three years, day in and day out, I had been living with war. Everywhere I went outside of Mexico City I saw scenes of pastoral peace. No wonder they seemed so beautiful. They were unbelievably welcome to my war-weary soul.

But even though the personal factors that made me so responsive don't need specifying one by one, I do want to speak of them as a group, for the fact that this particular roster of vision sharpeners was far longer than either of the other two was profoundly instructive. In the chapter on the camera eye I spoke of the role of the mind in selecting from among the hundreds of details the eye photographs, my chief point being that we pick out details according to our interests, and I elaborated a bit by speaking of the discoveries of the psychologists. But when I was combing that list of vision sharpeners, I had scarcely dipped into those psychologists. I already knew the role of interests, but what that list brought home was that our selecting is also enormously influenced by our emotions. And I came to understand that it is not just our brains that operate that valve, but our whole emotional and spiritual beings.

After discovering that the subjective element played a far greater role in seeing than I realized, I found that the subjective component can be divided into factors that bear on us from without and those that condition us from within. And often the two sets of factors operate in an interacting way. In Mexico I was always on a vacation (an external factor). Because of this I was relaxed (an internal factor). Being freed of duties by external circumstances, I found myself in possession of internal things, like energy and the will that directs the attention; and having them when my time was free, I could utilize these internal elements for the purpose of observing. In Mexico, then, I had the relaxation, the time and the freedom to use my eyes. Having the opportunity to observe, however, does not automatically mean one takes it. Normally one looks only when one wants to look. And my list also helped me here, because it revealed that among the factors working within me were certain hungers which made me want to feast my eyes on Mexico. I have already mentioned the one that was particularly gnawing just after the war: the hunger to see scenes of peace. I also hungered to watch people who were in harmony with their environment. After so much industrial civilization, with everything around being so new, I hungered, too, for old things, for a sense of the past and my own connection with it. And later, as my work kept me increasingly confined to the city, there was hunger to gaze on mountains, trees, fields and sky.

Bit by bit one is changed by what the eyes take in. I did not always know this, but my list of vision sharpeners brought it home by mirroring the emotional and mental changes I went through in the course of observing more and more eagerly.

The worst effect of the wartime experience was to turn me in on myself, and when I emerged from the Army I was miserably self-involved. As well as nursing a sense of deep hurt, my problems weighed on me like lead. And my feeling of bitterness at the war for playing such havoc with my own life was intensified by my awareness of all the pain and suffering it had brought others.

Mexico, with its unfamiliarity and its manifold worlds, excited my mind, regardless of my will. And mental occupation with this fascinating country was part of the process of becoming disengaged from self-absorption. Being led to self-forgetfulness was vital because self-concern is apt to hang in the human mind like an obscuring cloud. Thus the more excited I grew by what my eyes were taking in, the less I thought about my grievances. The more they dwindled, the easier it was to observe, and as my self-concern dissolved, my faculties were freer to drink in the world about me. Finally I began to see it with a mind unobscured, untroubled and, best of all, disembittered.

Recognition of disengagement from self as a major sharpener made me aware that the subjective element was more dynamic than I thought. Or perhaps I should say I became aware that the whole visual experience was more dynamic, for the sparks fly both ways. The eye of the beholder, because of its subjective charge, sends sparks across the gap to the object beheld. That other electrode, in turn, sends sparks back.

When I had this figured out, I suddenly had a horrid recollection. Perhaps my lovely metaphor was not so apt after all. For I recalled from the electrode experiment that sparks always leap from the negative to the positive pole. And the names for them even came back: the cathode and the anode. It was true that the direction of current could be reversed by altering the polarity of the electrodes. But without specific intervention, the flow of the current was always in one direction.

My metaphor therefore was not versatile enough. With their relentless one-way flow of current, the electrodes do not illustrate the oscillating interchange, the free give and take of the sparks in visual experience. I realized I had encountered the same difficulty with the electrode parallel as with the valve metaphor — and for the same reason. I had tried to explain a living process in terms of a mechanism.

Having found one flaw in my metaphor I began to suspect another. My experience had shown that the psyche behind the eye that receives the sparks is changed by the electrons flowing into it, for what we see influences our inward states. Our observing, in turn, is conditioned by the changes in those states. Was this particular process illustrated by my metaphor? In other words, when the current flowed through them, were those two electrodes changed in their inner natures as humans are under the influence of creative visual currents? I went to Frank Algier, a mechanically-minded friend, with my question. In silverplating, he said, one pole was coated with silver, but in the ordinary circuit the current left the electrodes chemically unchanged. So my suspicion was confirmed. Actually, I should have known it without asking. In the human situation, what arcs back and forth between the poles is more complex and wonderful than electricity, and, after all, human beings are not metal conductors.

I felt considerably chastened. When I read the psychologists, however, my faith in my metaphor began reviving. They did not use my terms and they were considerably less inclined to endow non-human things with out-going dynamic force. Nevertheless, I recognized in their discourse the features I had been trying to describe. With their talk of the forces in the field, the Gestalt psychologists even came close to the world of electricity. Certainly in Koffka's vision-influencing Ego I recognized the electrode that I first called the eye of the beholder. Just as surely, in his discussion of "Object-Ego Organization" in the visual act, I recognized the tension of two poles dynamically charged in relation to each other. In what the psychologists classified as the "circumstantial" and the "psychological" I recognized my distinction between charges from without and charges from within. And their "selector tendencies" and "reaction sensitivities" were clearly charging elements. Some psychologists even came close to my own mechanistic vision in speaking of the beholder's "tuning." So I knew what I had been talking about was a reality. And as I struggled to interpret the prose of the psychologists and grew increasingly tired of their self-conscious terminology, I came to feel that, thank you, imperfect as it might be, I preferred my own metaphor.

CHAPTER 9

The Vision Deadeners: Personal

Wᴇɴ you have an out-of-town visitor, you generally do what your guest wants. Take visiting a museum. Ordinarily, when I go to the Metropolitan I like to look at paintings. But my visitor from Boston, Edward Dell, was interested in ancient Egypt, so it was to the Museum's Egyptian wing that we went.

The wing is effectively arranged. With its sphinx in front and its two seated Pharaohs at the entrance, you get the impression you are entering a temple at Luxor. The hall of the tombs of the Fifth and Sixth Dynasties is particularly good. The tomb of Per-Neb, with its massive stones and narrow corridors, is reconstructed in its entirety. But the tomb chapel of Kay-Em-Snewy, the overseer of the granary, and his brother, Wer-Djed-Ptah, the judge, is represented by only its west wall, placed, appropriately, on the west side of the hall.

My impressions, however, did not have this sort of clarity on my visit with Ed, and when we stood in front of the chapel wall I did not identify it. All I saw was an expanse of limestone, covered with hieroglyphics.

When Ed remarked, "Isn't that an odd-looking bird?" I had to ask, "What bird? I can't see any bird."

"You mean to say you can't see a bird?" he asked incredulously.

"No. Show me where it is."

At this, Ed moved nearer and pointed directly at one of the chicken scratchings on the cream-colored wall. My eye followed his forefinger, and, sure enough, it was almost touching a beautifully incised little bird.

In fact, it might have been one of the chickens that had made the scratchings, for it was obviously a chick. Ed thought it looked odd because, despite its Easter outlines, it had outgrown a normal chick's size.

The moment I discerned the chick I had a curious sensation. It was as if a whole flock of birds suddenly fluttered into the room, flew to different lines on the wall and instantaneously transformed themselves into little drawings. For there must have been well over a hundred birds carefully incised on that wall. And with my eyes opened to one, I could see them all.

As well as more chicks, there were owls, ibis, hawks, ducks, and turtledoves. As the birds became visible to me, so did all the other figures on the wall — the red-torsoed overseer of the granary, with his small squared beard; his yellow-skinned wife, standing affectionately in profile beside him; their young son; the judge, who was the overseer's younger brother; the tables of food before the judge; and a variety of isolated objects like jars, bowls, eyes, legs, hands, and hanks of rope twisted in three loops. And when I saw that nearly all the features on the wall were depicted intelligibly — that is, so realistically that you did not need to be an Egyptologist to recognize them — I grasped the cause of my blindness. I had been blinded by fear.

It was not that I thought the wall was going to topple forward and crush me. It was a more subtle fear — fear that I could not see, or rather, fear that, through lack of understanding, I was incapable of discerning what was before my eyes.

When I entered the room, the wall had seemed vastly esoteric, and, being unfamiliar with Egyptian picture writing, I had leaped to the conclusion that there was nothing on the wall I could understand. This conviction was so deep that when I looked at the wall I had a sort of blindness. I could not even make out that it was the side of a building. All I could take in was a confused mass of incisions that suggested an expanse of petrified sand, marked like a barnyard floor.

That visit to the Egyptian wing took place in 1952 when my awareness of subjectivity's role in vision was just beginning. It proved a landmark, because until then the only subjective factors I had recognized were positive ones: those influencing our selection of visual material, those sharpening our vision of what we select, and those coloring our perceptions so that what we select appears as it does.

The sudden appearance of those Egyptian birds dramatized that subjectivity also has negative influences. I was slow in coming to this realization because negative influences, being dulling rather than eye-opening, are hard to grasp. Sooner or later, positive influences obtrude themselves on you. Parallel images as vision stimulators are a case in point. But even after you become aware of the positive role of the second level, it takes you a long time to recognize that single-level perception, comparatively speaking, is playing a negative role. It is the old difficulty: How can you become aware of what you don't know exists?

Once on the track of negative visual influences, I became increasingly aware of how powerful, as well as pernicious, they could be. With positive influences that tend towards distortion, the countervailing photographic evidence of the camera-like eye places some check on the fancy. But what is not observed is not visually present to be assessed.

In pursuing the negative influences, I was surprised at how many I found. My phrase about the "sharpeners" led me to label the new elements the "deadeners" and ultimately I came to the conclusion that in the lives of most of us our vision deadeners outnumber and outweigh the positive influences. We reject, I think, more than we select.

Certainly, I found too many negative influences to encompass in a single chapter; which is why I have split them in two. The influences themselves suggested my cleavage; for like the positive ones, they divide into those that come from within and those that come from without. The vision deadeners that are individual I have called "personal"; those that are environmental I have called "cultural."

Once I had isolated my own fear of visual incompetence as a strong personal vision deadener, I questioned others to find if they were blinded by the same fear. To my relief, I found everyone understood what I was talking about, and nearly everyone confessed to similar visual inhibition in one field or another. Some confessed to having it in all difficult fields that were strange to them. But people, I found, varied in the degree to which they were afflicted by the fear. On the whole, those with long experience of machinery seemed to be the ones who suffered from it least.

As my friends talked, I realized that complicated things presenting a multitude of impressions, all unfamiliar, are what induce such fears, and that the emotions in moments of panicky blindness range from mild cases of feeling flustered and bewildered to being so deeply confused as to feel helpless. As I listened, I realized that not only does this fear blind us from seeing, but it tends to prevent us from looking.

Some friends said that, if interested, they would try to puzzle out what at first glance seemed so confusing. But many said they immediately admitted defeat and turned away. It was common, I found, even for those who started boldly, to screw back the case of a defective radio and call in a repairman. In other words, the blinding effects of the fear of visual incapacity are often compounded by another great vision deadener: visual impatience.

Fear of visual inadequacy, I learned, is often unnecessary. My fear before that Egyptian wall was. And many friends who were not mechanical said that, when there was no repairman for miles around, they had found themselves capable of repairing frightening mechanisms when the sheer necessity of getting them working again had left them no alternative. The trick was to calm down and patiently examine the function of one moving part after another. As they spoke, I realized that those afraid of not being able to make head or tail of the complicated must learn to have fuller trust in the eye's capacity to see. With confidence in the eye's ability to explore convoluted intricacies established, something else happens. One learns to trust the eye's capacity to lead.

Normally, it is the intelligence that leads the eye. And experiences of apparent visual incapacity are generally instances when the observer has the awful feeling that his intelligence is powerless to direct the eye. Yet to be lost does not mean you have to remain lost. And what my patient friends taught me was that even where the intelligence can not prove a knowing guide, the visual safari does not have to come to a halt. Because of the eye's seeing power, the intelligence can fall back a little. From second place it can follow the eye's leadership and try to make deductions from what the eye takes in. For the intelligence does not always have to be teaching the eye; it can learn from the eye, too. And the man who calmly trusts his eyes to be able to pick their way observantly over unfamiliar terrain is not likely to be frightened into panic blindness.

Other personal vision deadeners can be discussed in a briefer manner by taking a new line. Up to now I have tended to treat the visual system in isolation. Our eyes, however, are by no means our only sources of cognition. Our ears, noses, mouths, hands and skins also help us to knowledge of the physical world, and the visual system is only part of what has been aptly called the perceptual system. Thus many vision deadeners can be ticked off by citing things that impair the perceptual system as a whole.

In this class come those conditions that lower the body's physical vitality: illness, intense pain, emotional shock, tiredness, drunkenness, grief, worry, fear, and so on. It is true these do not work consistently. Sometimes they can make vision almost freakishly intense (as can drugs). But often they work negatively; and it stands to reason that when they block memory, blur perceptions, reduce responsiveness and numb all the sensibilities, they have their deadening effect on vision — as well as on the appetite, on hearing, on feeling, on attention and on thinking.

Because of the basic inseparability of the being, other factors which obstruct thinking, such as ignorance, inattention, disinterest, and carelessness also play their role in deadening vision.

Because the ego is very much part of the system, it can also play a negative role. It can do this by blinding us to what might be undermining to our self-esteem, to what might go against our purposes and to what might destroy our illusions. Besides making us feel incapable of seeing difficult things, it can prevent us from looking at things we consider unsafe, improper, or disturbing. If we are insecure, the ego can check us from looking at the uncertain. If we are hidebound, it can prevent us from looking at anything new. It can also lead us to cut off the outside world to preserve our privacy.

Again, because of the fundamental unity of the human system, it stands to reason that vision is also deadened by those things that lower the vitality of the spirit. In this class come such factors as unhappiness, bitterness, resentment, depression, overwhelming disappointment, the feeling of isolation, the sense of having lost one's bearings, boredom, awareness of being totally uprooted, feeling helpless against fate, loss of love, loss of faith, and all the other factors that lead to emotional numbness and the conviction that nothing matters.

More ticking off can be done by reverting to the vision sharpeners. For many a deadener is merely a vision sharpener in reverse, and understanding the working of the one helps explain the eclipsing power of the other.

Take self-concern, which by definition is being turned in on one's self. Obviously, when the attention is turned inward, there will be little observation of the outward world. Relaxation is another case in point. In referring to it earlier as a sharpener, I implied a lot about the deadening effect of its opposite — being unrelaxed. For our seeing is always disturbed when we are upset. Again, the process is not consistent. Being upset can heighten vision, but generally it inhibits it. Certainly to see with objective clarity we need to be calm, patient, untroubled, confident and concerned with outward things. One has only to name such opposites as being flustered, disconcerted, bewildered, confused, agitated, fretful and irritated, to realize how they interfere with careful observation. And these are just the relatively minor deadeners. When anger at the height of its raging, acute anxiety, and prolonged nervous tension are counted too, the vision-deadening can be almost total.

Companions were also cited as vision sharpeners. Yet since what we notice and how we respond to it are influenced by those we are with, an unobservant companion can dull our seeing just as surely as an alert one can sharpen it. He can discourage vision by such comments as "Oh that's not worth looking at!" or "What do you want to look at that for?" (By being very attractive, he or she can divert our attention from anything else.) Or the unobservant one by "talking our head off" can prevent us from seeing by forcing us to listen. Becoming sympathetically involved in the troubles of others can be as blinding as becoming too deeply involved in our own.

What we are focused on, in fact, can be taken as the heading for a host of vision deadeners. Besides distracting friends and such concerns as have been touched upon — illness, loss, our ego, and anger — the list includes other elements, such as our fears. For when we are terribly anxious about something that may happen, the eventuality looms so large that we have little attention left for anything else. Similarly, the center of the visual stage can be hogged by fixation on biological needs, ambitions, sexual desires, material cravings, daydreams, determination to surpass others, emotional needs, etc. In fact, almost any kind of mental preoccupation with what is non-visual can be, and often is, a vision deadener.

Concern with economic problems, worry about the future, puzzlement over how to handle something a child has done — these are among the preoccupations that can so grip the mind that one can walk down a street and not remember having seen a thing.

And even when one is not thinking about a specific problem, one's vision of one's surroundings can be cut off by preoccupation with such general sensations as feeling weighed down by responsibilities, absorbed by duties, and burdened by hundreds of details clamoring for time and attention. For deadeners of vision divide in the same way as the sharpeners. Some are circumstantial and some are psychological. And by circumstantial I do not mean the cultural influences of the total environment (which will be discussed in the next chapter), but circumstances in our particular lives: like the report that has to be ready by next Tuesday; or the sore on the cheek that does not seem to be healing. The blinder, then, can be a dread from within, or a duty from without.

Vision deadeners can also be divided into those that prevent us from looking, and those that prevent us from seeing.

Some of the factors that halt looking — such as grief, pain, anxiety, or preoccupation with inescapable problems — are often not our own fault. They are brought upon us by unavoidable and generally unwelcome circumstances. Yet much of our not looking is our own fault; in many instances, we deliberately refuse to look.

This refusal to look, however, is not always fully conscious. By and large, the three classes of things we choose to look at are the useful, the interesting, and the sensuously pleasing. The classes we refuse to look at are their opposites: the useless, the boring and the repulsive. In the long run, I am convinced that much that seems repellent is not really so, yet at this point I don't want to campaign for a closer examination of the obnoxious. However, I do want to lament our refusal to look at the unserviceable and what we deem the unworthy.

The tendency to overlook the unserviceable is a result of what I call the law of visual utility. Stated briefly, this is the tendency to look most at what is useful, least at what is useless. Though often we have no awareness of its operation, the law works ceaselessly. Generally it reveals itself frankly when one is about to make a major purchase. Say one wants to buy an automobile for the first time; suddenly one starts looking at all the automobiles around. Or perhaps you have undertaken some do-it-yourself work in the house; you find the problems involved give you a passionate interest in things you never bothered to notice before, such as how the floorboards are laid in friends' houses, or how their windows are trimmed.

Note that the working of the law reveals itself most strikingly when something previously useless shifts in value: when the useless becomes the useful. Therein lies the key to the law's danger. Utility is a variable thing. Even with the same person a matter can vary, being useless at one time and essential at another. And sometimes fate, by ironically twisting one's situation, makes something long considered useless come in wonderfully handy.

An object's utility can certainly sharpen our vision of it, but confining one's looking to the merely useful can be terribly restricting. It can also foster the mental habit that already does too much to keep us from seeing actual appearances. I mean conceptualizing. And if this sounds too big a word, it can be defined as transforming a reality into an abstraction.

To understand its image-obliterating force, one has only to remember the reading practice already discussed: the suppression of the image of the type in favor of the concept of the word. For what we do with groups of letters we do repeatedly with objects. We read them rather than see them; that is, we dismiss their appearances the moment we have identified them either by class or function. Often, for instance, a lovely piece of eighteenth-century workmanship will be relegated into visual limbo the moment it is classed as a chair. Or a nicely designed mechanism will be visually wiped out by being recognized as a can-opener. Or a graceful natural conformation will be made to vanish by sizing it up as a plant. But there is a great deal of pleasure to be gained from the appearances of particular chairs, particular mechanisms and particular plants. Nearly every object — certainly every natural one — has its own visual interest and especial charm; and a great deal is lost if it is not appreciated as a concrete and individual specimen, but instead is regarded only as an easily dismissable representation of an abstract concept.

Observing for only utilitarian reasons, then, besides dismissing what it considers altogether useless, also tends to exclude the "useless" aspects of the admittedly useful. Insofar as it does, it can be a vision deadener. Nevertheless, it is not as deadly as its companion killer: advance visual judgments which predetermine that certain things are not worth looking at.

To prejudge that something is automatically boring is a form of visual snobbery. To realize how it has blinded past generations, one has only to think of men who looked with interest at things their predecessors considered unimportant: like the swing of a pendulum, the imprint of a seal on wax, the flying of kites, keys as conductors of sparks, and the bobbing of a lid over a saucepan of boiling water. Such observations led to significant inventions. Denigration, in contrast, can blind us even to the appreciation of invention, as is witnessed by how my scorn of the lowly candle long blocked realizations that came easily once my eyes were opened to the inventive wonder of the domestication of a single flame at the tip of a wax rod that could be held in the hand.

So beware of advance visual judgments. Many are just traditional attitudes, uncritically stuffed into the great grab bags of unexamined ideas we all tote. Not deigning to examine what one thinks unworthy of attention can be as shortsighted as it is snobbish, for too frequently we are wrong about that unworthiness. Each of us, then, should try to be open-eyed, as well as open-minded. And we should recognize that being one often leads to being the other.

The failure to see what we don't look at, naturally, is not a bit mysterious. However, there is something profoundly strange in failing to see what the eye gazes at directly. This second type of not-seeing, then, is the more interesting. And it is a common phenomenon: so common, in fact, that one is tempted to assume that we have two sets of eyelids: the physical ones with the hairy fringe that we close consciously, and the psychological ones that we close unconsciously.

The second lid theory may be verbalizing the same cutting off of vision I spoke of when, in accounting for seeing sketchily, I referred to a valve opening and closing in the mind. But the shift in metaphor is deliberate. Here I do not want to suggest a cutoff behind the eye, but an interception that seems to take place in front of it.

That images which confront the eyeball should not register is indeed strange — so strange, as to deserve further analysis. This phenomenon of looking and not seeing is partially explained by vision deadeners we have already discussed, such as lowered physical vitality, grief, anxiety, and preoccupation. Prejudging also plays its part, for we tend to drop those psychological lids when our eyes accidentally light on what we have written off in advance as being boring. The law of visual utility applies here too, for we can not totally avoid what seems useless to us. What we do when forcibly confronted with objects of mixed value is make a selection, seeing only the utilitarian part that we want to see.

The case of the face cards is proof enough of this. In a game the only thing that matters is a card's value, which is determined by its suit and number. Ruled by the law of visual utility, we look at nothing else. In bridge, for instance, the fact that the queen of spades has a sceptre has no utility whatever; what matters here is that she'll beat the jack. In the game of hearts, that sceptre isn't any use either; here what matters is getting rid of the queen of spades so she won't cost thirteen points for being in your hand when the winner goes out. And the reason so few people have noticed what the card nobles carry, even players who gaze at cards year after year, is that they have steadfastly chosen to lower their psychological lids on what they dismiss as useless pictorial data.

All the things we have listed — fear of not being able to see, conceptualizing, rejection of the useless, etc. — still do not fully explain this failure to observe what is so often under our eyes. But perhaps the electrodes of vision, having helped account for exceptional seeing, will be equally useful in explaining the reverse. Remember that for sparks to leap between the eye of the beholder and the thing beheld, the two poles, besides being close, must be properly charged in relationship to each other. The converse, obviously, is that, even if the terminals are very near, no sparks will fly if the charges are reciprocally wrong. And doesn't this explain much non-seeing? Or as the psychologists call it, "selective inattention?"

No one can be equally interested in all things. Even the man who is potentially interested in nearly everything visible is sure to prefer one area to another. If an object belongs to a class in which he has no interest, clearly it has no charge he responds to. Or if a thing is poor in contrasts that stir double-level perception, its charge will be weak; and if our own charge is weak, too, the two feeble charges won't bridge the gap. Or suppose the object has a heavy charge of ugliness, and we are so charged with distress that we do not want to absorb anything that will make us feel more miserable. Again there will be no sparks.

Earlier, in commenting on the vision-sharpening benefits of travel, I spoke of the liabilities of its opposite: remaining stationary in the midst of familiar sights. In this situation, I said, our eyes become coated with film. This was an earlier way of describing the psychological lids, and it leads to a factor that causes us to lower them. Inevitably, it seems, we come to take accustomed elements in our lives for granted. What we take for granted we cease to esteem. Lowered in our estimation, the object loses the qualities that make for visual charging: newness, foreignness and transience. Thereafter, it neither strikes nor intrigues us, and we postpone observing it carefully because we are confident that, if we want to take the trouble, we can examine it tomorrow. We tend, then, to drop the psychological lids before the objects we look at habitually.

Habit — or perhaps I should say routine — helps to deaden our vision in another important way too. If our lives are very much dominated by habit — and modern, machine-based civilization makes this more and more the prevailing mode of life — we become bound in a given working orbit, and usually in its related social orbit. Both confine us to viewing only objects within circumscribed fields which quite naturally become tiresomely familiar. What are the consequences? Because they are almost the only things our eyes fall on, we cease to see them with any freshness.

Because being in harness generally means wearing blinders too, we fall into the wretched habit of observing nothing freshly during the hours when we are duty-bound. And if those hours of duty are long and exhausting, we often find ourselves further incapacitated by being too tired to do any visual exploring in our hours of relaxation. If we lapse into the habit of being unobservant in both periods of time — the working and the free — we become further victimized. Seeing, because it brings so much interest into our lives, almost invariably stimulates further seeing. Deprived of that chain reaction, the habit of not-seeing grows even stronger. As a result, we can be improperly charged for visual experiences by having become both habit-bound and habitually unobservant.

And the story isn't through. When one thinks of the various conditions of being unrelaxed — being angry, bewildered, upset, nervous, tense, etc. — the picture of an overcharged individual springs almost automatically to mind. Yet the performance of the electrodes shows that, no matter how high the voltage, there will be no sparks if the disposition of the charges does not allow completion of the circuit.

On the whole, however, being overcharged is less vision-deadening than being undercharged. Anger, at the moment of its flaring, might, as the saying goes, be "blind rage," but a prolonged resentment can often be a vision sharpener. Anxiety can make one very alert to anything threatening. With hatred, one will grasp at everything justifying dislike. And, as Arnold Bennett has wittily pointed out, suspicion is a great gatherer of evidence on its own behalf. Even unhappiness, providing it is not too crushing, will not deaden vision, for it tends to alert us to further unhappiness through sympathetic attunement.

More often than not, unhappiness is the result of unsatisfied emotional hungers, and as I have shown, such hungers can be great vision sharpeners. It is the reverse of them that is the great deadener. This might be defined as having no charge at all; for it is the emotional numbness that results when the vitality of either the body or the soul is impaired. Then, sunk in lassitude and indifference, the benumbed individual, withdrawn and unreceptive, fails to reach out with his eyes for anything. Combining the two figures of speech, one might say it is the absence of all feeling, negative or positive, that truly closes the psychological lids.

The Vision Deadeners: Cultural

THE Army's basic training, literally, was eye-opening. Take that second lecture on the rifle — the one on its nomenclature. "This," said the instructor, touching the metal front of the rifle, "is the barrel." I thought he would then tell us about the trigger, the bolt, and the butt and let it go at that. But I had reckoned without his thoroughness.

"The end of the barrel," he continued, "is the muzzle. On the muzzle is the front sight. Notice it has wing guards to protect it.

"See this wood that is held around the barrel by two metal rings. This is the upper hand guard. It protects the hand from the heat of the barrel. The rings are called ferrules. The first one has a bayonet stud and a stacking swivel. The second ferrule has the upper sling swivel. The lower sling swivel is in the butt. You'll notice the sling has two leather slides. These are called keepers. There are two metal hooks, called frogs, to adjust the sling."

I listened in amazement that even the parts of the sling were so carefully named.

Relentlessly the instructor continued. "The opposite end of the barrel from the muzzle is the chamber breech. Here is the bolt, and this piece of metal that projects to the side is the operating lug. This is the rear sight, and it has wing guards, too. Then we come to the stock. The small of the stock is behind the bolt."

Surely, I thought, when we get to the butt, things will get simpler. But the butt had a butt plate, the butt plate had a long screw and short screw and within the butt, once the plate was removed, was a well to store cleaning equipment.

Up to this point, I had followed everything successfully. For the sergeant was still dealing with external parts easily seen as he guided our eyes by touching the parts he named. But when he took out the striking assembly and began disassembling it — well, in the welter of the cocking piece, extractor hook, ejector, groove-locking lug, main spring, sleeve spring and spring guide, I got lost.

I was not scornful, however. Far from it. As one minute part after another was carefully named, my respect for the sergeant increased. I realized that never in civilian life had any of my teachers tried to show me anything in such detail.

As I looked around at my fellow G.I.'s and saw how many were similarly lost, I realized that most of them had never before been asked to observe anything so closely either. From a few murmurs, I learned something else. Besides being unaccustomed to such scrutiny, some were fed up with what they considered a silly business.

The lecture on the rifle was followed by a session of drill. While I was obeying commands semi-automatically, I thought further about the visual exercise we had just gone through, again struck by its difference from any previous school instruction. Because it had made me aware of new possibilities of seeing, I realized hundreds of objects could be observed with the same sort of detailed care as that rifle.

"To the rear, march," "by the left flank, march," "halt," "forward, march," "hup, two, three, four, hup, two, three, four," "left oblique, march," "hup two, hup two" — as I obeyed the orders, my mind kept returning to the lecture. Why had those other fellows resented that detailed exposition? Granted it went on too long, and that, to men who have never needed or used one, a rifle is not yet an object of interest. But perhaps that lecture ran counter to one of their fundamental beliefs? We live in a world that likes to take things for granted. Could those men have felt such resentment because they believed nothing was worth looking at with such minuteness?

Training began at eight o'clock in the morning and went on till five in the afternoon. Much of it was physical. Hardly a day passed that we didn't scramble over an obstacle course, and there were always sessions of calisthenics and even longer sessions of drill. Sandwiched between these physical activities were the lectures. Many were so dull sergeants had to go up and down the aisles keeping us awake. But one. . . . Never will I forget the first lecture on camouflage.

"The eye is built to see movement," said the instructor. "Not only does the eye see movement easily," he continued "but movement repeatedly catches the eye. A flickering light, for example. And even a creature as tiny as an ant reveals itself when it moves."

The lecturer then discussed a problem we had all had: trying to make a friend pick out a certain object we had our eye on, from among a number of things in the distance. If the object was still, and hard to distinguish from its background, the communication of the identification, he reminded us, was all but impossible. But let that object move, and the work was done for us. All we had to do was exclaim, "See, that's it! The thing that moved!"

The eye, he said, was so enamoured of movement that it would follow the deliberately distracting gestures of a magician rather than concentrate on the object that the mind knew full well the magician was going to conceal. As the instructor spoke I had a sensation similar to the one at the rifle lecture. In telling me about the eye's affinity for movement, and its skill in observing it, the army lecturer was giving me something I had never been given in a civilian school: fundamental information about the character of the eye; something that was obvious the moment it was pointed out, but which, in my case, had never been pointed out before.

I had no chance to reflect further, however, for the instructor had gone on to discuss how one hides from enemy eyes that catch movement so easily. Under observation, he said, you froze. And you tried to avoid observation by a number of means — a chief one being to exploit shadow.

"A shadow," he said, "is the darkest thing on earth. You can't make anything as black as a shadow."

"Do you know why tall grass looks darker than short grass?" the instructor asked. "It's because tall grass casts more shadow. Actually tall grass is the same shade of green as short grass, or grass lying flat. But when tall grass is standing upright, the eye sees both the grass and the shadow and blends them into a darker shade."

I listened in fascination. This, too, became obvious the moment it was said, but I realized that until then I had never been given a single lecture on the general appearances of nature. At a summer camp, I had been told to look at the stars to identify the more obvious constellations, and I had been asked to note certain barks and certain leaves to identify trees. But that was not aid and encouragement to observe appearances in general.

"The reason you have to think so much about shadow in this war," continued the instructor, "is because of the airplane. Aerial observers will always be on the lookout for you. To a plane, if you are in a field in the late afternoon on a sunny day, especially if you are wearing fatigues, your shadow will be much more conspicuous than your body. Your shadow will be long and black, whereas your clothing will blend with the earth. One reason for falling prone is that you cast far less shadow lying down than you do standing up."

But if our own shadows gave us away, he said, we could use the shadows of other things for our protection. And again I was fascinated by his illustration. If one wanted protection from a strafing plane, one should not duck thoughtlessly under a tree. It was better to lie out in the open in the ball-like shadow cast by the tree's foliage. By crouching behind a tree trunk one might cast a telltale shadow of one's own. When shadows were long, he said, a man could even find a hiding place in the shadow of a fence post.

Hardly had the lecturer finished with shadow, than he passed on to the use of natural materials: one should not turn oneself into a big pile of brush, but one should take advantage of leaves and branches. However, one should be careful to drape oneself with leaves of the area: if among evergreens, evergreens; if among dead leaves, leaves that were also dead. One should watch, too, that the undersides of the leaves were not exposed. And when the leaves wilted they should be exchanged for fresh ones; dying leaves changed color and in so doing became conspicuous.

Implicit in all this specific counsel was an urging to have a visual alertness greater than we had ever had in civilian life. This sort of urging, I realized, was something I had never experienced in the peacetime world. And I marveled at all the observation of nature that went into the courses he suggested. How closely these men had studied the visible in order to understand and simulate the invisible!

Scouting and Patrolling was another eye-opening Army course, especially in the demonstrations. Generally they were held on a great treeless hillside. After the perfectly flat fields on which we drilled, did push-ups and ran obstacle courses, that huge slope was always a welcome relief. That it was outside the post meant, too, it was not sliced into monotonous rectangles, each bounded by identical barracks, mess halls, lecture rooms and supply shacks. To be marched out the west gate toward that hill gave one a happy sense of coming marvelously into the open. Free of the wretchedly restricting buildings, the spirit expanded, and the vast sky changed from an oppressive lid to a blue empyrean.

Our camp was fifteen miles from Salt Lake City. From the slope, if we looked back, we could just make out the city, nestling in a bay of the great wall of the Wasatch Mountains, which in late spring were still snow-crowned. When we reached the top of the slope another range came into view farther west. These mountains were brown, however, for, high as they seemed, they were lower than the Wasatch.

I well remember a particular day when we were marched to what was called the camouflage area. There was a haze over the eastern mountains, but the big sky was cloudless and we cast sharp shadows on the road as we marched. First, on the lower part of the slope, we were given a lecture on "Crawling, Creeping and Crouching."

"Keep your ass down. Raise your head real slow," said the instructor. And as this less literate lecturer droned on, I watched ranks of soft clouds beginning to form over the blue mountains in the east. We had not been up on the hill in almost two weeks and I was amazed at how much the grass had grown since our last visit.

After instructions in how to be catlike, we were marched to the scouting range on the flat top of the slope. Here were four markers, each a hundred yards beyond the other. To make his trick especially effective, the sergeant picked four of our tallest men. They were instructed to walk to the markers, the first one stopping at the first marker, the second at the second, and so on. Once there they were to stand still. At the first whistle, however, they were to kneel. At the second whistle, they were to lie down.

We watched them go. When the last man had reached the farthest marker, all four stood clearly against the sky. A sharp whistle and suddenly the two farther men were hard to see. The sergeant watched our surprised faces with pleasure. In kneeling, he said triumphantly, the men presented only half as big a target. Then he blew his whistle again. The men dropped to their stomachs and as they did so the far man disappeared completely and the other three became almost invisible. We were all properly amazed.

For me it was the rifle experience all over again. Once more the Army had done something that had never been done for me at school, at camp, or at college. It had taken me into the country and shown me conclusively what happened to the appearance of human beings at different distances in different positions.

And the outdoor instruction with living models was not finished yet. The sergeant took still further advantage of the markers. As soldiers, he said, we had to learn how to survey the terrain before us. It might be so we could move over it ourselves, or it might be so we could pick off enemy scouts trying to approach. The trick was to divide the terrain into belts.

"Look," said the sergeant. "See that man at the first marker. Take him as your first limit. That is, look far to the right and then swing your eyes in an arc so that you observe the whole belt of ground between him and you. When you've reached the left extremity of the arc, lift your eyes and then swing them back in a belt containing the space between the first and the second man. At the end of this swing, lift them higher and swing them back over the ground between the second and third man. Then take the area between the third and fourth man as your next band of vision; and finally swing your eyes back like a pendulum over the band between that last man and the horizon. In this way, you'll be sure there's not a bit of ground your eye hasn't traveled over."

The device was simple enough, but, so help me, no one had ever before taken the trouble to give me this system — or any kind of system — for looking at a scene.

In all of the instances cited, the Army was motivated by the law of visual utility. Its soldiers were necessary to it for victory and it wanted its soldiers to live to fight another day. I have given instances, then, not to praise the Army as the best of schools, but to illustrate the sort of thing that conventional schools might teach but don't.

That our regular schools do not have courses in observation seems to me profoundly revealing. Surely it proves that, fundamentally, our society does not care whether its members are observant or not. This apathy, in its turn, reveals that our culture, which, after all, shapes our values, does not esteem seeing.

Seeing in general, that is. But we are a practical people and we do esteem seeing for specific purposes. Students of the natural sciences, for example, are taught the value of being observant in their special fields. There is stress, too, on certain concentrated seeing in technical training. But the early age at which drawing is usually abandoned is indicative of the prevailing attitude, for drawing is the one school subject conducive to a general heightening of observation.

Our practicality, however, is not our only characteristic making us apathetic to contemplation. Our interest in theory also plays a part, because theory keeps wanting to cut through the particular to an understanding of general laws. Theoretical people, therefore, are impatient with individual differences. They do not want to sit and look at objects for their form alone. Wherever they can, they take visual shortcuts, which means they are constantly conceptualizing, seeing plants instead of azaleas, chairs instead of Hepplewhites and Chippendales.

Our practical, theoretical culture does not stop with being merely indifferent to observing for its own sake. It is actually hostile to it — which I will go into when I come to our vision-deadening Puritanism. But for the moment we can say it is partly because looking, for the sake of looking, is considered to go against what our culture tends to value most — activity.

A consequence of the premium set on activity is the opprobrium heaped on its opposite — idleness. This goes so far that many admittedly silly activities are considered more productive than "doing nothing." They are esteemed above idleness partly for the very fact that they are activities, and partly because they are "fun," whereas idleness is that horror of horrors — wasting time.

Puttering or loafing are perhaps tolerated, but looking around just for the pleasure of looking is a prime example of the worst kind of idleness.

So far, then, in our examination of our environment, we have isolated three main discouragements to general observation: that our culture does not value it, that our schools do not teach it, and that our mores disapprove of it. The sad thing about these cultural vision deadeners is that they work together to perpetuate and intensify each other. The equating of looking with something socially reprehensible like idleness nourishes the notion that looking should not be esteemed. The low estimation of looking supports the idea that it is not worth teaching. That it is not taught prevents its virtues from getting known. That they are not known leaves the prejudice reigning undisturbed. And the continuing prejudice against looking perpetuates the notion that it is sound judgment not to esteem it.

That our society does not encourage general visual alertness, however, does not mean that it is indifferent to all visual activity. On the contrary, it has strong views on the matter. It cares a good deal about some visual activity, and is almost equally firm in what it disesteems. Its attitudes come out in what it judges visually significant and in what it considers should be overlooked.

Clearly, the visual activity it values above all others is reading. Again we can look to our schools as the revealing index. The millions of dollars and hours of time spent teaching school children to read is an obvious indication of the value placed on the skill. We value literacy just for the sake of literacy. We value it so much, in fact, that, besides preaching its gospel to our own youngsters, we insist on spreading it among all the illiterate people of the world, regardless of how it might disrupt the social systems of the countries who have gotten along for centuries without it. At home we spread it with an almost equal disregard for the worth of what is read: bus posters, billboards, paperbacks, comic books, scandal sheets, trade journals, newspapers, magazines — what does it matter, as long as it's reading matter?

That reading can be, and often is, a vision deadener was implied in discussing its rivalry with seeing. And from my own experience I know that reading — or perhaps I should say the stress on reading — can be vision-deadening in still another way. For my addiction to books was not fortuitous. As a boy, I was deliberately broken of the habit of using my eyes as a means to educate myself. In my mind's ear, I can still hear the voices of all those adults.

"Don't try to figure it out by examining it. You are sure to be wrong. Read about it and you'll get the right answer." . . . "The outside world is not worth attention. Things that you see are not important. The important things are the things in books. Study them. Latin conjugations, French grammar, historical dates, chemical formulae, theorems, facts about Shakespeare and Wordsworth, famous poems — these are the things you should concentrate on." . . . "Your powers of artistic judgment are very poor. Don't look at pictures for yourself; read what the authorities say."

And so it went. Not only was I given no eye training, but I was discouraged from practicing any on my own. Education perhaps is not so bad today, but I'm sure many of the old authoritarian, book-centered ideas persist. That they do is, in many respects, ironic, for in working against the professed aims of education, many of them are self-defeating. Could it be that teachers have a vested interest in the matter — perhaps thinking of their jobs? For it seems obvious that with more training in how to be observant there would be less need for teaching. People with powers of observation could teach themselves; or at least get so curious about what they see as to track down the necessary explanations. And of course they would go to books as one of their sources.

For I know that reading can be used to aid vision — and later I will show in what manner. But in the way most people read it discourages observation. And our society contributes greatly to the deadening of our vision — by the enormous stress it places on uncritical, undirected, and usually escapist, reading. Such stress on reading obeys the law of visual utility. Schools teach reading, not only as a skill needed for living in our particular society, but as a basic educational tool for teaching all the other subjects they want to teach. And our society wants its children to read partly for the sake of the children themselves and partly so they can do the ever-increasing amount of white-collar work needed to run our economy. Advances in technology and science, and the increasing role played in our lives by both, also contribute to the utility — indeed the indispensability — of reading. Reading, then, is seriously valued by both our schools and our society as the key to useful knowledge. Much lip service is also paid to it as the key to the world of literature. And though our democratic society pretends not to, it obviously values reading for its assistance in getting propaganda of all kinds circulated and swallowed.

The utilitarian value of reading brings us to our utilitarian age. It is part of its materialism to value the useful so highly, and the visually useful comes in for the general approbation of all things contributing to what we call our standard of living. This explains what we have already noted: the esteem in which seeing for specific purposes is held. This, in turn, accounts for that stress on certain concentrated seeing which has led to the creation of research laboratories, and to our making sure that institutions of higher learning offer courses in which students are taught to be observant of what will be useful to them in their careers as it simultaneously makes them useful to our technological society. Metallurgists are taught to observe minerals, geologists to observe rocks, doctors to observe anatomy, botanists plants, mechanics machinery, and so on. But men trained to be alert in one visual area do not automatically become so in others; in fact, it is often remarkable how unobservant specialists can be outside their own field. Then, too, men whose chief use of their eyes is in a professional capacity often do not do much looking for pleasure. And the reason students in specialized fields at first find their work of specific observing so difficult is that they have had no preliminary training in the general art of observing. Thus at the beginning, young medical students are as uncomfortable as the G.I.'s at our lecture on the rifle. And young specialists in every field have to learn to observe at the same time as they are obliged to learn the difficult names for all their eyes have to get to know.

We have seen how utility varies with each individual at different times. It also varies from person to person. What is useful to the mariner is not useful to the typist. What is useful to the tanner is of no use to the business executive. And our culture's valuing the useful does not mean it esteems any specific class of visible objects under this heading. That it places value on use rather than on appearance, in fact, implies automatically that the object is considered more worth looking at for the purpose it serves than for its design or comeliness.

However, there are objects we do esteem for what they look like. They can be ascertained by examining three classes: the objects that are openly professed to be worth observing; those things which, having been seen, enhance social prestige; and what is unrelentingly advertised.

Our museums give the clue to the objects of the first class. And what does one find in museums? Art above all, but also historical relics and stuffed animals. And the money spent on museums shows we are not hypocritical in proclaiming these things worth looking at. The buildings and their devoted staffs are evidence that we care about these things in action as well as in words.

Perhaps it was a little unkind to speak of the stuffed animals; for after all, in maintaining zoos, our society also proclaims the visual worth of live animals. But the taxidermist reference slipped out as the easiest way to conjure up the contents of a museum of natural history. For nature is something many elements of our society esteem visually. The existence of botanical gardens is further evidence of this. So are our national parks. But there are also elements in our society, it should be noted, that care more for profits than for nature. The unending battle of conservationists for the preservation of wild life and natural beauty is evidence that, on the question of nature, our society is of two minds. Some forces play on the individual to regard nature, others to disregard it.

The equally unending battle of historical societies to preserve old landmarks is evidence that in this matter, too, our society is divided. "Treasure the houses where your great men lived," says one voice. "Gangway!" yells the man giving orders to the bulldozer.

On art, however, particularly the art of the past, there is no division. Works of art, our society constantly says, are visually significant. Witness our practice of excusing children from classes to be trooped out to museums regularly. Naturally, our awe of art has played a large role in determining our ideas of what things outside museums are worth observing. We should esteem, we feel, what the artists of the past have depicted most frequently. Beautiful landscapes, beautiful people, beautiful bunches of flowers, and collections of beautiful objects in front of rich hangings.

Notice the recurrence of the word "beautiful." Visually, we esteem the beautiful. Though perhaps, because society as a whole tends to be somewhat limited in its aesthetic sensibilities, we would be on safer ground if we said we esteem the pretty. From this, follows the converse: We have little use for what is not obviously pretty. Our delight in flowers and our relative lack of interest in leaves (except in autumn) are examples. Another is our dismissing many plants with a word that implies our visual scorn as well as our horticultural disapproval — weeds. A further example is our tendency to stop everything to look at a sunset when we don't feel we should bother to look at the sky during the day. And many women's horror at aging — at showing crow's-feet and gray hairs — is evidence of the value placed on remaining perennially young and, by implication, pretty.

Coming to the second class of objects that are valued visually — those that are socially advantageous because they bring prestige — we find some overlapping. Works of art are a case in point. Because culture is so often equated with prestige, there are many works of art that boost our social stock once we can rightfully lay claim to having seen them. Of course, if we own them, we are elevated even higher. There is overlapping too, in famous European buildings — say, Chartres Cathedral, or St. Mark's in Venice — for they can be classified both as works of art and as sights, that, having been confronted, bestow distinction. Paris streets, Riviera beaches, chalets in the Dolomites, castles along the Rhine, shopping centers in London — these too, or so we are assured by society, bestow distinction on their beholders. In our own country there is also some prestige to be gained — though notably less — from having seen the canyons, etc., classified as "scenic wonders," particularly those where luxury hotels have been established.

If the world of fashion has been evoked by the foregoing, so much the better. It means there need be little laboring of one of the chief weaknesses of prestige-bestowal as a criterion of visual significance.

Obviously there is a close connection between what is fashionable and what gives prestige. In our age, in fact, they go hand in hand, and what gives the most prestige is what is the most fashionable. New fads can be visually stimulating insofar as they lead us to look in new directions. But the swiftness with which crazes come and go is proof of their unreliability as indicators of true value. And think of fashion's negative effects. One has only to mention the phrase "old-fashioned" to conjure up what is no longer considered worth looking at. And one shudders at the vastness of that visual cemetery.

Another weakness of the prestige touchstone is society's peculiar attitude toward objects of the prestige class. It does not value your looking at them so much as that you have "seen" them. Actually, society's encouragement to get you to famous sights can even hinder your looking because it is likely to make you want to take in so many that you end up having no time to see any of them well.

The question as to what is advertised relentlessly answers itself. Obviously, it's merchandise. And there is unending pressure to give our attention to objects whose sale will profit those who manufacture them. But notice that word "attention." Giving something one's attention does not necessarily mean looking at it closely. Our ever-increasing emphasis on colorful packaging makes the distinction clear. In the case of the eye-catching package, one can even say there is an attempt to distract inspection. Things are done up in pretty packages so one won't look at them; so one will buy for the sake of the container, rather than for the sake of what is contained. With the case of products put up in vessels that have secondary uses as household containers, the emphasis on the packaging — and away from the contents — is even more flagrant. And can one honestly say that a picture of a long sleek automobile about to be entered by an elegant young woman is an encouragement to examine the car's motor for its mechanical efficiency? Instead, it is an attempt to discourage honest examination by exploiting the visual appeal of a pretty girl and a status symbol —

both of which are classed by our society as visually significant, and continually vaunted as such.

As advertisers increasingly exploit the objects society deems worth looking at — and think of the use advertising is making of works of art — the visual values of those objects are continually enhanced. Or rather one gets the sense that our culture esteems them ever more highly. In the long run this cannot help but influence our judgment. But advertisers, fundamentally, do not want us to look at their pictures — at least not for their own sakes. They want us to read their copy. And the pictures, after capturing us, are calculated not only to lead us to their copy but to dispose us favorably toward it. Advertisers, then, have a vested interest in our ability to read, and in persuading us that nothing is so worthy for our eyes as reading matter. Proof of their calculated interest is their subsidizing newspapers and magazines, knowing that the carefully fostered appeal of articles, news, and stories will get readers to buy the publications in which their advertisements appear. They want us to become habitual and indiscriminate readers in order to seduce us.

In telling the rifle lecture story I spoke of the widespread belief that, for the average man, nothing is worth looking at minutely. That is, not unless he wants to tinker with it. And that our society feels strongly about this is evidenced by the fact that the tinkerer, though he is tolerated, is regarded as a sort of nut. For it is part of the mocking anti-intellectualism of U.S. popular culture to lump earnest hobbyists with egghead professors.

There are aspects of visual discouragement, then, even in classes of objects society encourages us to look at. Forces work on us to disregard nature and history. With prestige objects, the emphasis is on fashionableness and on having collected the objects rather than on having examined them. With merchandise the emphasis is on being bewitched by the glamorizing presentation rather than on actual scrutiny. And all classes of approved objects suffer from the prevailing notion that, even though you are supposed to look at them, you are not supposed to look at them carefully. The prejudice against studying things too minutely, especially when added to the notion that random looking is time-wasting, intensifies the pall of visual discouragement that hangs around us. But our society does not merely discourage us generally; it apportions specific discouragement for what it deems unworthy of visual attention.

When I spoke of visual snobbery, I suggested how it could be a vision deadener to the individual. I also mentioned the eye-closing influence of comments like "What do you want to look at that for?" Generally when a friend speaks like that it is not because he has examined the inferior object and found it wanting. It is usually because, without knowing it, he has been blinded by the preferences of others. Having unthinkingly absorbed their verdict that only certain accepted things are visually significant, he makes the same advance visual judgments as the society in which he grew up. And at the same time as he reflects his society's visual snobbery, he spreads and fosters the sort of visual exclusion it sanctions.

Snobbery is always the result of intellectual climate. That social snobbery is caused by the mental climate in which upperclass people live is now widely recognized. Less recognized is that mental climates, as well as influencing what we think, influence what we observe. And just as socialites can be swayed in their judgments as to who should be acknowledged socially and who should not, so we can be swayed in what we look at and in what we choose not to look at. Widespread social impulses push us to observe certain things; whereas to observe other things we have to break through conventional attitudes. But even though it resembles social snobbery in being more unanimous in what it considers outside the pale than in its evaluation of what it respects, visual snobbery tends to express its negative judgments in subtle and indirect ways.

Thus there are no hard and fast rules about eligibility, but in the main there is agreement on the classes that should not be invited to the visual cotillion. And what is frowned upon for observation is often merely the negative of what is valued. Thus there is a tendency to consider that anything that is not art is not worth looking at. As already suggested, there is even stronger feeling against what is not pretty. And many have shut their eyes to what is not historical. City scenes are often dismissed for not being landscapes. Untold groupings of objects are not looked at because they don't resemble still lifes in art museums. And many vistas and buildings are ignored because there is no social prestige to be gained from having seen them. Defined more positively, the things we tend to think unworthy of inspection are objects of humble function, sights we pass every day, things that seem ordinary because they are widespread, and things at close range near to the ground.

If any one doubts that we tend to scorn with our eyes anything we are likely to kick or avoid with our feet, consider the lowly status of the puddle. Even its name betrays our disdain. Yet, as those who have discovered the ocular delights of puddles will testify, these irregular mirrors, that bring down such odd bits of the sky, are wonderfully varied in their visual interest.

Since the objects scorned form the bulk of our daily visual experience, one can estimate how much our visual snobbery interferes with our looking. When one adds to this another result of social conditioning — the amount of time our eyes are engaged in reading — one comes to realize the extent to which cultural forces shut our eyes to the world about us. And the arraignment is still not complete, for there is another way modern society tends to shut our eyes.

Much of what it has thrown up is so hideously ugly that the eye flinches before it. Box-like factories, cheap housing, smoke-spewing industrial works, railroad sidings, automobile graveyards, slag heaps, dumps — one has only to name them to recoil. And the creation of these horrors has generally meant the destruction of what was pleasant in the area before. As industry expands, too, not only does it encroach ever more widely on nature, but it spreads its blight over places of human habitation that before were quite passable. Thanks to overcrowding and neglect, housing developments become slums; pleasant byroads become mazes through miles of used-car lots, billboards and hot dog stands.

Nature tempts the eye to observe, to wander through its groves just for the sheer pleasure of it. But what industrial civilization has done in its inhumanity to man and to man's environment is in many areas so appalling that the eye refuses to wander. It resolutely seeks a book so it won't be obliged to see. In saying this, of course, I may be swayed by visual snobbery of my own. But surely there is a difference between the homely and the ugly —

especially the environmentally ugly, for this involves a wounding of the human spirit. Conversely, among homely surroundings, as the word itself implies, we feel at home.

So far I have not spoken of either the accuracy or inaccuracy of our seeing. That it has taken us centuries to get it as exact as it is will be discussed in the chapter on art books. But that it must be influenced and limited by the spirit of our time is inevitable. Studies of primitive societies of the present and our knowledge of the past both point to this conclusion. In fact, it is now a truism of anthropology that all human beings are deeply influenced by the values of the society in which they live. And what applies to values in general applies also to visual values, which, like the larger complex of which they are a part, of necessity include concepts, theories and ideas. Or if you want to state it less flatteringly — preconceptions, notions and prejudices.

In every society the time spirit tends to condition how the world is seen. We are no more exempt from this rule than are pygmy tribes in Africa. The difference is that in their lives it is easy for us to see the time spirit in operation; in our own lives it is difficult. Two factors give us an advantage over them: we are outsiders, and our time spirit is different. With our own visual conditioning, however, we are handicapped in the same way as the pygmies. We are insiders, and our time spirit is so pervasive — so undiscernible from the air we breathe — that it is difficult to imagine different outlooks to serve as touchstones to reveal the limitations imposed by our own.

But if we cannot discern the limitations and distortions of our time spirit, our traveling and our studies have made us aware that they must exist. Renaissance illustrations provide particularly good proof of how men always see "through the eyes of their own period." The phrase is Erwin Panofsky's and in his brilliant essay, "Albrecht Dürer and Classical Antiquity," he shows how those illustrations prove his point. By contrasting photos of classical antiquities with representations of them by Renaissance artists, he shows how those later artists distorted and changed the original appearances. His demonstration is particularly telling because he gives both Italian and German examples, revealing that nationals of both countries, besides being inexact in their perceptions, were inexact in different ways. In other words, they were bound so closely by the perceptions of their time that, besides the general period influence, they were even bound by the subtle distortions of their particular cultural area.

Those of us who live in the New World can test the period coloration of those sixteenth-century illustrations in still another way. We know the scenery of our own continent and we know what the Indians of the Americas look like. Thus we know that those illustrators, who were not very accurate in seeing the old, were even less accurate in seeing the new. For obviously the Indians here never resembled those Renaissance nudes in the first engravings European artists made of the New World. Nor could these artists have seen our landscapes clearly or they would have captured them more closely. Then, shifting from artists to period-bound colonists, how, in the name of precision, could the first settlers have ever called such obviously brown-skinned people red?

When one thinks further about the inaccuracies of those first observers of our scene, one realizes how the inaccuracies came about. Besides their vision being shaped by the art style of their day, the human tendency — no matter what the period — is to see things through our preconceptions. Thus often we see imperfectly because we have definite notions and we discern only what we expect to see. And unless we look very scrupulously, we fall into the habit of seeing only what confirms what we think is there.

Inescapably, then, we are subtly governed by forces that go unrecognized as shapers of seeing. Some of the forces are those of selection, for nowadays different things have different utility. But undoubtedly some of the influences spring from a vast number of partial perceptions inaccurately interpreted. In a sense, we are all like passengers in an airplane who have just heard that there may be some delay in landing due to restricted visibility. To come closer to the ground of reality we, too, have clouds and fog to penetrate. And this brings us to the matter of visual skill.

I know that in my own case, when objects are not before my eyes, it is often difficult to visualize their relationships in space — how the earth and the moon are related to each other as they rotate in the solar system, for instance. This is because grasping spatial relationships is a particular type of visual skill. Even when a number of buildings are standing upright before your eyes, it takes skill to infer their spatial relationships just from the way they appear.

Wayward forms, such as those assumed by clouds or smoke, also require considerable skill for their accurate perception; for, in this case, our schools' emphasis on geometry and geometrical terms tends to make it hard for us to see things that are irregular, asymmetrical, discontinuous, and unenclosed. The Gestalt psychologists discovered that the total context draws our attention away from details, so details take skill to discern. Subtle contours that are outlined only in light, the effects of atmosphere on colors, objects that are in motion, complicated patterns in which there are no sharp differences of color or texture to provide good emphasis for the salient elements, structures that are not intelligible in terms of known forms, small features in over-all compositions of much vibrant activity — all these need skill and practice for their discernment.

Visual skill is still another aspect of our seeing that is shaped by cultural values. A society that does not esteem observation as a general acquisition — that does not provide the sort of visual training, say, that we got in the Army — is not likely to produce a breed of skillful observers. Perhaps most other generations have been equally purblind. But this does not exonerate us. If we are going to turn out citizens capable of educating themselves more by being able to use their eyes better, we need detailed lectures on articles of common use. We need explanations of why things appear as they do. We need to understand the character and capacities of the eye. We need schemes of systematic looking. We need to be taken out of doors for demonstrations of the reality of appearances in the natural world. And we need to have it brought home to us that we must have a wide concept of what is visually significant.

That our society has enormous pressures to conform, both in thought and in behaviour, is well recognized. It is part of the time spirit, too, that there are also pressures towards conformity of vision. Unfortunately, most of us have been too unobservant to sense those visual pressures. For one thing, our visual exploration has not been adventurous enough to bump against those pressures. We haven't felt their restrictions because we've been happy in the ocular limits set for us. And it has been both a proof of, and a part of, our visual torpor not to notice our blinkers.

In fact, if you were to ask a cultivated citizen to classify his liberties, he might say — that is, if he could acknowledge how much of his thinking was deliberately shaped — that his greatest liberty was in a less molested mental area: the freedom of the eye. He might support his theory, too, by arguing that observation is the activity least hedged by legislation. When reminded of movie censorship, he might shift to say that, of all his freedoms, using his eyes was least controverted by economic considerations. And he might be right. Nevertheless, we have far less visual independence than we think. Scarcely recognized visual interventions are all about us. They influence how much looking we do, what we look at, what we ignore, how accurately we perceive what comes to our attention, how we interpret what we see and how much visual skill we have. An outcry is needed against them, for alert, exact, unstereotyped seeing — visual non-conformity, that is — is perhaps our surest means of offsetting the stultification of other conformities.

Part III

PRACTICAL AIDS FOR BETTER SEEING

CHAPTER II

Curiosity, Knowledge, and Time

We have reached a turning point. Fundamentally, the last seven chapters have had a single purpose: to gain enough understanding of the visual process to explain why we so seldom have the degrees of intensified vision described in the first three. In a sense, it is because we are victimized. For there are forces in ocular sensing itself, as well as in our environment and our mode of life, that, optically speaking, conspire to keep us in low gear. I have spent time on visual habits and psychological factors, too, because the conspiracy is a complex one and it is necessary to understand the conspirators to outwit them. Fortunately, self help is easily available, and Part III will be devoted chiefly to practical aids. Showing how they operate, by illustrating seeing in action, will elucidate the visual process further; demonstrating at the same time that we have by no means exhausted vision's potentialities.

Fundamentally, our greatest allies are curiosity, knowledge, and time. I mention them in a lump partly because I do not know which should be singled out first, and partly because they work together in an interacting fashion. However, let us start with curiosity.

Curiosity is a form of response. It can range from a sense of wonder to mere nosiness. Essentially, though, it is an awareness of partial knowledge accompanied by interest. And both wings of the definition need to be stressed. Obviously there must be some knowledge, for one can't be curious about what is completely outside one's experience. But just as obviously that knowledge must be recognized as being no more than partial, for with complete knowledge curiosity dies in being satisfied; and there is no sense of puzzlement, no feeling that there is anything more to find out or to check, in order to explain the initial sensation of not having the whole answer. Why interest must be present is to distinguish the sensation of curiosity from the feeling — or lack of feeling — we have for any number of partially known things about which we have no desire to speculate at all.

When a phrase is widely used one can be sure it corresponds to some reality. The phrase "idle curiosity" is an example. As well as suggesting a particular kind of curiosity, it also suggests that different sorts of curiosity can be classified. Its logical opposite, disciplined curiosity, was the first I thought of, but I abandoned these extremes when I saw a more useful subdivision could be worked out by classifying a curiosity by its intensity. I found four main degrees. I call them latent curiosity, idle curiosity, active curiosity and, again borrowing from the popular treasury, consuming curiosity.

Objects that catch our eye are not, of course, the only things that stir curiosity, for sometimes curiosity is the cause of vision, rather than vice versa. But no matter whether a curiosity causes you to look and so to have vision or whether something that catches your eye prompts your curiosity, once the stimulus has begun, the relationship is reciprocal. Curiosity can lead to more vision, which in turn can fan greater curiosity. The stimulus of one on the other grows greater in each of the four stages. And the subject matter, accumulating substance by contributions from both the eye and the brain, can always move upward through the stages if it is given time. And time is so staunch an ally that it does not operate merely when actively applied. Time, in its passive capacity, also aids the ascent when we just let it lapse.

The process — or perhaps one should say the interaction of the processes — was illustrated in detail in the chapter on the face cards. Because I began playing card games in childhood and have continued to love bridge, I had a latent curiosity about cards. There was therefore something in my consciousness for that riddle to stir. The stirring was enough to step my curiosity up from latent to idle. Then, as I had the day off, I had the opportunity and inclination to indulge that idle curiosity by taking the time to get out a deck of cards to see if it was actually true that the diamond monarch was the only king with one eye.

In this case, then, it was something non-visual that started the curiosity. But it was the visual that made the idle stage so brief. Because the moment I looked at the kings with a motive beyond determining their suit, my vision of the face cards was galvanized, and in that instant my idle curiosity became active.

I got on the phone. My artist friend increased my curiosity with the suggestion that the kings and queens might be actual persons. And when I borrowed another friend's eyes and we looked at three decks comparatively, my curiosity passed into the consuming stage. With each shift I observed more.

Perhaps every curiosity does not pass so quickly from one stage to another, yet basically the experience is representative. Curiosity does lead us to look at what has aroused our inquisitiveness. Looking leads us to further features, which often increase our curiosity. If we then apply reason, question others, or go to source books, we gather the knowledge that reveals that things which piqued us were even more interesting than we dreamed when we began our tentative investigations.

Curiosity, then, helps us overcome the eclipsing effects of single-level perception, flash glimpsing, habitual indifference, long familiarity, and preoccupation with abstractions. But note that we have to give time to the satisfaction of curiosity; time for the second and third look; time for the observing of something comparable to establish what is unique in the chosen object; time to question friends; even time to read books and visit libraries.

Curiosity, too, is an ally against the vision-deadening fears that we are visually incompetent or that we will come up with the wrong answers. It aids in this battle because there is nearly always an element of disquiet in curiosity. The feeling of being stirred up is often very slight, and sometimes it is exciting. Nevertheless, it has its troubling side, for the mind is uncomfortable not knowing. And often this degree of discomfort will be enough to enable us to march through our fears in order to free ourselves from the displeasure of being baffled.

Because of initial discomfort, curiosity can also be one of the strong allies in overcoming two of vision's greatest enemies —

lethargy and mental laziness. It can also help overcome impatience. And, if you are too turned in on yourself, it can pull your attention in an outward direction.

Nowadays, with so many libraries, and so many librarians willing to help, no one needs to feel helpless about his curiosity because of inability to find needed information. So when you feel the stirring of curiosity, let me urge you not to choke it off. Instead, let it develop, follow it up, pursue it. Speculate about it. Bring your imagination to play on it. Discipline and direct the investigation by formulating the questions the curiosity prompts. Seek the answers, and be prepared to devote some energy to the search. Even be bold enough to consult experts. The hunt itself will be pleasurable, for satisfying curiosity is one of the greatest joys in life.

There are particular joys, too, in pursuing a curiosity started by the eye. For if it was something visible that stirred the first glimmer of curiosity, you can be sure that you'll end up by seeing what caused the glimmer more fully and richly. Also, because the eye is restless and less fixed in judgment than the mind, vision has a way of opening new areas for curiosity. Some may prove truly original, and often the unexpectedness of the byways down which the eye leads us is part of their pleasure.

Information gained through an eye-started curiosity, too, has the vitality of all knowledge acquired in pursuit of curiosity. For there is always something particularly living in the three-way relationship between a man, an object of curiosity and the information he has gleaned in finding out about it. When we hunt with zest, part of us goes into what we track down, and the adventure of acquisition and what we acquire, in turn, become part of us. Then there are all the advantages of facilitation of learning and durability of retention. For just as no painful effort is needed to pick up what satisfies curiosity, so no special effort is needed to retain it. It clicks magnetically to us and it remains with us because it was not something a teacher wanted us to know, but something we wanted to know for ourselves.

Curiosity can be divided into solitary curiosity and gregarious curiosity. The latter, I think, is the more common, for often people will tell you that what arouses their curiosity most is what they find other people interested in. It will range from a personality who is being much talked about in the news to whatever happens to be at the center of an unwonted crowd. Gregarious curiosity helps the social wheels turn, but as long as it remains merely idle it is not especially fruitful, either for society or for individuals. It is not until an individual makes a curiosity personal by seizing on it and translating it from idle to active that it begins to be a generating force. Then it starts leading him to discoveries that are sure to be exciting to him personally; and which, if they are not discoveries others have made, might become important to the world at large.

The history of invention is studded with examples of men who got on significant tacks by noting things whose strangeness caught their curiosity. Probably every individual, too, can point to a curiosity that began when, in the course of aimless looking, something began to seem worth a little investigating. I know my own life was profoundly influenced when I noticed that, after watering a philodendron, the tips of its strands reared higher than the day before. This unexpected movement in a piece of vegetation that I had thought was motionless shifted my curiosity from idle to active. I ended by learning so much from the plant that it required a book to tell the story.

Knowledge can aid vision even more than curiosity. One of its manners of help is the way of curiosity itself, for a body of knowledge is like a powerhouse that keeps generating new curiosity. If you doubt this, take a walk in the country with a naturalist. His knowledge of everything about him does not make him blasé. On the contrary, it makes him alert to things you never noticed, and you will find his curiosity is aroused by all sorts of unexpected things. Similarly, if you go to a museum with an art expert, you will find him moving forward to examine details that escaped you altogether. And when you stop to think about your own curiosities, you will find the most active are likely to be in the fields where you are best informed. Those fields are our "interests." And the very word acknowledges the presence of curiosity, for to say we are interested in something is to say it excites our continuing curiosity.

Knowledge, in fact, is one of the chief agents that translates idle curiosity to active curiosity. For often it is an extra bit of information about something to which we have been exposed that makes the barely heeded object seem suddenly remarkably interesting. Once any interest has been securely established, it becomes a magnetic nucleus that keeps drawing to itself further information, which as it accumulates turns into knowledge. All knowledge tends to want to augment itself, and this is particularly true of the sort that has been acquired through satisfying personal curiosity.

A clear instance of this was provided when chance led me to show George Kubler some of the stones and scraps of pottery I had collected in the Mixteca Alta. I had come to know the Yale art historian through an interest in sixteenth-century Mexican architecture and he came to my apartment in connection with that architecture. I did not realize how much he knew about archaeology at the time; so I showed him my sherds not because I thought of him as an expert, nor because I was particularly interested in them, but because they came from the region of a monastery in which we were both interested. I was in for a number of surprises. The first was the extent of his curiosity, for not content with knowing merely what town they came from, he wanted to know what part of the town.

I had picked up the sherds on different walks and just dumped them into a cardboard box. So I was embarrassed when I could not remember whether a certain piece had come from a mound to the west of the village or whether I had found it on flat ground. Then he pressed me as to how deeply the items had been buried when found. That was easy: they all had come from the surface. But this question, even though I could answer it correctly, embarrassed me too. It showed me how uncurious I had been not to think of digging to find if there was pottery of a different kind in a lower stratum.

Then his curiosity led him to do something I had never done: to examine each sherd on both sides, as well as to hold it up in profile. What followed, I felt, was a remarkable example of knowledge increasing the possibilities of vision. Those scraps of pottery had seemed to me merely meaningless bits of baked clay, some decorated with a little abstract drawing. If I'd thought of their curvature at all, it was merely to think that perhaps some of them had curled a bit through lying so long exposed to sun and rain.

"This piece," he said picking up a coral-colored sherd, "is part of a bowl that had all its decoration on the inside."

"How on earth can you tell that?" I asked.

"By the curve," he said and held the piece in his long fingers for me to see its profile. "Can't you see it is part of a fairly deep bowl. I would say its sides ran up at about a forty-five-degree angle." And he waggled the sherd a bit till I could see what seemed its logical slope.

"But how do you know you've got it right side up?" I asked.

"Oh, that's easy. You can see the top edge is smooth. That's not a fracture line. Look at the way it is rounded, and see how that finished edge compares with the angled edges and the porous roughness of the breaks. Besides, the decoration shows you it's the top. There's a reddish-brown line running along it."

It was another instance of kings reformulating and birds flying in. The fragment of pottery remained unchanged; and I knew the stimulus pattern the sherd had registered on my retinas was

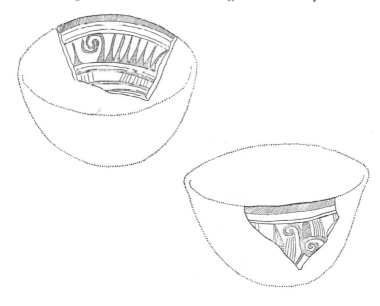

unaltered. But, oh how differently it appeared! Prodded by George's words, my imagination had done what his had done the moment he saw the sherd. It had conjured up the rest of the bowl.

The bit of clay, no longer meaningless to me, was now a segment of a whole I understood. And I could see how George was so sure the bowl had been decorated on the interior. That spit curl and those reddish lines that looked like golf tees were painted on the concave surface of the sherd. Similarly, I could see how he knew the bowl had a plain exterior, for the convex surface was as naked as an eggshell.

"Now this bowl," he said, taking up another sherd, "shows you the opposite type of decoration. It was plain on the inside and painted on the outside." This was now easy for me to follow, for the rim could be easily discovered, and here it was the concave surface that was plain, the convex one that was painted.

In my initial amazement, George had seemed a sort of wizard. But when I picked up still another sherd and figured out the likely form of the vessel of which it had been part, I realized such identification was not so difficult after all, especially with simple, symmetrical vessels. I realized, too, that one reason entire bowls were easy for George to conjure up was because he had seen whole bowls with shapes and decorations like the ones from which my sherds had been broken. And even if he had not seen their exact prototypes, I realized that, because archaeology relies so much on pottery to aid in the reconstruction of lost cultures, his basic instruction must have included the study of vessel shapes.

Knowledge, then, besides giving us the curiosity to look, can help us see by supplying us with the completing aspects of things that are visible only in part. This mental provision of the missing parts is more important than is generally recognized, for whole concepts are needed for understanding and very often the things we need to discern are only partially exposed. This is particularly true when the light is poor or the object far off. An extreme instance is that of a soldier who detects the presence of a sniper because he knows what the barrel of a rifle looks like. For to the retina — which merely records — the object revealed only in part is as much a fragment as the bits of pottery we had been examining.

A moment later, George began inspecting the two sherds in a

new way. He set them side by side, their decorated surfaces facing up. As he studied them I benefited from another dividend of his basic studies.

"See," he said, "you've got two different types of ware here. The one decorated on the outside is brown on cream. The other is red on pink."

I could recognize the classifying terminology as standard archaeological lingo and I could see the colors he specified, but I was puzzled as to how he was so sure of the superpositions. "How do you know which one is 'on' the other?" I asked.

"By the slip," he replied. Then with a dunking motion he suggested how each bowl had been dipped into a solution first. The coating it acquired in this way, he explained, was called the slip, and after he had pointed it out as distinct from the raw clay showing at the fractured edges, I could see this coating — cream in one case, pink in the other — did underlie the decoration. Just as clearly, I could discern that the painting was a later addition. So, literally, the brown was put *on* the cream. And I realized the visual aid of a new kind of knowledge: knowing not only what a thing was made of, but how it was made.

Another object I had picked up in the Mixteca was a cylindrical bit of stone about an inch and a half long that was tapered at one end and beveled at the other. I had been attracted by its bullet shape, its olive-green color, its smoothness, and the fact that it had obviously been fashioned by hand.

"This is probably a scraper for smoothing clay," said George, as he curled in his fingers and started planing the beveled face of the stone over the rounded outer side of his wrist.

I had seen modern Mexican potters polishing damp clay vessels with a similar movement, so I understood what he was talking about. When I tried it on my own wrist, I saw how comfortably the tapered stone could be held with the thumb and first two fingers, and how silkily its flattened surface moved over the taut skin. Obviously its nose would scrape off any lumps from a clay surface that was not as smooth as skin.

Here was an instance of knowledge aiding vision in a further way. What it brought to that stone was awareness of its function. Subtly this transformed it. No longer was it an abstract object, nor a stone bullet (the metaphorical name I had given it in hopes of fixing it in my mind). It was a tool. Seen with this comprehension, it was vastly more interesting than it had been before, especially when the archaeologist told me that in being a pre-Conquest item it was more than four hundred years old.

Combining the lessons Kubler taught me through the sherds and the polishing stone, I came to understand still another way knowledge aids vision. Though using different means, he did the same thing for both the sherd and the polisher. By supplying, in fancy, the missing aspects of the former, and by explaining the function of the latter, he made both intelligible.

Why this contributed so much to vision is easily understood if one remembers what has been said about the visual system. The mind, we now know, is not like a camera taking in everything that hits the retina. Instead, whether one interprets it as operating psychological lids in front of the eyeballs or a valve behind them, the mind tends to admit only what it chooses. And one of its leading principles in deciding on its invitations is intelligibility.

This can be observed operating both negatively and positively. Again and again what the mind ignores or refuses to absorb is the unintelligible. And what is true for passages in books or arguments in debates is also true for objects within the visual field. Conversely, the mind receives the intelligible hospitably. And the easier the material is to grasp the more it is welcomed. Witness the way bookish men turn involuntarily to billboards because they are easier to read than the more subtle signs of spring.

The dividends from Kubler's visit continued long after that morning in April, 1956, when it took place. Unknowingly, he had done a lot to transform my curiosity about Mexican archaeology from idle to active. One of my active steps was to visit the Museum of the American Indian. There I learned that his interpretation of the function of my stone bullet had planted in my mind an even greater curiosity about that stone than I knew. For my eyes lit up when I saw, lying under the glass of a case, a number of similar stones.

Naturally I read the labels avidly. The smooth stones were all tools. Some were said to be polishers; others were said to be chisels. I remembered Kubler's element of doubt, and it occurred to me it might have been justified. The polishers in the case were all rounder and chunkier than my stone. Perhaps, I said to myself, my stone is a chisel, for it was closer in shape to the objects classed as chisels than to those called polishers. And my uncertainty led me to think further of the benefit of doubt as a stimulus to vision.

Theory — which might be said to be knowledge in its incomplete state — is perhaps even more stimulating to observation than complete knowledge. For theory, like curiosity — having an element of uncertainty — makes you much more energetic about the two aspects of investigation that Jerome Bruner has called "cue search" and "confirmation check." For visually, I almost clawed my way through that glass to search for cues in those stone tools which would give me the checks to confirm the category to which my stone belonged.

My knowledge of my stone, then, had helped my vision in the museum in one of the best ways that knowledge can: by creating alertness to new examples of a class in which a preliminary interest has been stirred. The fact that my stone was almost the whole length of Manhattan away from the stones in the museum was instructive, too. It showed that knowledge can be brought to bear on vision under different conditions of time and space.

With my stone, I now had two instances of how knowledge had been brought to bear: as I looked directly at it at home (while Kubler was demonstrating it); and as, in the museum, I recalled it to the mind's eye. So whether an object is under your eyes, or only an image in your memory, it can be enriched by knowledge — that is, providing its image was taken in sharply and clearly in the first place. And whether present or remembered, it grows more interesting as it attracts more knowledge to it. More knowledge, of course, can often mean information about related subjects. And as far as pre-Columbian stone tools are concerned, the magnetism of my stone at the museum helped establish two other magnetic nuclei. Now I'm equally interested in scrapers, polishers *and* chisels.

Since then, my curiosity about Mexican archaeology has passed into the consuming stage, and I have gained enough knowledge to use another archaeological object to illustrate further ways in which knowledge facilitates vision. Besides helping to complete the incomplete, to provide the awareness of manufacture that accounts for exact appearances, and to bring the understanding of function that makes for intelligibility, knowledge — by helping us to interpret — helps enormously in observing the intricate, the detailed, and the visually ambiguous.

In a sense, two of these are different aspects of the same difficulty. For, by its very definition, a complicated object is one that consists of many intricately interrelated parts. One way knowledge helps with objects of this class, of course, is that it eliminates the sort of panicky blindness I felt with the Egyptian hieroglyphics. Another is that it helps the mind untangle the details by taking them up one by one.

Let us see how it works with my chosen object — a bas-relief from one of the friezes decorating Pyramid B at Tula.

I am not sure how this drawing of the Toltec relief struck you, but, if you are like most of my friends, you've done a double-take, shaken your head and had a feeling of confused incomprehension, not knowing whether it is man or beast. Whatever your response, you will admit, I think, that it qualifies as an example of what I am talking about — ambiguous complexity.

To the observer unversed in pre-Columbian lore, it is what the Gestalt psychologists would call an "unstable" figure; or to quote Koffka, it is "a stimulus constellation which can give rise to several perceptual organizations." This is so because it contains so many kinds of ambiguity. Because there is little in it that is familiar, or unmistakably structured, it is hard to tell which details pertain to the figure, which to the ground. It is hard to tell, too, whether it is a man or a beast; and if a beast, if it is a single beast facing you, or two beasts in profile facing each other. In fact, what it means to you will depend on how you organize it perceptually; or, as the Gestaltists say, how you segregate the elements. It will alter, too, according to the way you conceive the relationship of the parts.

A man familiar with Middle American art has two great advantages in segregating two of the chief constellations correctly. He knows that artists of that era often depicted personages with great feathered head-dresses. He also knows that the artists often represented human heads within the mouths of beasts. Let us, on the next page, take off the creature's hat and pull the man out of his mouth, and see what we get.

When shorn of his panache and deprived of his lunch, the iguana-like monster is clearly visible. Also, now there is no longer the compelling attraction of those human eyes, the beast is easy for those with a little experience to recognize as the Earth Monster. For this image, like all of man's religious symbols, contains more than meets the eye, being partly its visual self and partly its idea.

Split down the center, the Earth Monster suggests two creatures facing each other. This ambiguity — one beast or two — I'm sure is deliberate, just as I think there is purpose in depicting the long, lolling double tongue so it might be the monster's *or* the man's. These elements suggesting two-in-one, or one-in-two, I think are meant to convey a concept of the ancient religion that Zelia Nuttall, one of the greatest Mexican scholars, emphasized: "the unity, yet the duality" of the Supreme Being. And, if two beasts are seen in profile, note that the heads suggest serpents rather than lizards. So the figure has not been completely explained. Enough has been said, however, to show how understanding, by the logical segregations it allows, considerably reduces confusion. The demonstration shows, too, how knowledge can make a complicated figure, if not fully intelligible, at least visually manageable.

The bas-relief may be an extreme illustration, but in many basic respects it is a valid one. For in general terms, as distinct from actual appearance, it is like many things one sees: Its boundaries are not well defined, its forms are cohesive only if they are understood, and its parts have equal value to the uninformed eye, without essential aspects being given any more stress than subsidiary ones. One sees the same phenomenon with a wall of trees on the edge of a clearing when the light is particularly flat. The man ignorant of trees can hardly discern any of the tree outlines, but the botanist can see the maples and the beeches quite distinctly. Similarly, the radio technician, looking at a mass of outwardly undistinguishable wires can see which carry signal impulses, which go to tubes and which leave the transformer with current for various other components.

Knowledge enabling the eye to impose intelligibility on the complex brings me back to the story of the fire in the courtyard. Let me recall that my power to observe that particular fire was greatly enhanced by the application of three succinct bits of knowledge: that flame is burning vapor, that the rate of burning depends on density, and that hot air ascends.

In contrast to the sherds, the fire was an entity complete in itself; in contrast to the inert, unchanging stone tool it was a moving, constantly changing thing; and, in contrast to the man-made bas-relief, it was a phenomenon of nature. The fire, therefore, required different non-visual factors to make it intelligible. Because of its dynamic nature, what was needed was knowledge of its laws of being. My scientific touchstones were particularly helpful in observing the flames. Realizing they were vapors helped me see how they emerged from the solid logs much as one would expect vapors to emerge. Realizing that hot air ascends helped me see that those released vapors were not the wild, capricious, illogical creatures I had always thought. Instead, they were dabs of fire being bandied about in a perfectly explicable way by air currents, which, in turn, were behaving according to the laws that always govern them.

The fire story also illustrates another of my themes: the importance of time. I have already detailed how time worked to advantage during my observation of a church façade. But that specific case barely touched on time as a general visual aid; besides, it was confined to time bestowed by the accident of drawing. The experience before the fire is more representative, for then I was engaged solely in observing.

First, it should be noted I did not brush off the fire as if it were any old fire. I gave a whole evening to it. Once that commitment was made, I gave the time deliberately, beginning by gazing long enough for a clear picture of the fire to form in my mind. Once firmly planted, the picture of the flaming center and the black outer butts stirred my curiosity about that phenomenon of the best burning occurring at the point of contact. Once the question emerged, I did not dismiss it but gave it time to clarify in my mind. Once it was sharply formulated, I took the time to recall what I knew about the physical laws of fire in the hope that those laws might help in the answering. When a possible theory occurred to me, I took the time to reverse the logs to test it. Even when the heated butts began flaming too, I did not leave the fire. I gave it still more time and new hypotheses rose to be tested. And lest I seem to be blowing my own horn, let me point out how many of the fruitful results of that evening were due, not to myself, but to time. Perhaps its chief gift was to free me from one of the greatest vision-deadeners — impatience — which is the feeling that one lacks time. The gift of patience also freed me from the vision-deadener of activity — not all activity, of course, but the sort that makes observing difficult by preempting the mind's attention and exhausting the body's energy.

Besides allowing for the things I have detailed — leeway for speculation, the chance for imagination to come into play, space for the pursuit of curiosity, the opportunity for bits of past knowledge to rise to the surface, and freedom to find form-fixing words — time also gave me the freedom to look idly. This was in addition to the freedom to look purposefully. It was a great boon, for idle looking is often the more creative, for looking with a purpose, after all, is observing what we have already decided we want to see. It is an outgrowth of an old curiosity, whereas idle looking can start new curiosities. It needs to be noted, however, that the allotment of time for idle looking must be particularly generous. For the very fact that the looking is haphazard implies that the mind, generally concerned with its own purposes, is not likely to respond to what the eye has caught if the object does not have time to make a marked impression.

On that particular night in the courtyard, the greatest boon of idle looking was the unexpected vision of the candle. And the way I saw that candle leads to a gift from time that has frequently been implicit in this book, but not yet spelled out.

Knowing that I was coming to it, I deliberately hinted in the opening paragraph of this chapter that most of the time we are visually in low gear. Time's fortuitous gift on the fire evening consisted of passing effortlessly, and at first without awareness of what had happened, into a gearshift, which, visually speaking, was higher than usual.

Although again I would prefer a less mechanistic metaphor, I use it because each of the gears in an automobile has its own character, and I have long felt that our minds have comparable ones. When we are in low we go slowly and our mental motor seems to work with effort. When we are in second we move faster and the engine is quieter, though there is still a feeling of dragging. Yet when we get into high we seem to speed effortlessly along, with the motor silenced to a gentle purring. But even though an automobile can go into reverse too, it must be stressed that the mind is infinitely more versatile. It can shift in many directions — not just forward or backward — nor does it have to remain on one level. We can get into the aural gear, for instance, in which we do nothing except listen. If we want to jogtrot we can shift gears and our body will mechanically start us moving at a pace that is faster than walking, but slower than running. Besides this bodily shift, with the intelligence almost completely disengaged, we have almost equally autonomous emotional gearshifts. Then if we want to concentrate on thinking out a problem, say, we can shift into the brain gear, wherein our mental energies will all be engaged in work on the problem. We have a gear for daydreaming, too, wherein the world of our bodily existence seems to fade away. And, of course, we have an eye gear.

It might be argued that, as long as our eyes are open, they are, as gears, always engaged. But the common type of haphazard, semi-aware observing is not what I mean. Perhaps I should call it the looking gear, for what I have in mind is that gear in which we use our eyes exclusively in order to observe.

It is not always an easy gear to shift into, and requires more discipline than the chronic daydreamer possesses. Yet, oddly enough, it is sometimes easier for the daydreamer to shift into it than for the man of concentration. The latter is apt to be kept from it by his very concentrating, for as likely as not he is fixed on something non-visual — a business or family problem, an emotional ache or perhaps the pursuit of abstract ideas. However, even the most preoccupied man can shift into the looking gear if he will make a start at observing something concrete, and then use time as his ally.

With the fire, I kept my attention on it so long that, unknowingly, I moved into high eye gear. Proof of this is given by what happened subsequently. I was in the looking gear when I turned toward the candle, which in large part accounts for the sharpness with which I saw it. Then, being still in the looking gear, I noticed related objects: the electric light bulb as an extension of the candle in the glass chimney, and the big neon sign as an extension of the glass-protected lighting element of the bulb. I saw these things as I had never seen them before because I had gained such momentum in the looking gear that I remained in it even after I had decided to give up observing for the night.

The first of the many other examples in this book was the deck of cards, where the riddle in Proust clicked me suddenly into the looking gear. In most of the other instances, though, the shift happened only with time: the time I took concentrating only on colors during the winter train ride got me into the looking gear so that on a later visit to the washroom I was struck by the gold instructions; and the time I spent looking at objects from the plane in order to find similes also carried me into the looking gear. Here, too, I kept noticing things — like the resemblance between the snowy hills and my sundae — after I had abandoned deliberate looking; and again it was because I had not yet passed out of the gear.

I am sure you, too, can summon up many such instances. Haven't you noticed, for instance, how when you come out of a motion picture everything on the street resembles a scene from a movie? This is because, as you were sitting in the theatre watching the film, you shifted, without knowing it, into the looking gear.

However, the sensation that the world about you looks like something in a movie generally does not last very long. This is because the movie experience does not put us in the looking gear as securely as when the mind, too, is actively engaged. Because of the need for double engagement, time is a highly important aid. For it is not enough to start the eyes in a course of deliberate looking; the mind also has to come into play so that as you look you ponder what you see. And the mind, particularly if it is not accustomed to analyzing and interpreting visual phenomena, finds this an effort. Two conditions are generally needed: first, that the mind be disengaged from what it was thinking about previously; and second, that the mind get warmed to the new task. Time helps both. And the ease with which those similes began coming to me in the plane illustrates how much better the brain can function on visual material once it has got out of visual reverse and been running awhile.

Once the eye and the mind are working harmoniously, and with equal ability in the looking gear, you start seeing hundreds of things easily and excitingly. But there is still another obstacle to that nice interlocking of forces. The looking gear is an objective one, which involves both visual apprehension of what lies outside oneself and mental absorption with external appearances. To get into the looking gear, therefore, one must first get out of one or the other of the various subjective gears in which we generally run. Shifting from the subjective to the objective is never easy. But our eyes, because of their camera-like capabilities, can often aid us more readily than our inward-turning minds. The eye by nature is interested in objects and concrete appearances. So if we can be intelligent enough to let the eye operate on reality in its natural manner, and if we will allow it enough time to pull its reluctant mental partner into the act, we have the means of being transported out of the grinding low of subjectivity into the happiness of self-ignoring freedom that comes with contented absorption in the objective world.

Haven't you noticed that the most delightful companions tend to be those who go through life operating most of the time in the looking gear? They are the ones whose talk conjures up what they have seen. They are the ones who stir your imagination. They are the ones who give you new realizations of the fascination of life. And you can experience life in the same way if you will open your eyes and give those willing allies, your curiosity and your knowledge, the time to function creatively on your behalf.

And you will remember what you give time to. This is partly because, as scientists have found, what we only flash-glimpse fades quickly from the consciousness. But it is also because of the type of double operation we have been discussing. To truly receive a visual image, we must think about it at the same time as we look at it. Also, we must absorb from it what it has to offer as we give to it what we are capable of bringing. And this last explains why there must be passive phases in our looking as well as active ones. The need for receptive passivity in front of great paintings is well recognized by art experts. Repeatedly they tell us, to borrow Malraux' lovely phrase, that we must let the voices of silence speak to us. But works of art are not the only objects that have silent voices that we can hear, or seem to hear, if, in addition to our deliberate looking, we allow them time to join in the conversation.

Time, then, needs to be bestowed for the assimilative processes it allows to operate; and assimilation is important not only for its present pleasure, but also for the sake of memory. Memory, in turn, is important because visual memories become a sort of knowledge. Also, images that are well established in the memory have vital power. I have spoken of them as being magnetic nuclei, but they might also be compared to seeds that germinate. For those images grow by the thoughts they stimulate, as well as by the fresh visual material they attract.

The above applies generally to all objects, but there are certain categories of things which especially need time for their observation. They might be defined as the intricately detailed, which we have already mentioned, and objects of an unfamiliar class. When a single object falls into both categories, of course, the greatest amount of time is needed.

Why time is so useful in observing the unfamiliar is because seeing is a form of learning, and the same laws that govern the learning process also govern the seeing process. The parallel is attested by the fact that the same word — study — is used both for cramming and for examining an object carefully. In seeing, no less than in studying for exams, one finds that the mind can take in just so much at one time. In concentrating on one aspect, it can give scant attention to any of the others.

In visual examination, the first thing the mind wants to grasp is an object's general form. If the object is something of a new class, the observing task is twofold: You have to learn the forms of the class to which it belongs, as well as the individual form of the thing itself. And at first, absorbing the new form will require so much concentration that the energies of the mind will not be free for detailed observation too. This was certainly true for me in Mexico when I first saw those writhing, elaborate Churrigue-resque altars. Only after I had seen a great many of them did I become aware that most of them followed a fairly regular plan. And only when the recurring design was well fixed in my mind was I able to look comfortably at their inverted obelisks, cherubs' heads, volutes, foliage, symbolic grapes, paintings, saints, and canopies over the niches.

An object of an unfamiliar class, then, will require twice the time, or at least time and a half, because in the first round the effort of achieving an essential grasp will blind one to most details. Initial grasp of form, in fact, plays a far more dynamic visual role than most people realize. Think, for instance, how much harder an upright chair would be to observe, if before looking at each example you first had to figure out that it was a platform on four legs, with two of them extending curiously up one side to support crosspieces.

Objects of an unfamiliar class require overtime for still other reasons. When you lack knowledge of a thing, not only are you deprived of the eye-opening facility that knowledge brings, but you also have to give part of your observing time to additional chores. If no literature exists on its category, you have to give your imagination time to make up explanatory hypotheses to stand tentatively in place of the missing knowledge. Even if there are books on the subject, you have to take time to read them. And part of the completing extra knowledge you have to acquire is verbal. For every class of object has its own terminology, which means, if the class is unfamiliar to you, you will be obliged, like the medical students I spoke of, to learn many new and sometimes difficult words. For, as the sergeant who lectured to us on the rifle was well aware, to really know something you have to know what to call its parts. So study of the unfamiliar requires the time to learn its nomenclature, as well as the time to absorb its forms.

In studying the greatly detailed, a number of still unmentioned factors make time essential. One is the simplicity of our present

tastes in architecture and interior decoration. Since the same canons apply to fashion and to works of art, most of us have grown
up in an environment stripped of what we have dismissed as curli-
cues and gingerbread. In other words, we are no longer accustomed
to masses of detailed ornamentation. This means that such detail
confuses us more, say, than it did the Victorians. When confronted with a multiplicity of detail I have found that, as is necessary on entering a dark place, I have to sit quietly for a while until
my eyes become accustomed to the surroundings. And I have often been amazed at how the eyes, just as they will adjust to seeing
with unexpected ease in the relative dark, will come to new ease
of vision of the detailed.

On several occasions I have mentioned the gestalt psychologists, and their researches have uncovered a major factor that
makes details difficult to discern. The power of the gestalt is what
they call it. Literally translated, gestalt means shape-entity, and
what has been discovered is that shape-entities grip our minds in
a particularly compelling way. Because of this tendency to see only
wholes, it is often not until we have suppressed the gestalt of a
thing that we can start seeing the details within its boundaries.
Consider for instance how details of a painting will stand out easily once we have a photograph of the area they are in, and so have
the section released from the painting's over-all gestalt. Thus
with large, detailed gestalten we need lots of time: time to absorb
the gestalt itself so that we can take it for granted and so loosen its
grip; time to segregate it into sections that we can examine individually; and time to reformulate it so that we can get a new total idea
of it, with awareness of the working of its parts, as well as of
their integration in the whole.

If this implies a certain amount of effort, so much the better.
For the mind's need for rest after exertion brings up another reason
why time has to be given to seeing. This, too, can be illustrated by
the parallel with the general learning process. Modern educators
recognized something with clarity when they invented the phrase
"attention span," and they observed that such spans varied in
length from child to child, from age group to age group, and even
at different times of the day for the same individual. The eye, no
less than the mind, has its attention span. And I am inclined to

believe that, partly because of lack of training, the visual attention span in areas other than reading tends to be shorter than most other attention spans. Certainly most of us can listen attentively for longer than we can observe attentively. And I think most of the extraordinary fatigue that overcomes us in museums is due to the fact that we are not accustomed to looking so carefully for such long periods. We tend to think our legs give out and we joke about "museum feet." But generally it is our eyes that have given out. Or, phrased more exactly, we have worked our eyes beyond their normal attention span and are exhausted by the unwonted effort.

Because of the limitations of the visual attention span, after a while, we quite literally cease seeing. Thus to observe anything of any complexity or richness of detail we have to give it return time, as well as initial time; that is, we have to come back to such objects after periods of rest. This is really not the chore it seems, for return visits can be fascinating experiences. Interesting details, never noticed in moments of fatigue, will appear in miraculous clarity to rested eyes. Their mysterious emergence will give almost as much pleasure as their intrinsic worth.

Especially fascinating are return visits after considerable absences. Intervening experiences will have deposited new memories that will magnetically pull out previously disregarded features. It is certain, too, that the first looking, if it had any care at all, established some curiosity about the class of object. This curiosity will have led to the acquisition, either casually or deliberately, of further knowledge. And then, when one confronts the object again, this knowledge will make all sorts of things visible and intelligible that before were invisible and obscure. Besides its own delight, such an experience brings one of the greatest of all joys: the awareness that, thanks to the interworking of curiosity, knowledge and time, one's powers of apprehension have expanded.

CHAPTER 12

The Reporter's Eye

In the days before the United Nations, East Forty-second Street had a shabbier look than it has now. There were many dingy elements, especially after you passed the Third Avenue El. And the trolley that used to trundle along this dreary stretch compounded the sense of decay. It was joltingly noisy, its tracks narrowed the street, and its appearance underlined the feeling that most of the area dated from the turn of the century. Yet rising above the tenements on the south side was the *News* building, with the soaring white stripes of its walls accented by the brick-red blinds in its windows. In the contrast one saw two types of human indifference: that which allowed a neighborhood to decay because of neglect, and that which erected a giant building cynically devoted to making money through publication of a tabloid whose circulation was built by "legs and limericks."

In this setting of double callousness I saw one of the most poignant scenes of my life. The chief character was a newsdealer; not a regular newsie, with a permanent stand he could sit in, but an impoverished little man who on Saturdays would set a board across a couple of blocks to make a few dollars selling Sunday papers. The day I happened to pass was cold, and to keep him warm the man had a dark cap and a black coat that was long and baggy, like a clown's in a circus. He was interfiling the advance sections of the weekend paper. From somewhere he had obtained a couple of stones to hold the top papers from blowing away. But the wind was strong and it made the interfiling difficult. At one particular gust, the stone on top of the comic supplements was dislodged. Before the man could clamp his hand on the pile, the wind got under the top comics and lifted them into the air. Like a flock of big-winged awkward birds, they flew out into the traffic.

The distraught little man retrieved the stone, saw that it was steady on the pile, and, having lost his cap in the excitement, went after his flying comics. As he chased them the wind lifted the lock of gray hair that had been plastered across his bald pate. Cars honked, but he darted among them, regathering his comics. A streetcar began bearing down on him as one of the last comics settled on the tracks. He lunged for it. Brakes screamed and the street car jangled its bell, but the little man reached his supplement and the trolley stopped in time. Then, dodging the honking cars, he made his way back to the curb, holding the crumpled comics he had retrieved.

To me, one of the most hateful aspects of our civilization is the way it forces so many human beings into work for which they have no respect. Repeatedly one is confronted with men devoting great chunks of their lives, and perhaps their most precious energies, not to what they think is their best work, but to work that will earn the money to pay the butcher, the baker, the landlord, and the clothing store. That little man, desperately chasing those comics, seemed to me a revealing symbol. Because he couldn't afford to let those comics get run over, he risked getting run over himself.

It was an affront to human dignity to see a man so old reduced to that extremity. The setting, too, the canyon-like street in the decayed outer rind of the city, and the car owners, jeering with their horns as they angrily honked at him, heightened the scene's horror. The comics, too, seemed symbolic — symbolic of the worthless ends to which so many people are forced to devote their lives.

I am not sure what made me look as I did. Probably a combination of the upward flight of the papers, the darting movement of the little man, and the clamor of the brakes, the horns, and the imperious trolley bell. What I am sure is that grasping the incident's symbolic overtones was the factor that made it so vivid. And that scene has remained in my mind ever since, like a nightmare glimpse of a reality that is generally cancelled in my consciousness by the counter reality of the world being rich in goodness and kindness.

Because the man was not killed, the incident was not a "news story." Had the streetcar gone over him, however, it would have been my duty as a reporter to get those facts that newspapers find so important: his name, his age, his address, his marital status, and the number of children he left. The story would have read somewhat like this: "James Sullivan, 63-year-old newsdealer of 999 Brook Avenue, the Bronx, was killed yesterday on East 42nd Street when he was run over by a streetcar. The accident occurred when he ran in front of the trolley in pursuit of a newspaper that had blown from his stand. He is survived by his wife, a son and two daughters. Police did not hold the motorman."

And that would be about all. Being not much more than a peddler, the newsie would not rate a second paragraph.

At this point I can hear you protesting, "You wouldn't hold that up as an example of vivid reporting, would you?" I wouldn't. But it gives me the opportunity to reveal this chapter's purpose, which, frankly, is to advocate journalistic training as a means of improving vision. And my imaginary paragraph points up one of the first advantages of such training. A reporter does not see primarily for himself; he sees for others.

As a matter of fact, a professional reporter has to see through three sets of eyes: his own, his employer's, and his readers'. He therefore repeatedly benefits, not from double-level, but from triple-level, perception. And he is regularly obliged to be something most of us seldom are: an onlooker in the scene in which he participates. This duality of stance multiplies his angles of vision. Furthermore, his responsibilities not only frequently force him to make the effort of looking, but often hold him to that effort long enough so that, whether he plans it or not, he passes into the looking gear.

Journalism, therefore, is an occupation that fosters vision in many interacting ways, their interaction, of course, being part of their stimulus. For ease of comprehension, though, let us extract some of the occupational vision sharpeners and discuss them separately. Logically, the one to isolate first is the reporter's need to see through his employer's eyes.

I do not mean to imply the newspaper owner wants a biased

view. Bias has definitely been wanted in the past, but, fortunately, this is less common than it used to be. Now, so far as the reporter is concerned, the prevailing influence of the publisher is not on how the picture is to be slanted but on how much of it is to be given. Descriptions require space. Generally, where the story is small, as in the case of the newsie, the publisher does not want visual details. What he wants are the basic, non-pictorial, unassailable facts, such as names, ages and addresses. With a large story, however, the publisher wants columns of description, especially if it is a story, like a fire or a flood, where the physical aspect is the most dramatic element.

The cub reporter, with one small assignment after another, begins to feel frustrated by his publisher's lack of interest in the visual side of minor stories. When a story has to be compressed, description is generally the first thing to go, so the cub's frustration is likely to be intensified by noting again and again that his prized pictorial touches are cut. Unless he is a fellow with great natural curiosity — a curiosity that adapts itself to almost any new situation — he will tend to fall into the habit of seeing no more on an assignment than he knows his paper will use. If it is a boring testimonial dinner and the chief news is the speech of the guest of honor, the reporter will keep his head buried in the prepared text and come away with little visual recollection of the event.

In this case the law of visual utility acts in reverse. The reporter, with no personal interest in his assignment, will see only that aspect of a scene which he knows from past experience will be useful to his news story. However, if his assignment depends on a sharp eye, he will see everything very vividly. I know a reporter who will sit across from his wife at meal after meal with no consciousness of what she has on. But send him on an interview where he knows he must convey a sense of his subject's character, and he will come back and tell you what color the man's eyes were, what he was wearing, how he inflected his words, what sort of gestures he made, and so on.

More news assignments depend on the gathering of non-pictorial facts than is commonly realized. Nevertheless, because disasters, accidents, crimes, and incidents of violence keep recurring, and because the human love for pageantry leads to parades, in-augurations, and many kinds of ceremony, there are always plenty of assignments that need sharp eyes. And it is the type of visual training one gets on such assignments that I want to extol.

Having to see through the publisher's eyes, even on small stories, has its good points. For one thing, it does not allow one to see exclusively in the way one normally sees: merely subjectively. If an old newsdealer selling comics gets into newsworthy trouble one cannot see him as just a symbol of man's plight in a society where money is essential to survival. One has to step forward and get the facts that establish him not only as an individual, but as a particular newsie, the James Sullivan of Brook Avenue who sells papers on Saturdays. And even though these facts may not seem pictorial to the reporter, they will evoke definite pictures in the minds of all Mr. Sullivan's neighbors and friends. In fact, to those friends the single-paragraph story, with a definite name and address, would be far more interesting and moving than a philosopher's account of his emotions as he saw a poor, nameless, old man retrieving a comic section in the path of an advancing streetcar.

Reporting, then, leads to more objectivity of vision than is com-mon. It also leads to greater completeness — that is, completeness in a narrative sense. Note, for instance, that sentence about the police not holding the motorman. That was the result of hard ex-perience. As a young reporter I was sent out as a "legman" on the "district." I had to keep in touch with the police precinct houses of my allotted area. If any precinct had a story worth using, I had to get the facts from the cops and phone them to a rewrite man. On the whole, the assignment was boring, for night after night would pass with little happening, and in a city as large as New York a misdemeanor has to be out of the ordinary for a metropoli-tan daily to care about it.

One Saturday afternoon, however, a good story broke. A young laborer, who was out of work, held up a toy shop on Madison Avenue. As he left with the contents of the till, the saleswoman he had forced to the back of the store at pistol point screamed. The youth started to run. A cop started to chase him. There were many shoppers on the street, but the cop fired several shots. The youth, far from stopping, dashed across the street, ran east on Sixty-seventh Street, darted into an areaway and disappeared over a fence. A second patrolman joined in the chase and the young man, who had never committed a robbery before, was finally cornered in the cellar of a radio store. I got his name, age (twenty), address (an Italian tenement in East Harlem) and all the details of the chase, and I got on the phone with a sense of pride equal to my feeling of excitement. A rewrite man took all the colorful details I gave him. When I had exhausted my notes, I waited for his congratulations. Instead came the devastating question: "What court will he be arraigned in?"

It was a question I had not thought to ask.

"Go back to the station house and find out," the rewrite man ordered, and hung up.

I have since learned that veteran rewrite men like to play such tricks on cubs. And it taught me a valuable lesson. You have to use your imagination — or your knowledge — to figure out all the angles of an event so that while on the assignment you can ask the questions that will enable you to get the whole story with its chief dramatic consequences. And rewrite men are one of the educational advantages of being a reporter, for they help you see with other eyes. As old hands on the paper you work for, they know what the publisher wants. And insofar as they are deskbound and therefore not present at what is being reported, they form a kind of reader's eye. In collecting for them, you get practice in collecting for the public. Rewrite men, too, not being mute like most newspaper readers, offer the advantage of representing a segment of the public that says what it wants a story to contain. Particularly when you are inexperienced, these articulate intermediaries help you search out what they know readers want. On *The New York Times* there are still reporters who will tell you how much they learned about observing from Meyer Berger. When he was acting as a rewrite man, his visual imagination was fantastically alert. "What did the room look like?" he would ask, and he would insist on a detailed catalogue, including even the pictures on the wall. In fact, he would ask what everything looked like: the spectators, the illumination, the condition of the sky, etc.

There are, of course, lots of ways in which incidents can be seen and I would not hold up modern "police coverage" as a prize example of what has come to be known as "reporting in depth." A playwright presents scenes far more vividly than a reporter. And a sociologist is apt to give the situation more overtones because of his broader frame of reference. But the need for training to be a police reporter does illustrate new aspects of sketchiness of vision.

In discussing it in connection with the church façade, I confined myself to sketchy apprehension of architectural details. But it is now plain that this is just the beginning. Life is rich in other details too, and the picture we come away with is generally sketchy because it is almost invariably subjective. If we have no responsibility to see a scene other than as it strikes us, we will do a lot of selecting, some of it consciously, more of it unconsciously. The conscious selecting will depend in part upon how much time we spend, but, even in deliberate and careful looking, the unconscious plays a big role.

Witness my interest in what the personages in the face cards were holding. When I found none of my friends lit on this aspect, I felt the need to analyze my offbeat focus. I found it stemmed in part from interest in the symbolic meanings in heraldry, and, more importantly, from an interest in saints. Saints are identified by what they hold. Their attributes, too, reveal their stories; so that when one sees St. Barbara holding a tower one finds it is because she was locked in a tower, and so on. An understanding of the role of attributes in iconography, and memories of pleasures in identifying past saints, then, were unconscious factors influencing my seeing. The artist who noticed not what the hands held, but the hands themselves, was a woman who, as a little girl, always loved watching the hands of her parents as they worked.

As well as selecting subjectively, we reject subjectively, dropping the psychological lids on what we don't wish to see. Finally, there is the phenomenon of projection, wherein we actually impose meanings — even physical appearances — on a scene when they aren't there. Often, too, we can be deeply moved by what we feel we have seen. I know that when I watched that old man chasing his comics I was projecting into the scene my discontent with my own newspaper job.

It is because we tend to be satisfied with the subjective view that we so often fail to see the whole story. The motorman, suddenly confronted with a crazy old man running in front of his trolley, was as much part of the story as the newsie. He had to brake his car on a moment's notice and he must have had an agonized dread that the brakes wouldn't hold. If he'd had the awful experience of killing the man, his story would have been one of more prolonged drama than the death itself. All the motorists who had to slam on their brakes were part of the story as well, but we tend not to push our imaginations very far.

Out of publisher-induced habit, however, a trained reporter will think of the consequences for all the principals involved. Thus he will see more in an incident than a passer-by. And the scene before him will be supplemented by what passes in his mind's eye: the vision of bereavement in the front parlor of a Bronx apartment, and an anxious motorman standing before a judge.

Actually, a reporter, particularly a young one, hardly ever sees his publisher, much less speaks to him. Liaison is achieved through the city editor, the man who hands out the assignments. And another way a publisher, acting through his editors, can enlarge a reporter's vision is by the nature of the assignments. These, too, break into a reporter's subjectivity.

It is subjectivity's nature — as the word implies — to confine vision to what the observer, for subjective reasons, responds to. His deliberate looking (as distinct from his accidental looking) therefore tends to be limited to what he has an interest in. But when a reporter goes on an assignment he knows he cannot collect only those impressions that catch his personal interest. Artificially, if not actually, he has to have the sort of total interest the publisher wants. This is very healthy, for in forcing him to keep his eyes and ears open he may discover that, his own judgment to the contrary, many things considered interesting by his publisher actually are. His assignments, too, often take him to events whose interest he is aware of before he goes. Also many are events he could never have got to on his own hook. The publisher, then, by providing his reporters with a wide range of personal experiences that have to be observed fully, extends their seeing by paying them to be objective about many non-personally selected assignments. And often these assignments, by planting new nuclei of curiosity in reporters' minds, lead them to be permanently more observant of things to which, initially, they were exposed fortuitously by encountering them while out on stories.

Now we come to how a reporter's vision is sharpened by constantly having to see through his readers' eyes. What is uppermost in the reporter's mind is that those eyes are not present. He knows, in fact, that the very reason he has been assigned to the story is so he can describe it for those who cannot see it for themselves. Even if it is a story where the action is more important than the setting, the experienced reporter knows the action will not be intelligible unless the reader can imagine the setting. If the reporter wants to communicate the feeling of the event, he knows that his own emotion is not enough; he must convey what caused that emotion. He, therefore, keeps appraising the scene visually, trying to account for his own impressions, noting the inanimate objects that play a role in the narrative and keeping ever on the alert for what will help the reader visualize the scene. If the setting is one the American reader is almost sure to know — Madison Avenue, say — the reporter realizes the name will do nearly all his work for him, particularly if he throws in the East Sixties. Nevertheless, he must watch for significant details, little facts that will both evoke the setting for the reader and advance the story: a fact, say, like the newsie losing his glasses; or people in the *News* building lifting the red blinds for a better view of the hubbub in the street.

If the setting is so familiar to the reporter that he has come to take it for granted, the thought of the absent reader's unknowing eyes can bring the reporter into new freshness of vision. For in being forced to get outside himself to observe the accustomed on another's behalf, he can often come to see it with the dust sheets of familiarity removed.

If the setting is a foreign one, the reporter must still have his eyes peeled for significant details, but, in addition, he must size up the main outlines so that these, too, can be transmitted. He knows referring to the scene by name is not enough to evoke it in the reader's mind. It must be described in some detail. And besides doing his sizing up quickly, he must take in appearances with a sharp precision that he can recall. For when he is back at his typewriter, vague impressions will not be enough to reconstruct the scene accurately. And because his story must be on the wires that afternoon, he cannot revisit the scene to soak up its atmosphere and ascertain just what gave the setting its particular character.

Conveying a scene in terms that will make it vivid is his third problem. For neither a description of general outlines, nor a string of significant details is enough in itself. The reporter handling the unfamiliar — and that is what most news is — also has to find comparative images that will be meaningful for the absent reader. This involves fishing in his reservoir of visual images for analogies which he can be reasonably sure also lie in the minds of his readers. Sometimes this can be troublesome, especially if his visual memories are hazy.

Let me illustrate. Shortly after the Italian basso-buffo, Salvatore Baccaloni, came to this country I was sent to interview him. He was a fat, comic-looking man and his appearance, obviously, was a major element in the story. How to convey it to readers who at that time had never laid eyes on Mr. Baccaloni? I knew my salvation lay in a recollection of a movie comic of the custard-pie era. If I said the singer resembled that comedian, all those who remembered him would have a good idea of the fat Italian. But what was the comic's name? I reached about for it in my memory. It was John something. John, John . . . then it came — John Bunny.

The next problem was to check if the face I had associated with Bunny in my mind was really Bunny's face, for I was digging among memories almost thirty years old. Fortunately I had a picture library to consult and a little time before my deadline. A photo of Bunny showed my recollection was correct. But Baccaloni did not have that aureole of fluffy hair. So I wrote my description, saying the new singer looked like a younger edition of Bunny, but a Bunny who had lost his hair.

A second illustration will clinch the matter, as well as pave the way to the next step. I was assigned to a production of *Pagliacci* at Carnegie Hall. The description of the setting was important because Carnegie Hall is not an opera house and the production was ingenious. Because there was no pit, the orchestra had to be on the stage. In this case, it was placed behind the scenery, which meant, in turn, that the scenery had to be almost transparent so that a relay conductor in front could see the beat of the orchestral conductor in order to bring it forward for the singers.

Howard Bay designed that production and he hit on a novel device to achieve the necessary transparency: a gauzy scrim curtain with some outlines drawn on it that suggested an Italian hill town. *Pagliacci* is so often given with nondescript, hand-me-down scenery dragged out of some theatrical warehouse that the freshness of Mr. Bay's outlines needed to be described, especially since the church he suggested was distinctively Italian. It had a tiled roof and under the eaves of the gentle triangle at the top of the façade was a series of small, equal arches, with each arch being bricked up. I knew such blind arches were characteristic of a certain architectural style, and I knew I could convey the appearance of the church to the reader if I referred to that style by name. But what was it? I did not know. So before I started my review I dashed to the *Encyclopaedia Britannica* and opened it to the article on Architecture. Its illustrations, as I suspected they might, showed a church like the one Bay suggested. The caption gave me my name — Romanesque.

A reporter, then, must constantly be seeking words for visual appearances, which brings us to verbalizing as an aid to vision. Fundamentally, this need of the reporter to be always translating impressions taken in by the eye into words to be set in type is, I feel, the greatest visual stimulus of his occupation. It is greater even than seeing more completely, and observing more objectively; greater, too, than habitually appraising what is before his eyes, constantly being exposed to new experiences, and repeatedly being obliged to think of parallel images. And one reason it has this greater importance is because, in a sense, it embraces most of the others.

However, caution is needed, for I only want to praise the kind of verbalizing that sticks close to appearances. For words, as the experimental psychologists have shown, play a potent role in perception. They can make an observer lengthen a form into a "canoe" or squash it into a "kidney bean," depending on which is mentioned as a closed form with upcurving ends is flashed on a screen. Because of their potency, words are visual instruments that can work two ways. That they can blind has already been implied when I spoke about how an imprecise, generalized word like "chair" can obliterate a piece of eighteenth-century craftsmanship.

I brought up that illustration largely to warn against the way words blind us by riveting our attention on an object's utility rather than its appearance. But settling concentration on an object's function is only one of the ways in which words impede vision. To illustrate another, let me use a saying I found in Joyce Cary's *Art and Reality*: "When you give a child the name of a bird, it loses the bird."

This type of vision killing might be called the way of classification. For when a red-throated bird is classified as a mere house finch, it loses the marvelous individuality it had when it was an unknown bird. And anyone can summon dozens of instances in which he has dismissed items for being merely further examples of a class he has categorized as commonplace. For classifying can let down double shutters, and for this reason a warning should be made against knowledge. In the previous chapter I praised it as one of the great allies of vision — which it generally is. But when it is used to set up classifying rugs under which appearances can be swept, knowledge can also be blinding.

Imprecise classifying can be even worse than precise classifying, and words particularly to be avoided are the crude, generic ones — names that might include a multitude of distinct forms — as the word glass includes tumbler, goblet, brandy snifter, or wineglass.

Classifying, however, is perhaps not as great a villain as another vision killer that words do so much to strengthen. I refer to one touched on earlier: conceptualizing. Verbal classification, at least, is often accurate. But when a thing is reduced to a concept, it tends to lose more than its appearance, more than its individuality. It also tends to lose its living reality. As a result we can read about a "battalion" being wiped out with scarcely a notion that human beings have been involved.

"The names which denote things," says Proust, "correspond invariably to an intellectual notion, alien to our true impressions, and compelling us to eliminate from them everything that is not in keeping with itself."

Proust, being one of the great observers, puts his finger on what I am trying to say. He also points to the next danger. Words, having the power they do, fix the concepts they embody in our minds. And many such concepts, besides being incomplete, are inaccurate. Sometimes, indeed, they actually falsify. One has only to think of the insulting words of the racially prejudiced to see that this is so.

Words, then, can be visually dangerous because they make it so easy for us to cast our preconceived notions ahead of us so that they influence how we perceive. Sometimes those verbalized concepts veil reality altogether, and, when they do, we often mistake them for reality itself.

But if words can obscure, they can also articulate. Later, when I discuss art books and start giving reading its due, I will take up the visual help contributed by utilizing the words of others. The rest of this chapter, though, will deal with the help given by words you use yourself. That is, when you don't chip away at things to make them fit words, but instead conscientiously use words to try to make them fit things.

Some people, as we have noted, are more eye-minded than others, and some can take in scenes photographically, feeling no need of any intermediary words. Generally, they will only start translating their visual impressions into words when, later on, they have an urge to tell their friends about what they saw. I am definitely not one of these. If I want a visual impression to stick, I have to use words to help while taking it in.

In fact, I need words doubly: as flasks in which to preserve what I have seen, and to discipline my eyes. If I look on a scene with no intention of finding words for it, I tend to daydream — or else I take it in so vaguely that I can barely describe it afterwards. If I use words, however, I can impose a strict discipline on my seeing. Somehow I am enabled to move my eyes from point to point, and I can linger at each section until I have it fixed in my memory.

The type of verbalizing I enjoy most and which, if successful, has the surest power to make a scene indelible, is finding the telling simile. How well, for instance, I remember one particular summer rainstorm in the city when I had to take refuge under an arched doorway. What brings it all back to me — the street, the hour of the morning, my mission there, the friend I was waiting for — is the simile that came to me as I watched the pelting rain bounce back from the asphalt. The little V's made by the bouncing drops reminded me of plantlets. And, lo, the black pavement had suddenly sprouted thousands of silver seedlings.

Almost as much as the vivid simile, I love the single word that is magically right. For such words can be like monstrances holding a blessed essence. Beyond communicating appearances, they make you feel the magic of what is described. And once they have been applied to one visual appearance, they heighten your awareness in all future encounters with similar appearances. I mean such a word as Colette used in *Creatures Great and Small* when she described a fire on a hearth as a "glittering *bouquet*." Or as D. H. Lawrence wrote in *The Plumed Serpent* in defining the effect of an outdoor bonfire: "The air was *bronze* with the glow of flame."

But similes like the silver seedlings are generally strokes of luck. One cannot count on them. And unless one is a Colette or a Lawrence one can seldom find the word that is unforgettably right. But even if the perfect phrase refuses to appear, one can always fall back on standard words. Drab as they sometimes seem, if they are words of recognized precision that carry exact connotations, they will often conjure up more in other minds than you would think possible.

I know that whenever I feel defeated in achieving the alliance of object and metaphor that Proust extols, I fall back on the methodical use of plain words. First I use them to isolate the area to be observed. If it is a pillar, say, I will use the word "base" to train my eye on its lower part. Then, I will notice its base is like a square pad of clean-cut stone. Moving up, I will ask myself what its "shaft" is like. That word will help me see that the shaft is made of a single stone cylinder, with one ring at the bottom and two at the top. Next I'll use the word "capital" to fix my attention on the area in question, and reach into that drawer of my vocabulary that has the words for the different capitals. Then, having fixed the pillar's form in my head, I will seek the words to define its texture and its color. It might, for instance, be grayish-white and its texture smooth but at the same time a little porous. By rights, I should try to name the stone it is carved from. But here, knowing so little about different building stones, I tend to turn away in defeat.

This example of ignorance as an inhibiter of vision, leads us once more to that old friend of vision — knowledge. Every special branch of knowledge aids vision in two ways. As I have pointed out, it provides the parallel of similar forms that enable one to distinguish particular elements in new visual situations. Knowledge also helps by furnishing the words that enable one to designate what one has seen. An object's name is often the encasing drop of oil that enables it to pass easily through the valve between the sensing retina and the conscious mind.

Since conscious observing and naming things are both acts of intellectual comprehension it is not surprising that they are governed by similar rules. And it is worth noting that word-finding, like seeing, can be inhibited by lack of confidence. Before the difficult-to-describe, one gets a panicky tongue-tiedness not unlike panicky blindness. The two, in fact, are closely related, for each arises from a conviction of impossibility coupled with a feeling of inadequacy. But if the eye can lead the mind, as we now know it can, it can also loosen the tongue. For after all there is not so much difference between achieving a clear visual grasp and finding the verbal text that embodies it. Indeed, one aids the other, especially since our education's stress on reading has provided more experience in manipulating words than in analyzing visual phenomena.

That learning to look is in a very real sense learning to describe is evidenced by the common use of the word "indescribable." Some loquacious persons, it is true, use it merely as a synonym for marvelous and then go on to give a detailed description — the very thing they said could not be done. Others, though, both in company and perhaps even more frequently when alone, use the word differently. They apply it to visual situations that they feel are impossible to absorb, and, after such classifying they generally turn away from them.

But many more things are describable than is commonly believed. So tongue-tiedness is susceptible to the same sort of cure as panic blindness. First, one must get over the feeling of impossibility. Then, patiently and confidently, one has to allow oneself time to summon the aiding words. Actually, the very difficulty of finding words can be helpful for, in the search, one keeps looking at what one is trying to describe. The groping for specific words gives extra time for the contemplation of the image, with often an interacting stimulus resulting.

One tip I learned as a reporter is worth passing on. Don't be afraid of summoning up too many words, for the unnecessary ones can be cut away later. Thus you can look at a tropical sea on a sunny day, for instance, and say of its shallow water "it's a sort of green," and not worry if at first you do not have the right name for the predominant shade. Then you can say "it's not all one color" before you begin to get a precise description of the mottled jade and turquoise. Then you can concentrate on the water lapping the shore, noting how it is more sun-spangled, say, than the sapphire blue stretch beyond the distant reef. When your eyes rest on the reef, you notice that the waves are breaking even more whitely there than those over the dark brown rocks of the shore. Then, if it is a little windy, you notice the white caps out at sea. In shape they may suggest the rounded shoulders and the tapering line of a gull's wing as it flies obliquely towards you.

To get color ideas, you can stand and let remembered greens come to you: bottle green, emerald green, the clouded green of glass that has been tumbled about on a beach; the green armor of a certain fly as the sun catches it, bean green, nile green, apple green, the gleaming green of a freshly cut lime. When you find you've exhausted the greens in your memory, you can start looking at nearby non-sea greens in the hope of fresh words. Perhaps you'll make the discovery that accident led me to make: for all its varieties of green, a tropical sea can never quite give you the particular green of the long fronds of the palms that grow beside it.

If, at the end of your gazing, you still haven't come up with a succinct description, it won't matter. The effort of finding words will have helped the visualizing. In all probability, too, it will have got you into the looking gear. I know that on the morning that I looked at the sea in Puerto Rico my descriptive effort got me into the particular looking gear of concentration on colors. And it was because I was still in that gear that I was so struck by the differing green of the hitherto barely noticed palms.

Verbalizing, in fact, is particularly useful for getting into the looking gear. Not only does it enforce transition from the subjective mood to the objectivity that is one of the gear's characteristics, but it automatically engages the thinking gear in ocular perceiving, thereby bringing about the necessary interplay of mind and eye. An interplay, incidentally, that often needs help, especially if you want to define subtle nuances or delicate differentiations.

Actually, word-seeking is only part of verbalizing. For, because of the need of comparisons, it includes image-seeking, thereby obliging you to extend two vocabularies. The verbal one is extended as you search your memory for words so lightly seeded there that they have not taken root as part of your working vocabulary. And besides giving you greater control over the words you know, it drives you to dictionaries and thesauri for the unknown words you now find you need to acquire. The visual vocabulary is extended because verbalizing enforces memory search. Here, too, recollection for specific use brings new control of the lightly seeded. And because observing is concerned with appearances, verbalizing simultaneously stabilizes images already absorbed, and enriches the visual vocabulary for future use by planting fresh images.

If you say that all I am advising is to talk to yourself, I'll boggle at the "all," but I will accept the rest of the charge, for talking to yourself doesn't deserve its bad name. I will go further and say: Be like a reporter on an assignment. Talk to yourself a lot. And do it the way he does, either by taking notes or by interior monologue. The more you do it, the richer will become your store of visual images, and these images will be all the more useful for having been put away with their names sewn on them.

Perhaps at this point you are muttering: "All this about getting eye training as a reporter is all very well, but how does it apply to me? I haven't the faintest chance of getting a job on a newspaper, and I'm not even sure I'd want one."

The answer is that newspaper reporters are not the only kinds of reporters. News reporting has been stressed chiefly to give consistency to the chapter. But there are other and perhaps better types of reporting. In their evocation of character and their depiction of places, the great novelists certainly report circles around ordinary journalists. Yet you don't need to write fiction either. You can write letters. And writing more letters that recount what you have seen is something I urge. The effort of writing saves talking to yourself from deteriorating into idiotic babbling. Written verbalization, too, has an advantage over the merely spoken that one sees easily in the writing of others. Witness your response when you come across a description of something you have seen for yourself. Always you read it with the realization that the scene had more interest than you felt at the time. Your own writing can aid you in the same way. I know that often, when I wrote my regular Sunday letter home, an experience of the week, after being related, would emerge in my consciousness as being more worth writing up than I had thought when it was happening.

Thereafter, too, I possessed the experience more fully. This fixing process occurred so often, in fact, that when I first saw photographs being printed I rejoiced in finding the means of describing it. When I saw those pictures slowly darken into increasingly recognizable form as the apparently blank sheets of photographic paper soaked in the developing solution, I felt how much original experiences resembled such sheets. Mere exposure is just the start of the process. The true printing only comes when the experience has been dipped in the bath of verbal recollection.

In writing descriptive letters, therefore, you gain at the same time as you transmit — though the latter is the important part. This means that, like the reporter, you have the stimulus of having to observe for someone else. As in his case, you can't be just content with the sort of shorthand seeing that is adequate when you are looking only for yourself. And the influences that work on him work on you.

Having to evoke a scene for absent eyes forces you to cull your memories. Besides being a form of review, it makes you select the dominant elements so your account has the proper impact. It also makes you find the words to crystallize transient impressions. And

if you write such letters habitually, you will find your vision bene-
fiting from your letters as a reporter's vision benefits from his assignments. Some of the sketchiness will pass from your seeing as
you look at everything more objectively and use your imagination more fully to piece out or interpret what lies beneath the visual surface. The thought of those letters will give new visual utility to much that passes under your eyes. You will get into the habit
of seizing details that are necessary to conjure up scenes for others.

Practice in articulating your impressions, in turn, will enlarge
your visual vocabulary, not only by the greater number of images
you'll have to draw on, but also because you'll gain new words for
basic physical appearances — words like contour, texture, and
surface; like salient and recessed, like lustre and opacity; words
that give you the quality of objects, and words that direct the attention to the aspects of objects to which you want to refer. Besides helping you see more things more easily, this enlargement
of vocabulary will diminish those tongue-tying fears that prevent
you from studying what you think you can't describe.

You might protest that you have no friends so interested in
what you take in that they would want such letters. If true, this
still does not debar you from the practice I'm recommending. You
can keep a diary or, better still, a journal.

At first, keeping a journal does not seem to have the advantage
of reporting something for the absent eye. But this is an illusion.
Anyone who has reread a journal he made four or five years ago
is aware how much the memory lets slip away. Some entries, if
recorded telegraphically, will even be unintelligible, so completely
have the related circumstances passed from the mind. And things
one thought one would never forget are revealed as having been
forgotten by the turn one gets in having them unexpectedly res-
urrected. In keeping a journal, then, the absent eye you write for
is your own. You write to preserve a scene, an incident, or an impression for the person you will become in the future. You write
against the time when you have lost the power to recall, unaided,
the fullness of detail which did so much to give life and significance to the original experience.

If you protest that you have neither the time nor the energy
to keep a journal, you still need not miss the visual stimulus of

being a reporter. You can gain it, spared of all the pain of writing, if you make a game of pretending you are on an assignment. And you can influence your way of seeing by the type of publication you choose to imagine you are writing for.

In Puerto Rico I was covering the Casals music festival for *The New York Times*, so I had to be alert to the island's growing musical life to which the festival was a stimulus. Had I been an ordinary tourist, I could have assigned myself different areas of alertness. One day I could have pretended I was reporting for a liberal journal, thereby sharpening my eyes for the economic aspects of working-class life that such a journal would want. Or I might have stimulated my vision of the new luxury hotels by pretending I had to report on the island's tourist facilities for a magazine specializing in comfortable travel.

Where I have found imaginary reporting most life-saving is at boring parties. And the trick is easy. First you have to forget you are a guest. Then, once you have lost the sense of being a participant, you look around at those present not as friends or fellow guests, but as members of a certain social class revealing many things about their civilization by their response to this particular social situation. And once you have shifted into this particular eyegear, even a monumentally silly woman can become quite a fascinating specimen of a given type. Marcel Proust is the great example of the writer who had this gift of looking at parties with a reporter's eye. If you want to see its full potentialities, read him.

CHAPTER 13

Plants and Drawing

THE visual process is essentially the same, no matter what one looks at. In consequence we can learn a great deal about all observing by analysis of a single visual experience. Similarly, learning how to observe one thing thoroughly can teach a lot about how to observe all things. And because experience gained in studying a single object can develop observing skills that thereafter facilitates vision wherever we turn, in this chapter I want to urge study of only one grouping. Since one of the best ways to observe a thing is to draw it, I also want to urge drawing as the aid in the chosen study.

You are at liberty to select whatever you want. My own suggestion, for a starter, is a flower. Then you can move on and make your chosen province plants in general. And whether you select plants or not, I intend to use them as illustrations, hoping the possibilities they suggest will reveal the advantages of a single theme.

I hit on plants as a source of interest, and drawing as a means of studying them, not only simultaneously, but by accident. During World War II, I was a flight surgeon's assistant, and when the United States dropped its atomic bombs I was still at the desert airfield where I had questioned my fellow soldiers about the tent era. In a drive to beautify the post, some scrawny rosebushes had been planted around the sheetrock shacks that served as our medical installation. The bushes had not bloomed during the summer, so I had written them off for dead. The awful heat had nearly killed us, so it seemed understandable that it should have killed the roses.

What was my surprise therefore in mid-October, the time

when all normal roses are over and gone, to see blooms on two of those little bushes. The flight surgeon had a nice civilian secretary called Audrey Brady, so I decided to cut two of the roses for her. Why not cut one for myself, too, I thought? I did, and placed it in a tumbler on a corner of my desk.

That particular October was in 1945. The capitulation of Japan had ended the war and our field was shortly to be abandoned. Because many men had already been shipped away our work had slackened. Not being under pressure, and being bored with the records I was sorting, I paused every now and then to look at my rose. Being hardly more than a little ball, the bud's form was so simple. I realized it would be easy to draw, and I acted on the impulse to sketch it.

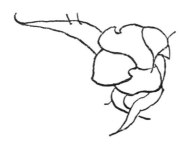

My estimate of the bud itself had been correct. It was easy to draw. But the leaf-like green things around it, which had formed its casing and which I had hardly noticed, proved trickier. The need to draw them accurately forced me to look at them closely. The casing, apparently, had been in three segments, but now that the green things were peeling back, two of the original shields were dividing in two.

Figuring that Miss Brady, being a woman, would know more about flowers than I did, I went to her office and asked if she knew what the green things were called. She said she thought they were sepals. To check, we looked up the word in the dictionary, where its entry was accompanied by an illustration. The picture proved Audrey correct about the name, and the entry gave us still another useful word. The casing the sepals had formed was the calyx.

Because my bud's petals were just beginning to come unsealed,

I had difficulty judging just how many outer petals it had. My sketch, however, had made me look carefully at the barely visible seams, from which I gained the impression of three outer petals, each one overlapping the next, rather like the webbing of a furled umbrella. The matter wasn't totally simple, though, because the span of the three overlapping petals did not quite encase the whole bud. On the right, I could see part of the petal of a ring one stage nearer the center. Much to my disappointment, the bud did not change during the day. I had expected to see those three outer petals lie back, one by one. The next morning they were still as closely joined as ever, but the sepals had curled back a little farther. I could judge precisely how much by comparing their new state with their more clutching one at the time of my sketch.

The third day was a Sunday and as I was able to get off the post I never looked at the rose. Came the fourth day and my return to the dispensary. Still no change in that blasted bud! Regretfully, I came to the conclusion that I had snipped it too soon. Clearly, it was never going to open now. And this conclusion was strengthened by the fact that the beautiful soft, deep red of the petals was assuming a slightly purplish cast. However, I didn't throw the rose out. Remembering how my mother had got good results with recalcitrant buds by "floating" them, I decided to try her trick. So I filled a saucer with water, cut away the entire stem of the rose, and set the still tightly packed bud afloat.

To my amazement, when I returned to work the fifth day, the bud had opened. Its inner heart was still sealed up, but fold after outer fold had spread back, and the inner faces of those relaxed petals were a paler pink than their red outsides. There was work piled on the desk, but I brushed it aside to make a careful drawing of the rose. Unknowingly, I had developed an attachment to that flower, and for a man living a monotonous and isolated life on a place as arid as the desert, the opening of a rose can be thrilling.

Something prompted me to be scientific. When the drawing was finished, I measured the span of the rose, counted the petals that had broken free from the heart and jotted down the fact that it was nine A.M. Then I got to the neglected papers. Glancing back at the rose a little later I was amazed to see that the closed

heart had opened. Four or five petals, that I hadn't been able to see only twenty minutes before, were now visible.

At ten o'clock I couldn't resist drawing again. Wanting to gauge just how much the heart had expanded, I ignored the outer petals and traced the little cleft pear the center had formed in the drawing of an hour earlier. Then, alongside, I drew its present form. In other words, what had been

this   was now this

The fact that the inner core of the flower had changed so dramatically led me to use my nine o'clock drawing as a reference to check if there had been a similarly striking change in the outer petals. There had not. The three outermost ones had lost their tension and were falling away, but all the inner ones remained arrayed in standing circles. An idea flashed on me. Perhaps, I said, I was totally wrong in my conception of how a rose opens. Those outer petals aren't lying back voluntarily. They're being pushed back.

Then and there I scrapped my long-held notion that a rose opened from the outside in. The core of a rose, I saw, tended to open like a fist, forcing the outer rings of petals to give way.

When I returned to my desk after lunch I made still another drawing of the rose which deepened my new conviction. As can be seen, at one o'clock the rose's heart was still larger than it had been when drawn in isolation at ten o'clock.

In expanding that much more, it had pushed out still more petals, which were now falling back to resemble wide pink collars.

Eleven days after drawing the rose, it was my turn to be shipped from the desert. I never forgot the discovery that a rose opened from the center, but in the subsequent whirligig of events many of the other lessons implicit in the drawing experience were swept aside without being consciously learned. In fact, they did not crystallize until two years later when I began drawing another plant.

This was a philodendron, which, as it happened, was the only thing left behind by the tenant vacating the apartment that I was eventually lucky enough to find after being discharged from the Army. I have already spoken of that plant, and of how my curiosity about it shifted from idle to active when I noticed its growing tips reared higher after I had given it some water. It was by drawing that I detected that rising, for having drawn the plant before the watering I had the evidence of the lower position to know the higher one was not an illusion.

Since that philodendron has had its own book, I do not want to repeat illustrations from it here, but I would like to show how experience with the flowerless plant helped clarify lessons of the rose.

My drawings of the philodendron, like those of the rose, were painstakingly exact, for I worked as hard with the leaves of the plant as I had with the petals of the rose to have the forms correctly related to each other. I also tried to indicate every irregularity of contour. That such exactitude again led me to new observations — particularly in noting subtle changes — taught me that, if you want drawing to aid you in observing, you must draw in a special way. You must isolate your subject, draw it close up, and completely eliminate background. Above all, you must not be merely impressionistic — that is, satisfied with a few rough lines that convey the idea of the subject. Furthermore, you should not be concerned about being artistic. If your drawings look pretty when finished, so much the better, but achieving a pretty effect should not be your aim. What you should be after is a precise record of appearances.

And I hasten to add that I do not consider such rendering a high form of art. After all, if exactitude of representation were the sole criterion of a work of art, a painting of strawberry shortcake in a food advertisement might be rated higher than an El Greco. So bear in mind that in advocating drawing as a visual aid I am not urging you to produce masterpieces, but rather insisting that you be as literal as your probably unskilled hand will allow.

Suggesting that lack of skill leads to the second lesson that was underlined when I saw what had been true of the rose was also true of the philodendron. Plants are excellent models. They have infinite patience and hold wonderfully still. Provided they are small potted ones, or cut flowers, they can be posed in any way they seem easiest to draw. They are uncritical. And perhaps best of all for the amateur artist, their feelings don't get hurt if they aren't flattered. They do not even insist that you catch a likeness; and if you've botched the job they do not make you expose your failure by asking to see what you have done. This tolerant indifference, coupled with the ability to remain motionless as you study them as long as you like, and from as many angles, make them especially good models for those who are just beginners, both as draftsmen and as observers.

In addition to leading to exact observing of parts, the drawing I advocate enforces complete observing of wholes. This is compelled by the curious way a gap in a drawing shows up much more vividly than a gap in one's seeing. Our habit of seeing sketchily is so strong, and generally so unrecognized, that when we look at an object we will not be aware of its parts that are not registering. But when you work on a drawing you see clearly which parts still have to be filled in, and you are forced to study that part of the model which you did not realize had to be in the picture. The sepals of my rose are a case in point. The task of drawing the bud made me aware that the unnoticed sepals were a necessary part of the total impression.

On the desert I drew the rose with a fountain pen, or directly in ink. In New York I drew the philodendron in pencil. Combining the lessons of the two mediums showed me the type of drawing that is most useful for observation of form. It is sketching begun in pencil so that incorrectly placed lines can be erased, but brought to completion in lines so sharply drawn that they can be inked over. Preferably, too, it is drawing without shading.

Knowing you must confine yourself to drawing only outlines has all sorts of good influences on your seeing. They begin even before you touch pencil to paper. This is because such drawing requires a particular type of posing. The object has to be placed in strong, clear light at an angle where all its main elements are displayed intelligibly. This involves sizing up those elements and then inspection of the object from different angles until the spot is found where the major parts stand fully revealed in characteristic aspects.

The posing process, then, is automatically an act of observing the whole. Because of the type of drawing to be done, it must also be a process of selection. For the artist—and this is especially true for the beginner — cannot hope to draw anything massive and complicated in this fashion. He has to select a significant segment that is relatively simple and self-contained. Choosing what to reject and what to include involves further observing. Then examination of the chief components selected is pursued more closely as the outlines of the drawing are blocked in. Although the blocking in should be kept rough and light, it is wise to make it fairly complete so that proportions and the relative positions of the components are properly established. The final stage, the close study of details, comes with the correcting and the darkening of the lines that are to be permanent, and the drawing in of the aspects neglected during the concentration on overall shape. This last stage involves counting petals, noting just how they overlap, how their edges are crinkled, and so on.

Because in life, shadow is the element that does most to dramatize the dimension of depth, trying to draw a solid object without shadow presents a particular challenge. Suggesting three dimensional shapes by line alone necessitates a more than ordinary comprehension of form, which is one reason why this kind of drawing is so good for sharpening your powers of observation. You have to look and look until you thoroughly understand the true form of what you are trying to depict.

Even if you do not succeed in conveying the form fully, it does not matter. The effort will spur you to the paramount objective: visual comprehension. You might object that so much concentration on form is a very one-sided type of observing. In leaving out color it eliminates a major aspect of reality. It also omits the influence of atmospheric effects on visual appearances. You might say, too, that the spirit of a thing is often not conveyed when the depiction is only a painstaking outlining of each part in exact proportion. This is all true. But remember I'm not advocating drawing as the only aid to observing. Painting an object is also a way of learning to observe it, especially its color subtleties and the way its appearance is influenced by what is around it.

A by-product of hunting for similes is also worth recalling: namely, that you cannot make careful note of one aspect of an object without automatically noting subsidiary aspects. The type of drawing I am speaking about brings out subsidiary aspects again and again. Take the different shades, say, of the inner and outer faces of a rose petal curling back on itself. That is something you cannot help but notice, and your very despair in trying to suggest, without color, a contrast that cries out for it, makes you as aware of the difference between that pink and red as if you *were* painting.

Remember, too, the role of time. Our concern is more with the impression left on the mind than the impression on the paper. Depicting anything meticulously requires time; and the more inexpert the hand the more time is needed. And this enforced time in front of the chosen object gives room for all the mental processes that help observing: the stirring of curiosity, remembering, speculation, testing of theories, etc. The combination of time and drawing-effort, too, leads to a relationship that is allied to friendship. Ever after one has drawn an object one has a particular kind of tenderness for it. And it remains in the memory in a unique way. Always there is a flash of recognition and a recall of the drawing experience when its counterpart — or even something only vaguely related — is encountered later on.

Drawing is a form of discipline that takes the eye methodically from point to point and which holds the eye on each small section for the length of time needed to represent it on paper. This is always long enough for that particular detail to be absorbed. It is certainly far longer than the naturally shifty eye could ever dwell on it without having a set task to hold it there.

The area of the paper to be filled also plays its role, by imposing a comparably restricted field of vision on the specific area of the object being drawn. How excluding everything outside a chosen area sharpens the eye was demonstrated by the easier visibility of the heart of the rose when it was drawn without its outer petals.

A drawing aids vision even after it is completed, for it provides a secondary image that induces double-level perception. When one holds one's sketch at arm's length and shifts one's eyes from it to the flower, for instance, one is likely to see a special grace in the plant. The perception, perhaps, will make itself known in what you mutter to yourself. "Well, it's not bad," you might say. "I did manage to get some of the balance and harmony between the flower and the leaves." Or you might say the exact opposite: "How stiff my drawing is. I didn't get any of the easy, interflowing grace of the lines I now see so clearly in the living plant." Whichever your reaction, you will find that the *sharpening* of vision induced by the task of drawing now contributes to your *heightened* vision after your pains are over.

Where a drawing is especially useful, of course, is in aiding observation of things that change. Because of the gripping effect of the present image, the exact way an object appeared earlier is hard to remember. But a drawing is immutable and provides the clear-cut evidence of a past aspect. And that aspect will dramatize the precise character of the change, just as my stage-by-stage drawing of the desert rose revealed that the opening process was like an expanding fist.

Several other postoperative benefits could be illustrated by the rose experience, but lest you have grown tired of the rose I will use a different plant in discussing them. And the evidence of the same lessons being learned from drawing something bigger than either a rose or a philodendron will perhaps convince you that plants are good subjects and that, no matter what species you se lect, drawing it will widen your eyes to the world around you.

Mexico is again the source of my illustration. I had written about a man harvesting corn and my thought was that I could dress up the story if I illustrated it with a stalk of corn. Thus when I set out to make the drawing I did not intend consciously to draw a plant, merely an object furnishing a Mexican motif.

On reaching the cornfield where I had decided to work, I set about picking my model. As I wanted to show a ripe ear, the model had to be a full-grown stalk — one at least five feet high. Obviously, a plant that large could not be clipped like a rose and placed in a glass of water. Besides, as the field wasn't mine, I could not have cut the corn even had I wanted to. So I had to find a representative stalk growing in sufficient isolation from its fellows to be clearly visible. A position nearby from which I could draw was another necessity. I was prepared to stand, so I did not insist on a place to sit, but I knew the site had to be level and it had to allow unobstructed vision from far enough away for the stalk to appear small enough to fit the page of a sketchbook.

Only at the field's edges were such conditions to be found, so I set about circling the planted area. Although my chief consciousness was of rejecting one stalk after another, the old law was still in operation. Drawing was stimulating observation even before a single line was set down. And this happens invariably, whether you remain fixed and rotate your model or whether the model is the stationary element and you move around it.

Some stalks, I found, were suitable in themselves, but had to be rejected because they were partially obscured by other plants I was not at liberty to cut away. Other stalks stood handsomely erect in clear spaces, but had to be turned down for being earless. But I finally found what I wanted, a stalk with a good ear in a convenient location. And because Mexican sunlight is so bright and all-encompassing, the stalk was lit in a way that made its details beautifully clear.

I set about the job with the exactitude of depiction I have advocated. Because it was a lovely day and I was inwardly content, I had lots of patience. After the first blocking in, I checked and rechecked each curve of each leaf, making sure that, as well as having the leaves correct in themselves, I had each one set in proper relationship to the others.

In drawing, observation is aided not only by the black marks you make on the paper but by the paper itself. Normally, the shape of an interspace is something we do not see consciously. When we look at a pitcher, say, we see its outlines and we note the curve of its handle, but we are not apt to take in the lozenge-shaped void between the handle and the curve of the pitcher's body. However, when you make a drawing, you find that the parts you outline do not look right if the spaces between them on the paper do not correspond with those before you. Because the drawn voids are almost as completely outlined as the concrete forms, and because they are not complicated by the presence of depth, the spaces on the paper are easy to see. They, in turn, help you to see the interspaces in your model; for, when you hold the drawing up to the model, you can see how you have made an interspace either too constricted or too ample, or perhaps you have made an interspace almost circular, when it should be oval.

The paper helps, too, in the way it provides white blankness around your subject. I touched on this in speaking of the area of paper to be filled imposing a restricted field on the object being drawn. To amplify that, one might say that the area that is *not to* be filled helps focus concentration on the area that *is* to be filled. The elimination of all the background isolates the object so that it can be seen on the page with the clarity that comes when every other element that might compete for the attention is blotted out. As the drawing emerges ever more clearly on the paper, one gains the power to see the model with almost the same distinctness, the same freestanding isolation from the surrounding factors that earlier shaped — and also confused — the original impression. In other words, the part of the page to be filled helps by the pre-selected area to which it confines the eye; and the part of the page not to be filled, by remaining blank, aids concentration still further by tending to remove neighboring visual temptations from the easily tempted eye.

I drew the rosebud life-size, but I drew the five-foot cornstalk reduced enough to get it on a twelve-inch page. Here the paper helped in a new way. By dictating that the stalk be represented in a relatively small area, the page scaled the stalk down so the drawing of it could be taken in with a single look. Though I still had to shift the foveae from point to point for close examination, I could easily see everything on the page; whereas in reality the stalk was so large that my impression of it was an assemblage of its various aspects picked up from a number of independent looks.

At this stage, I had better present the drawing. In the reproduction on the next page you can see what I began to discern in my own drawing. The closer my lines resembled those of the plant, the more I was struck by the extraordinary balance of the long leaves on either side of the stalk. I saw that the plant was almost like an old-fashioned coatstand on which coats and hats were hung opposite to each other so there'd be no danger of it toppling. Leaves so large, I realized, were obviously heavy — so heavy, in fact, that they could not remain rigid to their tips. Yet, heavy as they were, that stalk, which I knew to be very porous, was able to remain perfectly upright because the weight of the leaves was so perfectly distributed.

This was a significant discovery about corn, and the paper made it possible. For on the paper I could easily see the proportional relationship of the wide-spreading leaves; whereas on the plant itself I had to size up each leaf with a separate look, and in

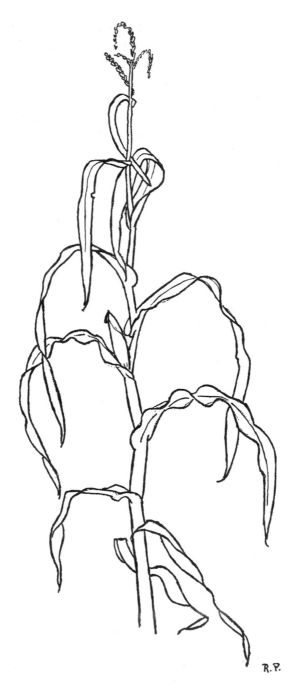

shifting my eye from the leaf on the right to the one on the left I lost the exact vision of the right one; and not seeing them simultaneously I could not see their exact relationship the way I could when they were together on the page in a span my eye could take in without shifting. What was true of the side to side relationship of the leaves held also for their top to bottom relationship.

When I had envisaged drawing a stalk of corn I had thought of the job as consisting only of drawing the central stem, an ear, and the wide-spreading leaves. But the plant before me forced me to note that there was still another element to be taken into account. At its very top were some little sprays that shot up and then drooped, rather like the jets of a waterspout. What were they, I wondered? I moved forward for a closer inspection. They resembled little beads strung on upright wires, some of which bent under the weight of their burden. The beads were beige-colored, and as I drew them, it occurred to me they might be flowers.

They did not look like flowers — at least not like any flowers I had ever noticed — but the possibility came to me because curiosity aroused by my desert rose had led me to read about blossoms. At that time I had been very ignorant, for I had never had any botany at school. Nor had the-birds-and-the-bees routine been used to introduce me to the mysteries of sex. Accordingly, I had thought flower heads existed principally so human beings could have beautiful table decorations, or spots of color for their gardens. But a dictionary entry had quickly disabused me, showing nature had something more primary in mind when it created flowers. The flower, it said, was "that part of a seed plant which bears reproductive organs." Elsewhere I read how flowers assured the plants' sexual propagation. Their bright colors and sweet scents insured that they would be enticing to bees, butterflies, and other insects. However, said the books, not all plants were insect-pollinated. Some were wind-pollinated; that is, the wind did the necessary work of transferring pollen from one plant to another. These wind-pollinated plants, which did not need insects as transfer agents, therefore did not need the allurements of bright colors and perfumes to attract insects.

Perhaps, I said to myself, corn is a wind-pollinated plant. If so, its flowers would not be scented and showy and these odorless, little beige beads would be adequate. Perhaps they are set at the top of the stalk so the wind can get at them most easily. Perhaps, too, they have an exalted position so their pollen grains will have a long way to fall before they are lost to the zone in which they might do their work of fertilization.

I have said one comes into a new relationship with anything one has drawn. The cornstalk was no exception. Accordingly, when I got back to New York I took advantage of being among books again to look up corn. To my delight, a botany textbook confirmed my guess about those drooping beads. They *were* flowers. And the book went further. It said they were staminate flowers, and added the information that because corn was a plant that produced both staminate and pistillate flowers it was a dioecious plant. The panicle bearing the staminate flowers was called the tassel. The pistillate flowers were on the ears and all that showed of them were the thread-like organs called the silk.

The book provided further eye-opening knowledge by bringing up a fact I had never thought of: corn was a grass. And the moment I knew, I felt sheepish for not having been struck by the obvious relationship between corn and grass before. The difference in scale had kept me unaware of how alike were corn leaves and blades of grass, corn stems and grass stalks, and the springing of the leaves from the stalks.

Corn leaves, said the book, were arranged *spirally* around the stalk. I examined the book's illustrations to see if they showed this spiral arrangement. The photographs were too small and fuzzy, so I thought of the drawing I had made in Mexico. Would it show the spiral disposition of the leaves? Almost tremblingly, I got it out. To my amazement, it did.

The leaves on my plant, I saw, were arranged around the stalk as if they were people standing at different levels on a spiral staircase. Through drawing, then, I had observed the plant even better than I knew. I had merely depicted the leaves where I saw them, without deducing how their points of origin were related. But because I had depicted them accurately, I had shown the unrecognized spiral disposition.

I rejoiced doubly at this discovery. First, it seemed a particularly striking instance of drawing's good postoperative effects on vision. For here the drawing had aided me to a new awareness of my model more than a month later. And then it provided me with evidence of one of the great advantages that drawing has over verbalizing as a means of visual apprehension.

In drawing, you can observe accurately without knowledge. With this in mind, I realized the experience with the rose had pointed to the same thing. For in those first drawings I had not understood that the rose opened from the middle any more than I had understood that the corn's leaves followed each other in spiral formation. Yet, because I sketched carefully, I took in a truth about the rose, just as I had with the corn. So in both cases I had recorded something of which I had no knowledge. And the recording had been the means of coming to that knowledge.

Allied to drawing's gift for fostering observation despite ignorance is the way it lets you observe without need of words. And in drawing, I realized, you can observe with an accuracy that exceeds either the generalizing of knowledge or the limited precision of words.

This is because the sketching pencil can tolerate non-understanding much more easily than the mind. The mind, as we have seen, tends to shutter out meaningless forms because of their unintelligibility. But the sketching pencil is satisfied with forms alone. To it, meaningless forms can be depicted with the same facility as understood ones. In fact, sometimes the absence of meaning can make the job easier, for the meaningless form can be seen more readily as pure form, unlike that which already has an identity as a leaf, a flower, or a stalk. So if one is careful to render exactly what is before the eyes, one can take into the mind an image that would be unlikely to get there otherwise. One can do it, too, without any fear of verbal inadequacy, and without any prolonged racking of the brain for the needed terms. For with the form present on the paper, it is safely preserved without verbal embalming and the pictorial record is more exact than it would have been if it had been verbal.

Notice, too, that the record is kept. For a drawn image has several advantages over one that has been merely committed to memory. Not only does it retain its accuracy unchanged, but it is an image that can be consulted — as I consulted my corn drawing when I looked for evidence of the spiraling leaves. And if you want the help of more than books to elucidate what you have committed to paper, a drawn image can be taken to experts who can bring to it the knowledge you did not have when you sketched.

Reading the botany book further, I reaped other postoperative benefits from my sketch. The book's language was so technical that its corn description would have been unintelligible to me — or certainly very hard to follow — had it not been for my drawing. But the drawing had implanted so clear an awareness of each part in my mind that I could visualize the aspects the botanist was discussing and be glad of the information he was supplying. As for the bareness of the style, the dryness of the language, and the exactitude of the nomenclature — well, the drawing had made my curiosity active enough to press gratefully through the stylistic jungle to the knowledge that sharpened my vision of the corn still further.

Awareness of the spiral disposition of the leaves heightened my sense of the wonder of their balance. In front of the plant itself I had thought merely of a hatrack with hooks at the cardinal points. But now I knew the balance was achieved in a far more subtle and ingenious way, a way that allowed for continuing balance as new leaves were growing. The botanist's words, then, gave me fresh awe at the mechanical ingenuity of the plant, which, in turn, redoubled my appreciation of the plant itself. But when I shifted my eyes from my drawing to his dry paragraphs, I could not help feeling that the sketch held some reality lacking in the botanist's description. The text conveyed little idea that a cornstalk could be a delicately balanced tower of glistening leaves, an object with the beauty of a fountain magically arrested in its fall.

This brings me back to the relationship of words and vision. It also brings up those assemblages of words — books. In the next chapter I am going to deal further with them, but here what I would like to suggest, is *when* to read. A lot depends on literary quality. Those books that enhance awareness of the visible world are good to read at any time. But with technical books, it is best to look first and read later. That is, gather your own impressions, using your eyes to take in as much as they can unaided, and turn to such books only after you feel you have observed all you can discern. This sequence transforms what would be dull stuff — hard to visualize and still harder to remember — into exciting material that explains what has been seen, extends comprehension of the partially perceived, and furnishes names for the parts that have been learned.

However, that botany book underlined some of the dangers I have mentioned. A word like dioecious might be one of the most exact names you could find for one of the plant groups into which corn fits. Yet it would be hard to conceive a more vision-killing word. And it does its deadly work in two of the ways I warned against. It classifies with a vengeance, and in doing so it stresses, not what is particular to corn, but what corn shares with all other species that have staminate and pistillate flowers in the same plant. And with its difficult Greek sound, the forbidding word, far from conjuring up the appearance of the plant, obliterates its living reality. And it is the piling up of such words in botanical descriptions that makes them seem, despite their exactitude, remote from the whole truth.

As we have seen with the child's bird, a thing that has been given a name tends to lose its particularity. And because particularity is precious, names that merely embody concepts or denote functions can be like cloaks of invisibility. Drawing, however, emphasizes and helps to preserve particularity. In fact, as one draws a given object one tends to become so concentrated on it as an individual thing that one even forgets it is a representative of a class. It becomes itself and nothing else. And the absorption becomes so great that at times one even loses sight of the whole object as one struggles to reproduce a particular part. Even its parts, then, become, for a time at least, themselves and nothing else.

In the epilogue I will speak a little more of the value of this apprehension of particularity. But here I want only to point out that when, through drawing, one absorbs a given feature with a detailed and accurate comprehension of its nature, that feature sticks in the memory as an especially creative touchstone. It becomes a more potent magnetic nucleus than an object that has been studied just by verbalization. The drawn thing, too, provides a secondary image so sharp and detailed that it enables one to see other objects of the same class with a realization of how they, too, are individual.

If one has drawn a large garden iris, one will carry in mind the precise recollection of its three tongues, its three upward-arching petals, and its inner ones resembling a tripod inverted in the chamber under the arches. This image will enable one to stand before a wild iris and notice that its tongues are leaner and that the arching petals are rudimentary little flaps that don't come even close to meeting overhead. In other words, one will find that careful drawing of a specific iris has brought the power to see the particular nature of a variant.

Even when the impression of what you have drawn begins to

dim, your drawing can still aid you. Witness what happened when on a trip to Japan I acquired a beautiful iris print two years after making my iris drawing. Comparing my work with that of the Japanese artist, I was able to learn in detail how our irises differed. I was also able to recognize and appreciate additional aspects of his skill. The contours of petals and leaves are so clean-cut that, in working in black and white, it is difficult not to make them seem wiry, which flower contours never are. The Japanese, working in color, solved the difficulty by bounding his masses with a line lighter in tone than the masses themselves.

I might add, too, that my iris sketch illustrates another of the advantages of drawing as an aid to vision. It is relatively simple to draw things larger than life-size. And just as reducing can aid in observing particular aspects of an object — as it did with the corn — so can enlarging. In the original drawing this flower was nine inches high, which is almost twice as large as any iris blossom ever grows. But by working on such a scale I was able to note and put in all sorts of details I would have been obliged to ignore had my drawing been small.

That plants are patient models does not mean they are necessarily easy to draw. Some plants with hundreds of tiny flowers, like lilacs, are very difficult. But the advantage of the plant kingdom as a chosen theme is that it contains specimens suitable to all degrees of graphic skill. It has forms of all sizes and forms simple enough for those who have never drawn at all. If you are a beginner, you should select plants of simplest form to start with, and preferably fairly large ones, since large objects are easier to observe than small ones.

Even when you have picked an easy subject, though, you will find yourself confronted with certain difficulties, the greatest of which will be conveying the impression of rotundity without using shadow. Another will be drawing a part whose long axis is advancing towards you. A third will be depicting something at the back of the plant that is partially obscured by parts in front.

The way you pose your plant can help with all three. You can manipulate it so that the contours indicate rotundity, so that the most characteristic features stretch crosswise in front of you, and so only the less important parts are obscured. And to aid in the latter, you can even strip away a few leaves. Nevertheless, these precautions will not eliminate all the difficulties. It is good that they should not, for these particular difficulties have much to teach us about the interaction of mind and eye.

The mind tends to see things as they are in concept, whereas the eye's tendency is to see things as they exist in space. There is a constant tug of war between the two types of vision, as one discovers in making drawings. Take the partially obscured section at the back of the plant: in one's first efforts one will find again and again that one tends to draw that part larger than it appears and more completely revealed than it is. Both mistakes are caused by the intervention of the mind.

The mind, with its prevailing thirst for full comprehension, tends to reduce the changes that space imposes on objects. One of those greatest changes is in size. At a restaurant, for instance, look at a woman seated far across the room. You see her in your mind as being the same size as the companion sitting across from you. Yet what is the far woman's size to our unbiased eye? Hold up your hand and see. If the restaurant is a particularly large one, perhaps one thumb will cover her entirely; certainly the whole hand ought to do the trick. In other words, you find your mind actually falsified what your eye saw. Your mind made her seem life-sized; whereas actually, at that distance, her image is smaller than a normal hand. Making her large when actually she is seen small is a triumph of the mind over the eye; and it is the same sort of mental triumph that leads us to draw back parts of plants so large that in our finished drawing they look grotesque. The discrepancy becomes plain when we revert to looking at the drawing with an unbiased eye and not the eye, which, while concentrating on the back part, had lost sight of the rest of the drawing.

The mind's thirst for comprehension also accounts for our adding aspects of an obscured part that can't be seen. We know the parts are there — for we've seen them from other angles — and we put them in because they are necessary to the completeness of our mental picture. Again, a glance at the finished drawing will often reveal the mistake, for we might even find we have split foreground parts too wide open in an effort to draw in parts that are actually overlapped.

The difficulties caused by foreshortening also illustrate what the mind tends to do. Somehow we feel things look most like themselves when they are squarely in front of us with their most extended axis running across our line of sight. Thus, when an object is represented with its longest axis foreshortened, we tend to feel it scarcely resembles itself. Witness the depiction of a forefinger pointing straight at us. Seen only as a fingernail edge with a rounded curve below, it is hard to assume the shaft of the finger behind the rounded tip. No wonder we tend to draw the pointing forefinger in profile. And because the profile view so often strikes the mind as being the characteristic aspect of an object, our tendency in drawing is to compensate for the head-on effect by drawing all foreshortened parts more in profile than they actually appear. Again we adopt the mind's view at the expense of the eye's.

The mind wants known forms to maintain consistent shapes, no matter what angle they are seen from. Actually, foreshortening is only one of the distortions that perspective seems to impose on reality. And I say "distortion" because an object whose shape does not conform to one's mental image of it always seem to be distorted. I had a striking instance of this in one of my first plant drawings. When I drew the philodendron in its pot, I wanted to include the saucer on which the pot rested. As things worked out, the plant itself was child's play compared to that saucer. Try as I might, I could not get the saucer to look right, because at that time I did not know the elementary fact that circular objects seen at an angle look elliptical. I was so obsessed by my knowledge that the saucer was round that every version suggested, not that the pot was resting on a dish, but that its base had a halo.

However, once I gained the elliptical clue, I got the saucer right. And when the drawing looked realistic I was amazed at this undeniable proof that the eye accepted the ellipse as a representation of a circle without any difficulty. Thereafter, I chucked out mental notions more easily and when I saw a leaf at an odd angle, I'd try to forget what it would look like pressed flat in a copy book, and, instead, to draw only the contours actually before me. It was not always easy to depict what I knew was a heart-shaped leaf as if it were a knife edge. Often, in fact, I felt I was drawing only meaningless shapes. Yet again and again, when the "distorted," unleaflike shapes were outlined on the paper the way they were in life, I would be amazed to see that, after all, the plant did look like itself, and the funny shapes undeniably looked like leaves, either advancing or retreating, or partially obscured by forefront leaves.

This should clarify what I said about the sketching pencil finding it easier to reproduce meaningless forms than identified ones. With the meaningless ones there are no mental concepts to take control of the pencil to shape the form into the mind's-eye-view. And learning to reproduce exactitude of form is so important that I suggest some practice by deliberately copying forms that have no intelligibility. Chinese characters provide one exercise: our ignorance protects us from seeing any meaning in them, so we can reproduce them without any notion that they must resemble known objects. They have another great advantage, too, for the mind seems to love simple, symmetrical forms; so much, in fact, that the forms we draw tend to emerge as far more smoothed out, regular and exactly balanced than they are in reality. Chinese characters, with their asymmetry and gloriously ragged edges, defy the natural tendency to geometrize. Copying them, therefore, heightens exactitude of vision.

Exact rendering of any kind helps us see the lines that are actually in the visual field, regardless of whether the lines seem correct or not. In other words, in helping us overrule intellectual ideas in favor of exact perceptions, it helps us distinguish between visual percepts and mental concepts. And if we make repeated drawings, depicting only what the eye sees, drawing the different parts strictly in the relative proportions they present to the eye, and accepting all of perspective's distortions of form, we will find that our drawings begin to look more and more realistic, more and more like what they are supposed to convey.

This experience is invaluable. Nor does it stop at helping us observe the things we draw. It helps with vision of all things, for it increases our confidence in the accuracy of our eyes and increasingly it allows us to accept the vision of the world they bring in. We start seeing reality more fully as it actually appears, instead of relying, as so many of us do, on a relatively limited number of mental concepts: concepts which in their crude forms — witness the drawings of children — reduce noses to triangles and hair to isolated straight lines that ray out from circular heads.

That our seeing is so concept-ridden, incidentally, is a factor in that sketchiness of vision that struck me as so odd when I first isolated it in roughing in that church façade. It is not just that the mind selects only a few salient features. It is also because the mind tends to go around with cartoon ideas.

Drawing plants, then, can not only lead us to examine details more minutely, but it can lead to something perhaps even more important. Besides enabling us to use our eyes more fully, it can help us observe the world more fully as our eyes see it.

CHAPTER 14

Museums and Art Books

In this chapter I am again going to advocate concentration on objects of a single class, only here it will be pictures. One reason for the choice is that, thanks to social conditioning, it is fairly easy to get into the looking gear in front of pictures. Art, as we have seen, is something our society considers worth looking at, so to observe paintings one does not need to break through conventional attitudes.

Pictures, too, have some advantages over reality. Like plants, they do not move or change, so one has more time to analyze and absorb their effects. Insofar as artists select their subjects from the welter of reality, paintings are nearly always less complicated, less crowded than actuality. And because their pre-selected elements are confined within a frame, they are gathered into an area that aids concentration. Finally, what is represented is depicted with artistic vision.

Up to now I have probably given the impression of being most interested in accurate vision. I certainly value it and am inclined to think it the gateway to the highest artistic vision. Fundamentally, however, I do not esteem mere accuracy of perception as much as perception with aesthetic overtones. However, such overtones are hard to describe, and as one can learn more about them by direct experience than by reading, I urge you, if you have an art museum in your city, to pay it a special visit.

And please set out with some resolutions: First, because too many impressions are confusing and overwhelming, resolve that you will only look at a limited number of pictures. Second, because flash-glimpsing is as inadequate with art as it is with life, resolve that you will allow enough time for the pictures to work on you and enough time for you to exercise your faculties on them. Third, resolve to nurse every little sprout of curiosity prompted by the pictures. Fourth, resolve to ransack your memory for similar paintings as you stand before the new ones so you can bring knowledge to bear on their appreciation. Under this heading, too, resolve to comb your memory for recollections of how the objects depicted have appeared to you in reality. Fifth, stop at the museum's postcard counter as you go in and buy what cards they have of the pictures you want to see.

If you claim this last suggests more advance knowledge than is generally possible, so much the better. The lack of advance knowledge can be a positive advantage. It may lead you to look until you have discovered which pictures interest you most. Then you can sample the card counter, make your purchases and *return* to the chosen gallery, postcards in hand. I stress the return to the gallery, not only because it extends the length of time given to the observing, but because you will find those cards will give you a whole new lease of vision on the very pictures you thought you had observed completely. Sometimes it will lift your sharpened vision to heightened vision. If you are lucky, it might take you close to transfigured vision.

Perhaps by now you have guessed why I suggested the postcards. That's right: to induce a form of double-level perception. And there are reasons why I have suggested collecting postcards rather than buying a catalogue. If you did with a cumbersome catalogue what I am going to suggest you do with the cards, it might make you so conspicuous that others in the museum would think you a crackpot. Besides, a catalogue sometimes has too much reading matter, and in the presence of paintings I want you to look, not read.

What I propose is simply this: When you get to one of the selected paintings, just hold its reproduction up in front of you, and then start looking back and forth, from postcard to painting, from painting to postcard.

If your postcard is in color, you may have noticed its colors on the way to the gallery, and perhaps been charmed by them. I hope so, for what is likely to strike you most about those colors, when you are before the original painting is that, pretty as they might have seemed on cardboard, they are wretchedly inadequate compared to the artist's original colors on the canvas.

Probably you will have a great many simultaneous impressions as you see painting and postcard in virtually the same eye gulp. For discussion, though, it is easier to consider them one by one. An early impression is sure to be that the postcard colors are not "true" — that is, they differ from the colors in the painting. The Virgin's cloak in both is likely to be blue, but you will see that the two blues are not the same. You will probably not have the words to define how the two shades differ. But it will not matter, the contrast will have been enough to open your eyes to the distinctness of the painter's color. Probably, too, you'll be struck by how much more beautiful is the shade he created than the shade the printer printed. And this is likely to extend to every color in the picture. If the artist is a great one, each of his colors will have a subtle individuality, defying exact definition; and each color will have a magical beauty that is equally indefinable. You will bless the drabber colors of the card that made you aware of the difference.

An attendant feature you will notice is that the artist's colors are also richer. This comparative richness is hard to define, but easy to detect; and richness is perhaps only a synonym for such qualities as depth of tone and subtlety of variation.

Perhaps one of the first things the original will make you aware of is the card's chalkiness. How does this happen? What makes the apparently richly-colored card suddenly look chalky? The answer is likely to be luminosity. This, too, is hard to define, and sometimes even harder to account for, but nearly all the great paintings are somehow luminous. And the importance of this luminous quality is dramatized by its absence in the card.

The search for the secret of luminosity will perhaps lead you to the highlights. The highlights in the card will be white enough, but you'll see they tend to be a dead white, whereas the whites in the original seem to shine.

Then, if you are wise, you will shift your attention to the shadows, where again you will notice marked differences. If the card is dark, you'll notice its shadows tend to be much blacker than

PLATE I. EL GRECO: *Christ Driving the Money Changers from the Temple*. Frick Collection, New York.

PLATE II. LA TOUR: *Education of the Virgin*. Frick Collection, New York.

PLATE III. SEURAT: *The Channel at Gravelines, Evening.* Collection of Mr. and Mrs. William A. M. Burden, New York.

PLATE IV. ZURBARAN: *The Immaculate Conception with Thirteen Angels.* Collection of Felix Valdes, Bilbao, Spain.

PLATE V. MASSYS: *The Entombment of Christ*. Koninklijk Museum, Antwerp.

PLATE VI. DÜRER: *The Festival of the Rose-Garlands.* National Gallery, Prague.

PLATE VII. FRA ANGELICO: *Coronation of the Virgin*. The Louvre, Paris.

PLATE VIII. FRA ANGELICO: *Coronation of the Virgin* (detail). The Louvre, Paris.

PLATE IX. Feathered Serpents at Teotihuacan.

PLATE. X. Feathered Serpent at Xochilcalco.

the painting's. If it is pale, you'll feel its shadows lack the richness of the shadows in the painting. And whether dark or pale, you will notice all card shadows swallow up detail. This will make you aware of another miracle in the painting: even its shadows are sufficiently light-filled for details to show in them clearly; and not just details show in the shadow pockets, for one also sees colors, variations in the shades of those colors, and beautiful subtleties of modeling.

Though they do not always happen separately, there are always two parts to the apprehension of a work of art: the sizing up, and the appreciating. The latter generally only really begins in the area of distinction. For sizing up is grasping the features a work of art has in common with comparable works, while the appreciation is realizing the features it has that no other work has. With paintings, one of the great areas of distinction is that of color values. And this is an area that can be greatly highlighted and isolated by the touchstone of postcards. The cards, as it were, show you common colors. The qualities of color in the originals that are lacking in the cards are the particular color values of the paintings in question.

If you try the colored card trick with a number of paintings, you will find something subtle happening to your own perception of colors. Having been made sensitive to subtle color values in paintings, you will begin to see subtle color values in scenes around you. No longer, say, will browns just be browns. They will be chestnut, tan, milk chocolate, bitter chocolate, bronze, copper, topaz, golden amber. And so it will be with all the colors before you, and you will notice new harmonies between them.

If there is a ring of familiarity to this, it is not accidental. When I spoke of the sea at Puerto Rico, I indicated subdivisions within the looking gear. Specifically, I spoke of the color gear. Now we can speak of a larger subdivision, which always includes an alert apprehension of color: the aesthetic gear. Museum visits, if we look at all conscientiously, nearly always shift us into this gear, and one gets especially well set in the gear of aesthetic looking if one uses cards as mediators.

Now let me cite a card influence I came to understand better after reading the gestalt psychologists. Cards have a way of liberating us from a force the gestaltists discovered: namely, that strong shape entities grip the mind so firmly that it is difficult to discern details "embedded" within the gestalt. And if this sounds fearsome, one only has to remember the Tula monster. With the bas-relief I deliberately broke the power of its gestalt — its overall impression — by pulling the head out of the jaws and doffing the monster's headdress. Once this was done the embedded details were easy to see. Well, great paintings have particularly powerful gestalten, and, for the very reason that their wholes can grip us so strongly, their details are often extremely hard to note.

Postcards of paintings, though, by diluting the genius, have much weaker gestalten. With them, the eye is often struck by parts in isolation. This is particularly true with odd shapes that arouse curiosity by being puzzling. And cards have many such shapes, not only because objects depicted are often engulfed in shadow, but also because, in the general reduction of scale, nearly all small objects become so tiny they can scarcely be recognized. Confronted with such shapes, we will often ask "What is that?" And this will lead our eyes to the original painting to seek the answer.

This happened to me standing before El Greco's "Christ Driving the Money Changers from the Temple" in the Frick Collection (Plate I). In the picture, the floor of the temple is checkered with brown and gray paving stones. In the foreground of the card, I noticed an angled brown thing that looked about the size of two paving stones. For the very reason that it was so hard to understand, I looked at the larger original for help.

Thanks to the greater color subtlety of the painting, I could see the flat object on an angle was not a double paving stone. It was a different brown. And I could discern the lines near the object more easily. Clearly, they were the x-shaped legs of a folding table, which showed the angled object was a table top. Recognition of the portable table that Christ had just overturned led my eyes to the object in the hands of the man in the orange vest who was bending, head downward, towards me. The clue of the table explained the chest-like object: a money box the man was lifting after it had been cast to the floor by the table's collapse.

In a flash, all the exact details of the picture's story clicked into place, including the nonchalance of the young girl on the right with the basket on her head. Being still in a transept of the temple, she had not yet come to the point where she could see there was trouble in the place where the money was normally changed. In the same flash, I realized something else. In its first impact, the painting, with its dramatic sky under the arch, its canary yellows, its acid greens, its pink-robed Christ, and its general air of flame-like agitation, had so dazzled me that its story-telling had made no impression. But being aware of that story-telling now, I noticed it extended even to the ear of the man who was raising his elbow to fend off the blows of Christ's scourge. Its lobe was bloody and there was blood on the floor, indicating that the ear had been flicked in an earlier flail of the scourge. Awareness that El Greco had told the story so precisely without impairing the dynamic quality of the design heightened my appreciation of the work. The same card that had deepened my feeling for the picture's color values, then, had also given me a sharper sense of how it fused story and form.

But postcards need not be colored to help in the appreciation of originals. In some cases, if the cards' contrasts are sharp, it is almost better that they should be in black and white. This is especially true for massive paintings crowded with figures.

The nature of the eye makes huge paintings particularly hard to grasp. The span of the foveae is not wide enough to embrace them entirely. Indeed, unless one gets very far back, one cannot even see the whole canvas in one look. Accordingly, one has to compile one's visual impression from a number of separate looks. First one looks at one corner, then at another; then, perhaps, the middle. If each section is full of interesting detail, sometimes the previously looked-at section dims in the memory. No matter how tenacious the memory, the total compilation is likely to be jerky and not very well put together. And it is here that the black and white card helps so much: It gives you the whole composition in a space small enough to be taken in with a single look; in fact, almost small enough to be covered by the foveal span. Thus with the card one can get a clear vision of the picture's overall organization, which, in turn, helps the isolated impressions fall into place.

Furthermore, the black and white card is likely to reveal the structure of the composition even more sharply than a colored card. It does this for the very reason that it excludes color. Always, the differing elements of the world compete for the eye's attention, and where there is lots of wonderful color, that color is apt to win most of the attention. So with a black and white card, with no color to complicate the impression or distract the eye, one can concentrate on the composition in a unique way. The grasp of form acquired thereby, besides organizing one's impressions, will enormously heighten one's apprehension of the masterwork as a whole.

What before seemed too big and unwieldy, too full of story content, will at this point become a great symphony, in which all the themes are marvelously interwoven in a structure so powerful and moving that its exquisite details blend without any fussiness into the total effect. One will see that the work has grandeur as well as richness, cohesion as well as variety, and strength as well as exactitude.

There is another facet of painting that black and white cards can highlight. Art critics are known for their fancy terms. Not all of them are meaningful, but there is one favorite that is perfectly valid — tone values. And such values can be magically demonstrated by black and white cards.

Tone values are part of color values, but they can be discussed separately because they are values of light and dark, regardless of hue. If this sounds too subtle, consider the word "pale." It can be applied to color after color, to blues as well as to reds, greens, yellows, browns, and so on. Pallor, then, is a tone property. And hues come in different tones, ranging from pale to dark.

What a black and white postcard will demonstrate clearly is that different colors can have the same tone. Say you are standing in front of a Vermeer, which shows a girl sitting at a green table against a blue wall. In the postcard you will find that the wall and the table are indistinguishable, both being an identical soft gray. You know from glances at the picture that the wall and the table cloth have different hues. What is your conclusion then? Obviously, that what makes them identical in the colorless card is that they have the same tone.

Then, thanks to the card, you will note an identity of tone among many different colors. A red, for instance, might appear as dark as a black. Also, you will see where the light tones are gathered in the picture, and where the dark ones. Probably, too, you will realize how meaningful is the arrangement of the tones. In a Rembrandt, for instance, all the light tones might very well be concentrated around the head. Some pictures might have too much uniformity of tone to be interesting in black and white. Others might have tonal values contrasted so sharply that they seem crude. Still others can be so subtle in their tonal relationships that on this count alone they are a joy to see. And oh! the pleasure of looking up again at a masterpiece whose tonal values one has come to appreciate! Not only are its colors just as wonderful as hues, but they are seen to have marvelous tonal relationships too.

Black and white cards can serve even better than colored ones in piquing curiosity, for the objects in them tend to be still more difficult to discern and so the cards provide more things to seek out for identification. Not only is there delight in mystery solving, but one's feelings for the painting's colors are heightened still further. For puzzling forms, once located in the canvas, are seen to have realistic colors that identify what they represent. Wine in a glass, say, will be burgundy in color. By contrasting with the surrounding hues, their colors will insure that the objects are clearly defined. And color coherence will enable the eye to segregate their particular constellations. In other words, shapes that were merely part of the ground in the postcard, become figures in the painting. And as they achieve this shift, they become so much more clearly visible that they seem to leap out. Thus at the same time as you come to relish them, you realize the painter has given them their identity, their differentiation, and their figure quality by using colors which, though different in hue from neighboring colors, don't differ in tonal values.

Cards can serve a further purpose in museum-going. If you go with a friend, cards can help make you both more articulate about what you look at together. This is important because articulateness before pictures is often difficult, for it involves something in which we are not practiced: translating impressions gathered by the eye, and therefore absorbed without words, into ideas transmitted to others by means of words. But, equipped with cards, you do not need much vocabulary.

Looking at a card, you can ask "What's this in the background?" and then point to it with a finger. Then your companion knows what you are talking about and can look for its counterpart in the original. Or if you want to exclaim over the wonder of a color in a painting, a color that you cannot name, you can point to the color in the card and say "See how much more wonderful *that* color is in the painting."

Or you can ask your companion to hold up a card to a painting and say what differences there are between the reproduction and the original. Conversely, you can hold up the card and start reeling off what differences you see. Either way, the tongue is likely to be loosened. The experience will be fascinating, for each of you will find you see different differences. And those the other picks out which you missed will augment your impressions.

I remember this happening at the Frick. Susan Comegys and I were standing in front of Georges de La Tour's "Education of the Virgin" (Plate II). She was holding up a colored card of it.

"All this background's too black," she said, referring to the card. "It swallows up things you can see in the picture. Look, in the postcard you can't see the shadow the basket is casting on the wall."

As a matter of fact, even looking at the original I had not noticed that basket's shadow. And as my attention was called to it, I realized it was one of the most marvelous touches in the painting.

Like most of La Tour's works, the picture centers on the effects of a candle. I had noticed what my friend had not — that La Tour showed how the flame caused a red transparency in the fingertips of the girl's hand shielding the candle. Yet I had not noticed how even the work basket on the table dramatized the light, doing this not only by the way its square meshes received the light, but by the way those meshes reappeared, enlarged and radiating more widely, in the basket's shadow.

Susan was much more alert than I in seeing the stories the pictures told. I, on the other hand, was somewhat more sensitive to color values and to the rhythmic patterning of composition. Aided by the cards, which were easy to discuss, and by features the cards made so apparent, we were able to exchange our respective visions in a way that would not have been possible without a device to help us communicate so many non-verbal perceptions. Because of the interchange of visions, each of us came to see the pictures we studied together with a fuller appreciation. We came away with more than happy memories of the paintings. We also had the memory that we had shared so intimately the sort of impressions that, before this experience, each of us had thought were unshareable.

Perhaps, with all this talk about studying cards, I have given the impression that I advocate making museum-going an earnest chore. I hope not, for going with postcards is not the only way to visit picture galleries. They can also be approached in a mood of relaxed receptivity, and the gains of this approach can be illustrated by what happened to me on Good Friday of 1958 at the comprehensive Seurat show assembled by the Museum of Modern Art. I was in a mood of open and sober sensibility, because I had spent the previous three hours in church listening to the meditations of an intelligent clergyman on the Seven Last Words of Christ. I was unhurried, too, because it was a day off and the long service had released me from the agitated gearshift common to those preoccupied with all the jobs they feel they must do.

The exhibit was on a single floor, and I began strolling through it in an idle fashion. Once I had found my way around the basic circuit, I began following it a second time, paying a little more attention to those sketches or drawings that had caught my eye on the first round. Because poor Seurat died at the age of thirty-one and because he spent so much time on each of his paintings, the exhibit was not large. Being easy to encompass, I kept circling through it, getting to know the contents through a series of repeated glances, effortlessly bestowed, rather than by diligent study of any particular picture.

Absorbing the show in its totality brought home a curious antithesis. Blackness was the chief concern of the drawings; for they included all the shadings from deepest black to, by contrast, the most brilliant whites. Yet in the light-filled paintings there wasn't a hint of black.

This gave me the idea that Seurat worked without color, not, as some artists do, for the sake of line, but to sharpen his apprehension of tonal values. Then, when he turned to colors, he brought to his work in them the extraordinary sensitivity to tone values that he had developed through working without colors. In the conventional sense, the paintings contained no draftsmanship whatever. They were built up by assembling tiny dots of color. The outlines that were suggested all resulted from the juxtaposition of dots of differing tones. The extraordinary subtlety of the paintings, I saw, came from his sensitivity to the minutest differences in tonal values. As well as being lovely in their hues, his colors were lovely for this subtlety of tonal nuance within a somewhat muted tonal range.

The huge central canvas of the exhibit was "A Sunday Afternoon on the Island of La Grande Jatte." And what gave added interest to the show was that it contained so many of the preliminary sketches, both in color and in black and white, for this great painting. One had the feeling of being admitted to an artist's workshop — with this difference: the preliminary works were hung and lighted with an orderliness and an amplitude of wall space that would have been impossible in an artist's studio. One could not escape being struck by the endless pains to which Seurat went to achieve his ends, and the amount of time he spent in working out his problems. This was underlined, too, by the number of preparatory studies shown for his other works.

Interesting as its assemblage was, "La Grande Jatte" was not the Seurat that won me most. The pictures that captured my heart were the twelve or thirteen summer seascapes in three rooms that opened off the exhibit's eastern corridor. As my circlings got slower and more concentrated, I stayed more and more in those three rooms. There was the familiar "Fishing Fleet at Port-en-Bessin," with its white sails dotted over a shadowed sea; there was the pier of Port-en-Bessin; there was Grand-camp at evening, and several others. At first, as I feasted on them, I could not decide which I loved the most.

Finally, because the picture, without my knowing it, stirred some memory, my heart settled on "The Channel at Gravelines" (Plate III); the painting with a pink sky, which has in its foreground a lamppost on the left and two anchors on the right, and, in the middle distance, a small two-masted sailboat — putting out, as I like to think, for its home berth.

What struck me about all the seascapes was that each depicted a specific scene at a specific hour of the day. Not one was a picture that might be a study of the ocean at any old time — in any number of places. There was nothing general about them. Rightly speaking, they were not even seascapes; they were channelscapes, for all were done from the shores of French seaports or fishing villages on the English Channel. And the effect of light, magically arrested in each one, was of such transience that it was clear each painting was a re-creation of a given vision that Seurat had at a particular moment. Each, too, was a record of a moment of transfigured vision.

I use the term in the sense I have defined earlier. That is, each vision was extraordinarily accurate, but at the same time it had the accompanying luminosity indicating that something more than the scene had been perceived. What was captured in all of them was the way, in certain high moments of summer loveliness, God's reaching down into the world seems to become palpable. Because of this, the paintings were simultaneously studies of momentary effects and glimpses of something eternal. One knew that, year after year, until the earth wore out, such moments would recur in summer off the Normandy coast.

Off other coasts, too. . . . And it was this that stirred the memory.

The moment of time captured with such imperturbable mastery in "The Channel at Gravelines" is a moment known to many people who have been on the shore of a sheltered seaport in summer. It is around seven o'clock in the evening, when the heat has gone out of the day and the sea is extraordinarily calm; when the day's work is over; when birds as well as men have lost their restlessness; when the sky is still faintly colored by the vanished sun and when those sky colors are mirrored in cooler, more silvery tones in the wide still waters of the bay; when a certain cool peace seems to lap at the edges of the soul and when one knows that soon summer darkness will be over the world.

Ringed to the north as it is with great oil tanks, the harbor at Salina Cruz on the Pacific coast of Mexico is by no means the loveliest port in the world. Its derricks, storage sheds, and dry dock for Mexico's few tiny battleships do not help. What one is likely to see putting out at evening is an oil tanker with a mocha-colored superstructure, rather than a picturesque sailboat. Yet, like Gravelines, it, too, has a breakwater. Its sheltered waters also mirror the colors of the sky when the sun has gone. Its people also know the joy of surcease from the day's labors. And it, too, knows that blessed interlude of evening calm.

Salina Cruz had been far from my mind when I entered the museum, and in my early looking I had been so caught up in Seurat's visual world that I had not thought of my own. Yet as I gazed at that tranquil painting, so gently flushed with diffused pink, I knew something in my own experience had been touched. What was it? Then, the memory of more than one happy twilight in Salina Cruz came back to me, and I realized I had experienced what Seurat had at Gravelines — and hardly realized it.

I, too, had been confronted by such a scene, filled with the same emotional overtones. Yet I had not gazed long enough to drink it in. I had let the moment slip by. Yet such was the evocative power of Seurat's art that it enabled me to savor in retrospect a beauty I had been too purblind to absorb at the moment of direct experience. And this is one of the great gifts the works of the master painters can bestow, especially the great Impressionists. They can enrich our lives by enabling us to salvage from the past moments whose beauty we did not properly apprehend.

At that moment I blessed Seurat for his gift. And with awareness of its value the gift increased fourfold. All of us at different times have periods of doubt about the ends to which we devote our lives. Other people's tragedies, other people's achievements, can fill us with the sense that our interests are trivial, and perhaps with the feeling that we are wretchedly complacent about our good fortune and small triumphs. In the months before going to that Seurat exhibit, I had been very much wrapped up in the earlier parts of this book. And often I had been swept with almost a sense of shame that I could be getting excited about such trivia as the pictorial aspects of playing cards, when such cruel things were happening in the world. In those moments, I had doubted the whole worth of what I was trying to do. Trying to get people to be a little more observant, say, of flowers opening, of the colors of the sea, or the wavering of candle flames hardly seemed worth a man's concern.

Yet what had Seurat done? He had spent days, weeks, even years on a handful of paintings. One might almost say on a handful of momentary glimpses, for each painting was clearly an attempt to reproduce a vision that would be so perfectly embodied that it would exist as an objective reality outside his own mind. He wanted to transfer his visions to canvas so they could persist in the world long after the eyes that saw them, and the heart that responded to them, were dust.

And here the visions were, being gazed at by throngs crowding into the museum, day after day. All his painstaking juxtaposition of little dots of carefully graded colors — which must have seemed picayune, if not odd, to his neightbors — was triumphantly vindicated. Sixty-seven years after his death those embodied visions were giving people delight, filling them with a sense of beauty, refining their powers to perceive the loveliness of transitory effects and helping them retrieve from slumbering memories moments of poetry that had barely brushed them in passing by. Clearly, his life-work had been worthwhile. This exhibit, then, was evidence that Seurat's faith was not misplaced. It proved that what one saw in an illumined moment was so worth communicating that a life devoted to the embodying of a few visions was wonderfully spent.

I came away renewed in my own faith that vision was a subject worth pursuing. I was enormously heartened, too, by Seurat's courageous persistence in carrying out his self-imposed tasks. And because of "The Channel of Gravelines," unknowingly, I carried within me a touchstone that within two months was going to make the museum visit a still richer experience.

It was the last day of May that the visit had its sequel. That was the day when the yachts sailed up Long Island Sound on the last lap of the Storm Trysail Club's annual two-hundred-mile race around Block Island. I happened to be invited for supper at the home of some friends whose back terrace overlooked a cove adjoining Stamford Bay. The terrace gave us an excellent view of the end of the race, as the finish line was just inside the gap in the Stamford breakwater.

The opposite arm of the cove was a wooded point that jutted like an emerald finger into the blue and white beauty of the day. After a long and rainy winter, the afternoon seemed especially lovely. And after so many months in the city, the great expanse of blue water, the clear sunlight, the freshness and warmth of the air, the fleck of red of the lighthouse beyond the breakwater, and the cottony clouds lazily piled at the distant horizon were all balm to my spirit.

The terrace was like the deck of a ship and it was easy to relax there, letting time slip effortlessly by. Not being a sailing man, I did not know the race was on; nor did I know (until I consulted papers the next day) that the first five sloops had already crossed the line. And I did not realize that — for sailing purposes — the wind had died. All I knew was that as evening drew on there was an ever-deepening sense of calm. The sun was behind us, obscured by houses and trees, so we never saw it set. In fact, the diminution of light was almost imperceptible. But we could tell the sun was down as the still water of the cove grew pink and faintly silver, like the lining of a pearl shell. There was a faint wash of reflected pink, too, in the eastern sky.

The scattered sails of various sailboats had added touches to the beauty of the afternoon. But now I noticed the sloops and yawls had assembled near the gap of the breakwater, almost as if they were a fishing fleet returning at the end of a day's catch. The sloops with their triangular sails, peaked at the head of a central mast, were so still they might have been part of a Seurat painting.

"They are having a hard time getting in," I overheard Stefan Lanfer say to another of his guests.

This did not tell me what was actually true — that these were the yachts that had fallen behind in the Block Island race — but it was enough to give the scene a story. I knew they were sailing men coming home at evening. "The Channel at Gravelines" came back to me and in my mind I matched the pink of this sky with the pink in Seurat's. His sky was a dustier, slightly richer pink, and the overall hue was more totally diffused through the whole scene. The moment he had captured, too, was a few minutes later.

As by now it's no secret that I sometimes talk to myself, I might as well confess what I said then. I was so anxious for something to happen that I addressed myself to the sky. "Get pinker, get pinker. And light, stay long enough so that before the darkness the whole scene can be suffused with that pink."

What I wanted was to have the scene take on the exact shade of Seurat's color. I was aware of some block in my apprehension of the beauty and the significance of what was before my eyes. I felt that if only that color would come into the sky I would see and feel what Seurat had seen at Gravelines. I wanted the transfigured awareness that I was convinced was so close and that would come with that particular soft rose.

Alas, it never came. Perhaps winter was still too near or the atmosphere too clear. Whatever the cause, the faint pink in the east faded without any general flare up of color, and suddenly everything was gray. I did not have the transfigured vision I had hoped for. Nevertheless, I am grateful for having neared its threshold. And I will remember those white sloops advancing ever so slowly towards the breakwater, even though my vision neither matched Seurat's nor satisfied me as an aesthetic entity.

In this instance it is not important that "The Channel at Gravelines" failed to bring me to the type of vision I wanted. What matters is that the memory of the painting acted as it did. Its treatment of similar subject matter made me aware that there were enormous artistic possibilities in the scene. And the rapture it had induced made me want to reach out to wrest a similar rapture from a Seurat come-to-life.

The failure was really in me, and the very fact of it, I think, lends humanity to this illustration of how the memory of a painting lives on in one as a creative stimulus. It is not only the poetry of a past experience that a painting can redeem. A painting can abide in one, like a philosopher's stone, ready to touch some experience still in the future and transmute it to gold. It is a touchstone that often allows one to see some glory that passes before the eye; and which, even when it does not succeed in revealing the gold, makes one sense that it is there and eager to reach out for it. This is a good deal. And when enough pictures are stored in our visual reservoirs we will find not only that we are seeing more, but also that more often we are seeing with the vision of the artists. Works of art, then, besides being sources of visual joy in themselves, help us to see the visual joys in the world of reality.

Starting this chapter, I cited five reasons for studying paintings as an aid to vision: "Finally," I said as I introduced the fifth. But I hope you realized the word was used partly to climax the enumeration and partly to stress the importance of that fifth reason — artistic vision. Actually there are many more than five reasons for studying paintings, even when they are viewed only as vision sharpeners. And the rest of this chapter will revolve around a sixth reason: Paintings are enormously helpful in aiding vision because so much has been written about them.

It is true that there are also many books about nature — and those books are not to be dismissed as auxiliaries in observing — but they are not as useful as art books. The reason is that nature is always shifting and changing; a painting is still. Thus, a description of a sunset is not likely to aid you much in looking at your particular sunset because the author's sunset was probably in some other country, certainly on some other day. But a painting that is carefully preserved does not alter radically with the years, and so in art books you can find reading material that describes the very thing you are looking at.

You might argue that technical manuals do as much for pieces of machinery, and that books on botany do the same for flowers, fruits, and other things that always conform to a set pattern in their growing. I would not quarrel with this. However, as I have pointed out, technical manuals do not pretend to stir aesthetic vision, and books on botany tend to wipe it away.

Besides elucidating artistic vision, art books can serve as substitutes for museums in communities without them. They do not equal the real thing, but they are far better than nothing. They can convey some of the glamor of art; whet the appetite to feast on pictures; introduce paintings into our lives that may later be known first hand; and give eye training that will prove invaluable against the time when one has originals to look at.

Some art books contain plates a good deal better than museum postcards, but on the whole their illustrations share such disadvantages as inexactness of color, loss of detail in the shadows, and absence of luminosity. And features like reduction in scale and intriguing obscurity — which are stimulating when we have cards in front of originals — can be serious drawbacks in plates whose originals we cannot consult. It is the texts of art books, then, that help most; or, more accurately, the interaction of text and plates as the two are studied simultaneously.

I experienced such interaction as I read Martin S. Soria's *The Paintings of Zurbaran*. Its first black and white plate shows "The Immaculate Conception with Thirteen Angels" (Plate IV). As I looked at the picture I was struck by the Virgin's childishness. She was not the usual young woman in the flower of her beauty, but a rather plain girl of about thirteen or fourteen. If I noticed the figures at the bottom of the painting at all, it was merely to think that they should have been called cherubs rather than angels. Then I came to Soria's comment on them. "The figures," he said, "are modelled in high relief rather than fully in the round." His words struck scales from my eyes. What I had not observed for myself was now perfectly clear: no doubt about it, those cherubs were like something sculptured on a frieze. And he further elucidated my vision by adding, ". . . the space behind them lacks realization."

In other words, as well as making the frieze-like impression apparent, he also accounted for it. His explanation has been helpful to me ever since, for the element needed in this picture is an element needed in all pictures that aim to depict figures in space. An interesting backdrop and realistically drawn figures are not enough; the space behind the figures also has to be realized.

The interaction in this case was actually five-way: It enabled me to see the particular plate with new vividness; it increased my powers of discrimination by enabling me to see which part of the painting was successful and which was not; and in doing so, showed me how paintings could be disassembled and their various aspects evaluated with differing verdicts; it gave me new articulateness; and it opened my awareness to a point worth looking for in realistic pictures — the artist's success or lack of it in realizing the space behind his figures.

Another example occurred during the reading of Max J.

Friedländer's *Early Netherlandish Painting: From Van Eyck to Brueghel*. Because by this time I had become interested in how painters handled space, I was fascinated by Friedländer's discussion of the Netherlanders' progress in discovering how space could be conveyed realistically on a two-dimensional surface. By the time of Quentin Massys (1466-1530), said Friedländer, the Netherlanders could paint beautiful glimpses of landscape in the background and foreground figures that were solidly constructed and movingly real. Yet they had still not got the hang of painting the middle ground, which Friedländer made beautifully clear in his comment on Massys' "The Entombment" in the Antwerp Museum (Plate V). Along the front of the picture are nine figures grieving over the dead body of Christ. In the distance one sees Calvary's hill with its three crosses silhouetted against the sky. "Everywhere," says Friedländer, "the eye comes up against the hedge of figures."

"Hedge" — what a marvelously chosen word! Poignantly as their emotions are depicted, that is just what those ten figures form. And this magically eye-opening word has stayed with me ever since. Besides making me see the Massys so sharply, it has enabled me to look at many subsequent paintings with an eye as to whether the figures are truly figures in space or merely a hedge concealing the fact that there is no middle distance.

Wilhem Waetzoldt's *Dürer and His Times* gave me aid of a different kind when I came upon its description of Dürer's "The Festival of the Rose Garlands" (Plate VI). Again it was a single word that led to the eye opening. That picture shows the Virgin sitting under a canopy with the Christ Child on her lap. On either side are figures that I took to be saints or donors. As I have confessed, I am not good at seeing stories in paintings, and, because this altarpiece resembled so many static groupings, I took it for granted it did not have a story either. The black and white reproduction helped foster the notion, for, being small and somewhat fuzzy, the little plate crammed with figures was hard to see. But in the chapter on the religious side of Dürer's art, Waetzoldt commented directly on the picture. The festival in question, he said, showed the "distribution" of the rose garlands.

It was the word "distribution" that did the trick. Instantly, I could see what was going on in the picture: The Virgin was placing a wreath of roses on a man kneeling on the right, the Child was about to give a wreath to a kneeling ecclesiastic on the left, and a friar, in black and white robes, was aiding in the crowning of the assembled worshipers. And comprehension of the story made the attendant cherubs much more charming, for besides doing some crowning themselves, they held extra wreaths which they were waiting to pass on to the three most important distributors.

Later passages in Waetzoldt's text made the painting still more interesting. The man being crowned by the Virgin was the Emperor Maximilian, and the ecclesiastic being honored by the Child was Pope Julius II. The friar helping in the prize-giving was St. Dominic. And there was logic in Dürer's painting this particular picture for the church it was designed for. The church was Dominican and the rose garlands were symbols of the rosary — an aid to worship that St. Dominic was believed to have invented at the Virgin's inspiration.

In analyzing the three examples cited, one finds that the first interaction of text and picture was caused by a bit of clear and precise description, the second by a brilliantly apt phrase, and the third by the addition of vital information. Sometimes the commentary does not even have to contribute this much. Often a writer can make you notice something in a painting just by calling your attention to it. And texts, provided they deal directly with paintings reproduced in their pages, can heighten one's vision of all possible aspects of a work of art — of formal patterning and story content, of color harmonies and emotional expressiveness, of tone values and symbolic significance, of technical achievement and period characteristics, of the handling of space and the type of brushwork, and the way the artist's individuality is revealed.

But note the proviso: The text must bear upon an attendant picture. And this leads to definition of the type of art book that helps most in sharpening vision. It must have more than pictures, for the type of interaction I have been speaking about does not take place where there is no commentary. On the other hand, the book must not be poor in illustrations, for nothing can be so boring as a detailed description of a picture that is not before one's eyes; and if the book is mainly on the philosophy of art, without reference to particular works, it may elevate one's concepts but is not likely to improve one's powers of observation.

The ideal book must have both text and pictures, and they must complement each other. Furthermore when, for the sake of economy in printing, the plates are gathered in one place, the text must always steer the reader to the picture being discussed, even if it means a parenthetical inclusion of the plate number every time the picture is referred to. Nothing is so maddening as struggling to follow comment on an absent painting and then later finding it reproduced after all.

References to plates (either in parentheses, margins, or via footnotes) tend to play havoc with an author's prose style; and the leafing back and forth from text to plate can be troublesome. Yet they cannot be helped. Someday, perhaps, we will have recorded books, with portfolios of loose plates at the back. Then it will be possible to hear the commentary with the picture before one's eyes. But until we can have such canned art lectures at home, we must put up with the drawbacks of our present art books. And provided a finger can be held at the point in the text that refers to a plate, the shifting back and forth, awkward as it is, has one advantage. It allows for the eye's natural desire to be always on the move. Thus one can go on reading and looking at pictures for quite a long time without the type of fatigue that comes from concentrating too long on a limited visual field.

In general, avoid a text that is vague, flowery and full of unintelligible terms. Pick one that gives specific information about the pictures it discusses — and this includes explanation of symbolism and identification of puzzling aspects. And pick one whose comments are sufficiently detailed to make one look at many different parts of a plate. Not only does detailed comment force one to give additional time to the picture in question, but it leads one to appreciate not just one of its aspects, but many. If, for instance, a text describing Fra Angelico's "The Coronation of the Virgin" (Plate VII) in the Louvre points out that there are two bishops and a king among the male saints on the left; that those are female saints on the right (Plate VIII) and that the one with the wheel is

St. Catherine of Alexandria; that the friar with the blood welling over his tonsure from the gash in his head is Saint Peter Martyr; and that the angel musicians include lute players as well as trumpeters — don't get exasperated. On the contrary, rejoice in what such information leads you to see. The old law will work here as well as elsewhere: Looking to discern a particular thing will lead you to see secondary elements adjoining it.

If you are a fairly passive viewer, you will probably be grateful for a text that leads you step by step. But if you are more independent, you will probably tire of always turning to the plates to verify what the author says. When you do, you can make a game of reversing the oscillation. When your leafing through your art book has given you an idea of the plates discussed in detail, you can deliberately fix on one of those plates in advance of the description, deciding to study it for all you can see in it before consulting the analysis. Besides letting it soak in naturally, you can use the Army technique of swinging your eyes in arcs across it from top to bottom. You can also try a variant of this by swinging a magnifying glass across it in the same arcs, and if it is an art book that provides magnification of its own by printing — as many do — enlarged details on separate plates, you can pore over those detached details as part of your study. Then, when you think you have exhausted the illustrative material, turn to the analysis.

The chances are that you will be as grateful for it as I was for that difficult description of corn in that botany textbook. Verbal descriptions, as I have said, are always most welcome *after* visual effort of one's own. And since not all descriptions in art books are easy to read, it is often only after one has looked for oneself that one can make much of what is said. Where this particular game will be most stimulating will be with pictures where comprehension of content is important. This includes not only pictures like "The Festival of the Rose Garland" and "The Coronation of the Virgin," but practically all pictures prior to the development of the theory of art for art's sake. For during painting's longest span, artists were deeply concerned with stories and symbolism. Formal aspects and aesthetic qualities — things one can discern through one's own sensibilities — may well be the most important features of painting, but in earlier works content was certainly important

— indeed, it generally informed and governed the formal aspects. And because aesthetic responsiveness alone is generally not enough to unlock content, one also has to have the key of knowledge. Art books hold many such keys.

You may protest that all I am asking you to do is study catalogues. There is an element of truth in this, and I would certainly urge it if art catalogues were more adequate. But most of them try to deal with such large collections that they lack space for much commentary. Also, unless the collection is a very specialized one, like a one-man show, the catalogue will contain a lot of isolated entries reflecting the gaps in the collection and the catch-as-catch-can way it was amassed. If it is an American collection it will not have a Giotto entry in the section dealing with Italian masters of the fourteenth century. And only the very richest collections have enough works by a single great painter to present him in their catalogues for his output to be judged as a whole.

But art books do not have to depend on single collections and they can draw on all the museums of the world. In consequence, their texts, instead of being circumscribed as to contents, can be ordered as intelligibly as an author desires. If he deals with a single painter, he is free to tell that man's life story chronologically, for he can count on illustrations for each period of the artist's life. Or if he wishes a series of groupings, the same freedom of assembling photographs will allow him to deal with the man's output class by class, with portraits, landscapes, religious subjects, and so on, each getting a separate chapter.

Humanity has produced so much art — and holding vast networks of facts without confusion in the mind is so difficult — that I would suggest choosing art books of circumscribed scope. Great panoramas of art history are invaluable, if what you are most interested in is history. But if you want eye training, it is better to select a book about a single artist or perhaps a single school.

Such a book can have a beginning, a middle, and an end. It can have narrative and biographical interest. It can introduce few enough personalities in sufficient fullness for them to remain in the mind as individuals. And it can be encompassed within the attention span normally allotted a single book. This last is important. Because an art book involves so much looking, we tend to have a shorter attention span for it than for a novel. If the art book goes beyond that shorter span, we grow weary of the effort of following it closely and cease enjoying the particular stimulation — the interaction of text and picture — that is its chief function.

Besides, as I have shown with plants, you do not have to study many objects of a given class to learn how to observe the class as a whole. You can sharpen your eyes on a number of paintings by one artist as effectively as by many paintings of different artists. And as you study a single artist's output you can see how his personality will emerge and how, even in an individual painter, styles change. And what you learn about looking at paintings by studying one painter with the aid of perceptively written, well-illustrated art books will ever after help you in seeing works by other painters.

Similarly, a grasp of the strengths, limitations, and particular characteristics of a single school will help you bring its images to confront works of a different school. This, in turn, will enable you to see the art of that differing school with the vividness that comes with perception on more than one level.

A personality, or a single area of painting well-planted in the mind, will also serve as a far more magnetic nucleus for further perceptions than difficult, scarcely remembered foreign names and a lot of incoherent, vague, unrelated painting impressions gathered by a superficial skimming over vast and little understood territories.

Where does one begin? Well, one of the advantages of art books is that they allow us to begin almost anywhere. And because, where possible, it is always better to do one's reading after looking, it is best to start with a painter or a school that has already caught one's fancy. This sequence, too, provides the advantage that comes because learning is always easiest when it follows the thread of what has previously aroused one's curiosity.

Since heightening one's power to observe is a chief motive, it is helpful, if one has no special pet, to begin with a painter who was himself a great observer — like Breughel, Dürer, or Gainsborough. Or another tack can be taken by starting with one of those painters who, to quote Berenson, "brought a new visual world into being" — Mantegna, Titian, Velasquez, or Monet.

Whoever is picked, and whether an individual or a school, the first book on the chosen subject should be followed by a second that covers the same ground, for the second author will present the subject a little differently. His work will make you review your own impressions and the impressions of the first author. It will also force you into choices between the two authors and perhaps into opinions of your own contrary to both. The second book, too, will get you on still more intimate terms with the painter or school you have come to know better through the first book. Besides bringing you into this new dimension of affectionate comprehension, the second book will also provide the multiple stimulus of two types of double-level perception: For one man's text will offset the other's; and the differing plates in the two books will enable you to see more in each set.

As a further note, I suggest that if you have done any painting or drawing, the logical artist for you to start with is one who has specialized in the very subject matter you have tackled yourself. For your preliminary working with the material of your chosen artist will not only increase your power to discern just what he has succeeded in observing, but will also put you in a position to appreciate fully both his technical means and his artistic power. Witness what I gained from the Japanese artist who depicted the iris of his own country.

A great boon of art books is that they allow us to begin *when* we want. We can start the moment we have bought them from a store or borrowed them from a library or a friend. So if we live in a town without an art gallery, we do not have to postpone our study of painting until such time as we can visit a metropolis; or, if our city does have a museum, we do not have to wait until we can get there at a time when it is open.

Painting, of course, is not the only branch of art that art books illuminate. They also deal with sculpture, architecture, drawing, furniture, silver, stained glass, tapestries, ceramics, etc. There are also a number of art books on what has been roughly classified as primitive art, a field that often requires specialized ritualistic knowledge, as well as somewhat different canons of appreciation. All such books, if they have interpenetrating texts and illustrations, aid vision in the ways that books on painting do.

They, too, provide many kinds of stimuli. Included, of course, is the basic one of making you want to see more. For as you read now an artistic evaluation, now an informative description, you experience instance after instance of having your eyes opened. These moments of excitement keep building two stimulating realizations. The first, which carries with it a little embarrassment, is the realization of how much there is to see that you don't see — even when it lies in pictures under your eyes. The other is that there is great enjoyment in seeing. And it is hard to say which prods you the more, the thirst for more such joy, or the desire to reduce your visual obtuseness.

Art books, besides making you aware that the objects they deal with are more interesting than you realized — in fact, that many objects are more fascinating than you thought — also reveal the exciting possibilities of vision in general. And as they make you note what their authors point out, they fire you, not only with the desire to be equally observant, but also to be as responsive and as articulate. For art books do not just make you notice more details. In the values they bring to your attention and the qualities they lead you to appreciate, they make you feel more deeply about art. And even if they sometimes make you ashamed for not appreciating more, they bring you the comforting realization that you have more visual ability than you thought. For generally, once something has been pointed out to you, you find that what prevented you from seeing it was not any ocular disability or lack of mental power, but such correctible things as laziness, inattention, disinterest, ignorance or impatience, and often just plain lack of visual confidence.

And this brings us to the promised praise of reading. In discussing verbalizing in connection with reporting, I said words were instruments that could work two ways: they could obscure, but they could also articulate. Which function they carry out depends on how they are used. For words themselves are neutral as to whether you use them to spare yourself the trouble of looking, or to make you look. And with books it is the same. They, too, can work for or against vision, depending on their use.

In dealing with reading as a rival of seeing, I concentrated on the use of books in ways that prevent seeing. And perhaps I seemed to blame books themselves for some of the vision-deadening uses to which they are put. If so, I have already used art books in this chapter to redress the balance. A few more illustrations will show beyond question that books, when used in the service of vision, can be one of its most wonderful allies.

Intentionally, but without comment, I gave a case study of the aid of books in my first chapter. Playing cards may be a minor art, but Benham's book on them showed what books can do. They can stir curiosity. Even better, they can bring those keys of knowledge that can amplify either self-started curiosities or those planted by books themselves. Best of all, books can help in the struggle to verbalize constructively — that is, to verbalize in the way that is eye-opening because it sticks to appearances.

The difficulty of such verbalizing was indicated in the chapter on reporting. There I cited various means of getting practice, most of them involving writing. And in the hunt for words, I spoke only of combing our own minds. But art books give us other minds to comb. And because art books deal principally with visual appearances, they are among the best books in furthering our skill in verbalizing our percepts of the visible world. This happens because in art books the authors account for their impressions. They have to, in order to communicate them. Thus when one reads art books, not only does one absorb those impressions, but one gains aids in sharpening one's own accounting powers by living vicariously with writers who, in some cases, are master verbalizers.

Pre-Columbian art is one of the provinces of art that has been brought into contemporary consciousness. Thanks in large part to art critics I have reached the point where I refuse to classify it as primitive. But once I did. Pal Kelemen is its champion who did most to help me change. An example of his aid can be taken from his *Medieval American Art*. Before I read that book, I had seen the serpents projecting from the famous Temple of Quetzalcoatl at Teotihuacan (Plate IX). I had also seen the serpents on the façade of the not quite so well-known pyramid at Xochicalco (Plate X).

Being so different, they had made different impressions. But I had been inarticulate before them. What was my delight, therefore, when I came upon Kelemen's comparison of the two. His account induced added vision of both because he supplied the words to describe what I had seen. The rendition of the Teotihuacan serpents *was* "even and static." And their rather rigid regularity was indeed in sharp contrast with — oh blessed words — "the vigorous movement and rippling feathers of the undulating bodies" of the Xochicalco serpents. I was especially grateful for "rippling" when applied to the feathers. Truth to tell, because I had not interpreted the Teotihuacan ruffs properly, I had not noticed that in both cases the serpents were feathered.

The verbalizing of writers on art, then, not only gives you new words — words of exact nomenclature as well as words of vivid aptness — but it also releases you from the panicky tongue-tiedness that so often inhibits verbalizing. For you find that, even though you borrow from those writers as you begin to articulate, you also bring new words of your own into play. Especially will this be true for the general words describing physical appearances, which I said were so basically helpful in urging the writing of descriptive letters.

Let me illustrate the process with a word I cited then — contour. In view of my own sketching I have been particularly interested in art books that discuss drawing. Rudolf Arnheim's *Art and Visual Perception* was one I found stimulating. Because I like drawing with line alone, I blessed Arnheim for making me stop to think of the difference between a boundary and an outline. A rectangular box facing you obliquely, for instance, will present several boundaries that are not part of its outline. Witness the juncture of the walls advancing towards you: certainly a boundary, but, being within the total impression, not an outline.

Outlines, then, are contours rather than boundaries. And Arnheim helped me further when he casually defined contours as "the areas farthest from the observer." It was said so simply. And when I looked around to test it, I saw it was true for all but base lines.

Then I read Roger Fry's *Transformations*, wherein he captured a fundamental characteristic of Chinese art by saying: "The contour is always the most important part of the form." Not only did I understand it, but I rejoiced in having the sentence to account for one of my greatest artistic enthusiasms. It enabled me to explain why I particularly love certain drawings, which, by stressing contour as they do, make it stand out more vividly than any other aspect. Fry's words also gave me the power, at last, to be articulate about what I strove for in my own drawings: not just to make outline drawings, as I had always put it, but by exactitude of outline, to throw the weight of the emphasis on contour.

Fry also helped me by saying some sketching "gives several slightly different versions of the contours." This shed light on why sketches so often strike us as adequate representations of reality. Because both objects and our eyes move, the contours before us are always changing. Sketches, having multiple contours, thus correspond with this particular phase of reality.

One reason writers on art have come to be articulate is that they understand how modern man, thanks largely to artists, has learned to actually see what his eyes take in. This means a further advantage of reading art books is the way that, taken together, they reveal "the conquests of vision." In other words, with their help we learn that all mankind has had to go through what we went through when we began drawing plants. That is, to break ourselves of habitually assuming our mental impressions were adequate representations of what actually appeared before us.

That people through the ages have believed their mental impressions approximated visual reality can be shown by studying each new step in the creation of realistic illusion in western art. Giotto's figures, which to us seem rather flat, amazed his contemporaries by their life-likeness. It was not so much that they resembled life fully, but that they resembled life so much more nearly than the figures painted before his day that they opened people's eyes to the fact that they had been observing crudely in accepting the earlier figures as adequate representations of reality.

Then, aided by studying anatomy, artists learned to see human figures clearly enough to depict them standing in well-modelled fullness at the front of their paintings.

Next came the effort to depict what was behind the hedge —

that is, to complete what Panofsky calls "the conquest of the third dimension" by learning how to represent the middle distance too. This meant working to see how people and buildings were changed by their position in space, which in the fifteenth century led to discovering the laws of perspective. But once artists learned how objects altered in size and shape when seen at different distances, they discovered there were still further barriers to realistic illusion that had to be broken. They had to learn what Soria showed me the young Zurbaran had to learn: how to depict space itself. For space, they found, was not successfully realized merely by making distant objects smaller. The pause at this barrier led to the discovery that if figures within paintings were to be integrated in their spatial environments — giving the impression that air was circulating around them — they had to be painted as if their appearance was influenced by what was seen to influence the appearance of humans in life: the effects of atmosphere. In the case of distant figures, this meant they had to be painted paler and more diffused in outline.

And still the eye's education of the mind continued, for around the same time came the discovery that hardly any form in nature had contours edged by line. Contours, it was seen, were revealed by color frontiers, so that in a portrait, say, a cheek's edge was defined not because it was contained by a line but because it was pink and the wall at the back was brown.

When the concept of things having dark outlines was seen as a convention imposed on reality by the mind, the way was cleared for a study of how contours were changed by light and shade, and by the tricks of atmospheric effects. By the time of Leonardo da Vinci — and in great part because of him — artists could see as they had never been able to before. And this new ability of the mind to recognize subtle effects that had always been before men's eyes enabled the Renaissance artists to paint those effects. Their paintings, in turn, made their apprehension of atmosphere and light and shade available to others.

Once the artists had learned how to create space within their pictures, the next step was to study figures in movement closely enough so that they could be depicted as moving about within the wonderful new roominess. And Baroque artists developed such sharp eyes for swirling draperies and moving bodies that they came to be almost too skillful. Now, in looking at their restless forms, one wishes they did not move so much.

The Renaissance masters and their virtuoso successors imposed their vision on generation after generation of Western Europeans. But that this vision did not comprise all there was to reality was revealed in the nineteenth century when the Impressionists burst on the world. Not only did they look directly into the sun, but they painted the outdoors as it looked in full sunlight. Clear-cut contours dissolved still further and many new colors were revealed. At first, men said nature was not as the Impressionists depicted it, and their vehement reception is worth pondering.

In speaking of cultural influences I quoted Panofsky to the effect that men always see *through* the eyes of their period. One can also say *with* the eyes of their period. And what needs to be added is that period eyesight, which is revealed by period art styles, is in large part the creation of art styles. That is, the vision of men and women in any era tends to be shaped by the work of the great artists they are accustomed to. This was true of those suddenly exposed to the new art of the Impressionists. The world of reality, they were convinced, resembled the scenery in Leonardo, Raphael and Poussin. Thus when they saw a world of nature in the Impressionists that was unlike the nature in their favorite pictures they were shocked. And because the Impressionist depiction of nature violated their concept of how nature looked, they said the Impressionists falsified nature. Now, however, we know better. The Impressionists painted more truly what the eye took in than any previous painters had done.

The nineteenth century was also when the camera was invented. The Impressionists were greatly taken by the new invention, and it helped them formulate their painting ideals. They, too, wanted to function like cameras in that they wanted to record isolated moments of stopped time. And in putting down their direct impressions, they wanted to record a scene's total appearance. That is, they did not want to act on mental judgments, favoring one element over another. Rather, they wanted to take in the mosaic of actuality with an innocent eye, and to transmit, in camera-like fashion, not what they valued especially, but the retinal images of what was before them.

Nowadays we do not think of their painting as photographic. Confronted with it, we find it too vibrant to suggest the camera. Perhaps it is because they constantly saw with heightened vision (and often with transfigured vision), whereas we generally see only with utilitarian vision, that we do not see the photographic quality in their work. Nevertheless, many art books effectively demonstrate that it exists by setting photographs of scenes the Impressionists painted alongside reproductions of the paintings themselves. It must be admitted that, when both are reduced to monochrome, the two are remarkably alike.

The first outcry against the Impressionists therefore is strong evidence that the valve mind does see differently than the camera eye. The fact that we have since come to accept the realism of the Impressionists so readily is proof that because of them, and because of the camera, we, too, have come to a better understanding — and a more complete trust — of the evidence of our eyes. And with every advance in seeing that artists have made possible — and there have been further advances since the Impressionists — the visual world seems to become more marvelous.

Scientists have used their eyes wonderfully, too, helping us see the world more fully and more accurately. I am certainly in favor of scientific seeing, especially when it leads to discoveries. In this book, too, I have repeatedly extolled seeing that reveals the interest of things. And the usefulness of utilitarian seeing needs no stressing. But my greatest concern is with pictorial vision. For I feel the deepest rewards from our eyes come from using them as artists, and that is why this chapter has featured museums rather than laboratories.

CHAPTER 15

Times Square in the Rain

Looking at something, knowing you must write about it for others, as I said in discussing reporting, makes you see what is to be described with especial sharpness. But perhaps even greater sharpness of vision is induced if you return to a scene you have written about from memory in order to check your description. And one rainy night I revisited Times Square to determine if I needed to revise the passage where, to emphasize the distinction between seeing and reading, I tried to suggest how ugly a pink sign looked when it was *read* as FRANKFURTERS, and how lovely it looked when it was *seen*, hanging inverted and unintelligible, on the glistening black of the rain-soaked pavement.

My purpose, admittedly, was twofold, for I also wanted to hone my wits for this chapter. I felt the foray into the rainy square on that winter night might put me in a position to convey with greater force ideas I had already formulated.

In the chapter on double-level perception I showed how postcards helped reveal the ruins of Monte Alban. That they served so well among archaeological ruins should give the clue that it is not only in art galleries that they can be used to sharpen vision. They are helpful for the observation of whatever they show. To demonstrate how and why was the aim I had in mind for this chapter. And so I armed myself with three postcards of the square, making sure that all three showed it in the rain.

They had not been hard to find. What should now, because of its multi-colored signs, be called the Great Colored Way has long been a favorite with New York postcard makers. Since its colors blaze doubly when its pavements glisten, professional photographers have been assiduous in seeing that drug stores, curio shops, dime stores, etc., are plentifully stocked with cards showing the square in the rain. And the cards I had with me were excellent ones, for color photography has advanced to the point where remarkable scenes can be reproduced quite stunningly for a nickel.

Trying to keep dry and at the same time examine my cards, I had to hug my umbrella at its upper catch. Moving about the square with the umbrella pulled down over my head, and constantly looking at postcards, I must have seemed daft. But I didn't care. I was a happy man. I found the reality upheld my original description and I did not need to alter a word of what I had written about the pink sign — so hideous in its legibility, so beautiful in its illegible reflection. Then, too, instances of the advantages of looking at a scene with a picture of it in hand joined the sky in raining on me. Not only was I getting the evidence I needed, but, even better, I was having realizations I had not bargained for.

The unexpected realizations are what I want to start with, but they did not come all at once, nor with ease. What was to prove a whole cluster of distinct discoveries came initially as one — namely, that, strikingly good as the cards had seemed before venturing out, they were inadequate in depicting the reality before my eyes. By wondering why, I gained the power to separate the contributing reasons.

One of the first striking contrasts was that the blacks in the cards did not have the qualities of the darks I could see. In the cards, the sky was a flat hard black, like a backdrop of shiny enamel. But when I looked at the sky overhead and down the side streets, I found the darkness infinitely softer; and, though equally impenetrable, it clearly conveyed two characteristics absent from the cards — depth and atmosphere. Far from being something that might have been painted on tin, it was space heavy with humidity that receded illimitably.

When I brought my eyes back to the lighted square, I found it, too, had areas of blackness that were a far deeper, richer black than the corresponding areas in the cards. Those parts of the pavement that weren't reflecting neon signs, for instance, were blacker than the blackest pitch, whereas in the cards they tended to be silvery.

Next, I turned to the light tones. Here the cards fell even shorter in doing reality justice, particularly in depicting direct sources of illumination. As I looked northward, for example, there was a tall cast-iron lamppost near the tip of the cement platform that runs up the square from the recruiting station. The post supports two globes that hang from either end of a crossbeam. In reality, the globes were brilliantly luminous; in the card, they were two white acorns. In reality, too, they gave off light which diminished in such infinite gradations that one could not detect its limits. In the card, each acorn seemed the hub of a whirling airplane propeller.

Seeing how the camera made clearly defined disks of the subtly spreading radiance enabled me to define another deficiency of the cards' light tones. For the camera, which could not convey a source of light as vividly as the eye could perceive it, fell equally short in capturing glow. What was before my eyes then led me to make a distinction I had never consciously made: the difference between glow and reflection. Glow is the effect of light spreading in air; reflection is the effect of light being batted back after encountering something solid. And I realized that, if there was to be a reflected image, the surface struck by the light had to be glossy.

The reflected signs are what makes Times Square so marvelous when it rains. On any night, the square, with its electric spectaculars, is something to make the tourist gape. But on a wet night when the pavement reflects those enormous signs, and when their messages, blessedly robbed of intelligibility, sprawl waveringly like great colored abstractions on black mirrors — well, it's enough to lift the heart of even the most blasé New Yorker. And the light underfoot, added to the light all around, makes the square one of the wonders of the world.

The thrillingness of the reflections brought home to me that here, too, the photographed counterparts fell short. It was not just that the card reflections did not give off light the way the reflections did in actuality. Their colors were inadequate too. There were reds, pinks, and electric blues in the cards, but somehow these colors were as far from catching the actual colors on the pavement as the colors in the museum postcards had been from catching those of the great paintings. In the cards, too, the reflected colors were not as distinct from each other as they were in front of me. The card that did most justice to the yellows, for instance, had too yellowish a cast for the non-yellows. Even what should have been blazing white was a little buttery. The overall cast of another card was too bluish. In it the flamingo pinks were almost lilac.

My first post of observation was just behind the recruiting booth. I took it because, after a little shifting to the right and left, I found it was the precise spot from which the photographer had taken the card with the yellowish cast. I sought the exact spot because experience had taught me that postcards are most stimulating as observations aids if you get to where they were taken. In this case, I knew I had the place when the tall lamppost cut through the same letters of the Canadian Club sign as in the postcard.

On other occasions postcards had helped chiefly by making me notice things I would otherwise have overlooked. And this was the type of aid I most expected when I ventured out, and, as I have indicated, found. In many other visits to Times Square, for instance, I had never noticed that Edwardian lamp with the scroll foliage and the acorn globes. In other visits, of course, I had noticed the Pepsi-Cola waterfall — one could hardly avoid that — but what I had not remembered was how Pepsi-Cola had advertised in the square before taking over that 120-foot cataract. The waterfall (fated to enjoy only one more year of life) was revealed as a second and bigger effort by the soft-drink company. This was disclosed by the 1948 postcard which, taken higher up the square, showed an earlier Pepsi-Cola sign under the Admiral Television sign. And when I looked to the head of the square for that earlier Pepsi sign I saw its old space under the television sign was dark. And I could calculate it had been dark for more than four years because it was also dark in the 1955 card I was using in 1959.

The 1955 card revealed another change by proclaiming, through a sign hooked like an upside-down L on the mansard roof, that the French Renaissance style hotel on the left was the Sheraton-Astor. Whereas the sign I could read in the same spot showed that the hotel's brief stay in the Sheraton chain had ended, allowing it to close its days as its famous old self, the Astor.

The sign over the entrance to the hotel bar was bright green, a common neon color whose reflection on the road was transformed into the incandescent green of young plants irradiated by spring sunlight. I deduced this sign must be new, for when I consulted the card I saw the 1955 sign was a routine blue: neon blue over the door, but a rich cerulean in its reflection.

With my eyes still on the card, I wondered what caused that red scribble dangling near the blue curtain of the reflected sign. As I looked up to find it, the scribble turned bright emerald. So that was it: there was a traffic light facing away from me at Forty-fourth Street. On a dry day only its stanchion could be seen from this angle, but when it rained the changing signals were revealed by their reflections.

In the card, as one looked up Seventh Avenue, there was a white-pink column of light far back in the long black vista. Perhaps that delicate pink pillar consisted of letters, standing one on top of the other; but the scale of the photograph was too small for them to be legible. Looking up, I easily read HOWARD, and recognized that the light column, which in the card seemed to hang in space, was the familiar sign running down the side of the building occupied by the men's clothing store.

And so it went. Thanks to the cross-stimulation of card and reality, I kept growing more aware of how things appeared, while at the same time I kept noticing more details. And identification of the causes of puzzling appearances tended to root the sources of the impressions more deeply in my mind. This was true for both their aspects: what they were and what they looked like, whether lamppost, traffic lights, or signs. And as my visual apprehension grew richer, the exhilaration of the scene grew greater. But my feet were getting cold, so I decided to warm up by moving to the viewpoint of the card that was bluish.

It was higher up on the west side of Broadway, and I knew I had the photographer's exact spot when the tip of the flagpole before the Father Duffy statue reached up and touched the orange "E" in the Hotel Victoria's horizontal sign. Simply orienting myself made me aware of that flagpole, and immediately the game began again, as the card made me conscious of an enormously long blue column. When I looked for its original, I saw the column was the up-and-down sign of the Brass Rail, doubled in length as it balanced on its own reflection. And this matching of sign and reflection made me aware that the effulgent whiteness glowing off Seventh Avenue in front of the newsreel theater was the mirror image of the Planters Peanuts sign.

In the card, there seemed to be a fire raging inside the office building above the Planters sign. I knew there wasn't, but as I looked up to see what caused the illusion, I saw a wonder of the square I had never noticed: at night, the spectacular signs on one side get reflected in the darkened windows of the office buildings on the other. Those oranges and reds were not coming from *within* the building; they were coming from across the street, and the panes, turned into mirrors by the blackness of the deserted offices were reflecting them back.

This postcard, like the other one, also made me aware of changes that had taken place in the square. The "big buxom beautiful musical" that had been showing at the Mayfair at the time of the photograph had gone. But the eight-story billboard, which bends around the corner of the theater building, was still there, still outlined in a frame of electric bulbs going on and off to give the impression of a revolving belt.

In the card, that belt gave off more radiance than you might expect, but it wasn't traveling and it wasn't made up of points of light. The bulbs were swallowed up in their own glow, pictured so crudely that the light trough was a static blur.

The inadequacy of the representation set me thinking. Lower in the square I had discovered that the human eye outdid the postcard camera in the range of tones it could encompass: at one extremity it could see deeper blacks and at the other, more brilliant whites. Here I saw that the eye could outdo an ordinary low-speed camera in shifting from one extreme to the other; that is, it could see first white and then black and then white again, not only with astonishing rapidity, but with such grasp of each extreme that it retained a clear impression of lights going on and off.

Having isolated this faculty of the eye to make quick shifts, I saw it was further illustrated by the cards' representation of the headlights of passing cars. There, the moving headlights blurred into streaks; in my vision they retained, without distortion, their identities as headlights traveling swiftly forward. This surely was because I could instantaneously see the darkness of the space they had just occupied without an overhanging image of radiance to blur it.

Those swiftly moving cars, I suddenly realized, were part of the magic of the scene. In the rainy darkness their lights shone especially brilliantly. Cars coming downtown flashed radiant white disks; cars going uptown made a chain of red jewels brighter than rubies. And these head- and taillights, besides illuminating the threads of rain, were reflected on the pavement as vividly as the show windows and the variegated signs.

Then I realized that movement of another sort — the changing colors of the signs — was playing a far larger role in the impression made by the square than I had thought. Color change, then, was something else the cards lacked: no wonder they did not do justice to what they pictured. I blessed them, nevertheless. Not only because at that moment they made me so intensely aware of the importance to the scene of all the elements they could not capture, but also because they had so vastly increased my sense of the wonder of the human eye. To think that it had those marvelous apprehensive abilities that the still camera, for all its amazing capacities, lacked! And to think that the eye could carry out its multiple functions simultaneously: grasping the entire range of illumination as it took in depth, and distinguishing between colors at the same time as they flashed on and off. As I felt this wonder, I shook my head ruefully at how seldom we make full use of our extraordinary visual faculties.

By this time I was ready to leave the square. I had been stimulated, dazzled, elated and blown about enough. But the night's visual adventures were not over. I had eaten my dinner at a Chinese restaurant down a side street. There I had picked up a colored postcard of the restaurant's façade, which I could not resist using for one more experience of the pleasure of contrasting cards with reality.

The card was not taken in the rain, but it served my purpose, because it was taken in otherwise similar circumstances: late in the evening, when the street was deserted and the restaurant closed. By this time I was beginning to tire so I did not bother getting to the cameraman's exact spot. I just stood across the street and started scanning the card with the idea of looking up periodically to check each feature. I used the card as the basic reference, for I have found it works best this way. Reality tends to be too large, too bewildering and too complex. It tempts your eyes to roam all over without taking very much in, whereas a card's elements are restricted by what the camera frames. By seeking out the elements in a card you have specific things to look for, a definite visual program, and a systematic way of confining your eyes to a selected segment.

One by one, I found the reality of each feature: the bandy-legged letters of pink neon that gave an oriental look to the name CHINA BOWL; the canvas canopy that sheltered the entrance; the circular gold motto, painted like a large Chinese seal on the glass doors; the framed recess to the left that held an arrangement of artificial white lilies; and the green valance hanging in the plate-glass window in front of the bar. And I might add that most of these were features I had not noticed when, intent on food, I had gone into the restaurant to eat.

Only one thing did not square with reality. The card showed something glowing from inside the bar that suggested a jukebox. I could see no such object in the bar and when I crossed the street and peered closely into that dark area, I could see nothing that, if turned on, would give the card's red neon circumflex accent or the blue disk. The mystery, I felt, might be explained if I overcame my lethargy and found the cameraman's spot. It meant going nearer Broadway and looking back at the restaurant at an angle.

When I reached the spot, I found, conjured up as if by magic, the blue disk and the red chevron. Knowing by now that they were not inside the restaurant, I realized that, like the apparent fire in the Times Square office building, they must be reflections. And the earlier experience gave me the clue that these reflections, too, might be caused by something across the street — something I could not see because it was at my back.

I made an about-face. Sure enough, I found the counterparts of the reflections. The Rustic Bar on the north side of the street, which I had never noticed before, had a blue clock in its window, and the gable over its entrance was outlined by red neon. The card, then, had unexpectedly led me to look more carefully at both sides of the street. But more important was something that dawned on me later that night after I was home.

The China Bowl card had dramatized how much the eye tends to discount one of the leading features in the world of visual appearances — reflections. The camera, lacking the eye's power to select among appearances, had recorded those reflected neons as vividly as it had the restaurant's canopy. I, on the other hand, had passed that restaurant many times and been so interested in what was to be see *through* the plate glass that I had not noticed what was to be seen *on* it.

Confronted with this proof of my obliviousness to these particular reflections, I realized I must have dropped my psychological lids on reflections many times. For instance, had I ever looked at the reflections in the spherical silver teapot that stood before me and that I had used so often for tea in the evening? No. And as I looked at the pot, I found myself ravished by the sight. Curving on the left of the silver sphere was an aquamarine shape — the reflection of a Mexican tumbler from Guadalajara. On the right was a gorgeous canary yellow. A shift of the eye showed the origin of this other color that went so beautifully with the silver and aquamarine. Was it anything precious? No, it was a saucer from a dime store. When I peered into the bowl of a spoon to see its reflections, I was even more surprised. My face was upside down.

The silver exterior of the cream pitcher was badly in need of polishing. But this proved an advantage, for the tumbler reflected in its gun-metal sides was a different shade of blue than its reflection in the shiny tea pot. Thanks to the tarnish too, the darker blue was touched with a rainbow-like irridescence. The gold lining of the creamer, I saw, also influenced the colors it reflected. And when, in an experimental mood, I dumped out the cream and half filled the creamer with water, I was struck by the fact that the reflections on the surface of the water differed from those on the gold lining. This time, however, the difference was not caused by the surfaces having different colors, for the clear water, letting color pass through it unaltered, was equally golden. Here the difference was caused by the fact that one surface was metal, the other liquid.

Reflections, then, often take added beauty from the surfaces on which they appear. The pot, the spoon, and the little pitcher like an Aladdin's lamp gave evidence that curvature, color, and texture are among the properties of surfaces which influence the appearance of the images they give back.

One can never look at reflections without also being struck by highlights. And as they glanced off at me from my three objects, I realized that the mind discounts highlights for the same reason that it discounts reflections. Knowing they are transient surface impressions dependent on placement, it tends not to accept them as basic realities. If they are on things that can be seen through, the mind grasps at what is beyond or within; or if they are on opaque substances, the mind seizes on the permanent shapes or, more likely, just the functions, of the forms that are so magically adorned with light.

I realized, too, that distortion is an element that prejudices us against most reflections. We certainly do not discount the undistorted reflections we see in mirrors, nor do we deny their reality. But few surfaces are as flat and smooth as mirrors. As a result, most reflected forms are in some way broken up and pulled out of shape. My yellow saucer, for instance, was so distorted in the silver sphere that I could not recognize it from its reflected shape alone. And as I thought of distortion as a cause of prejudice, it occurred to me that the very thing that sets us against reflections should make us all the more eager to study them. Their tricky distortions make familiar objects look so different that when we swing our eyes back and forth between reflections and objects we regain the power to see those objects with fresh eyes. The imagination, too, is stirred by seeing the same object in two aspects simultaneously.

The beauty of the reflections in the teapot, the creamer, and the spoon also brought into focus something dimly perceived in Times Square: that the shades colors assume in their reflections, tempered as they are by what they glance from, are usually lovelier than the shades of the original objects. I realized, too, that the rain in the square had done more than make the pavement glossy;

it had also stippled it with constantly shifting silver dots. And as I thought of the beauty of reflections, and of the interest they gain when they are analyzed, I felt how obtuse we are in noticing only obvious ones, like those of vast signs advertising peanuts.

In one way the Times Square experience was frustrating. Its visual stimulus was so great that what I hoped for — extra comprehension of the interaction between postcards and reality— did not come until later, and even then, quite slowly. Understandably, the stimulating factors that crystallized first were those which paralleled those I had already explored. Getting to the positions of the cameramen, for instance, took time; so did the constant checking back and forth between scene and card and the effort of thinking out what caused the differences between them. So the cards served as a mechanical device to make me give time to what I chose to look at. And time played its usual role of letting things sink in, instead of vanishing as do so many impressions of flash glimpses. The cards, too, shifted me into the looking gear, as was proved by the way observations accelerated once I became thoroughly involved in looking, carrying on through to the way I looked at my teapot, at home, seeing reflections in it that had never registered before.

The cards also gave me enormous help in achieving concentration. They made my looking purposeful by providing appearances to be sought, and this was valuable because choosing what to look at in a crowded, busy scene is a difficult matter. In this case, the process was further simplified because I was looking for the sake of checking, which, because it does not involve verbal effort, is much easier than looking in order to define. The cards, too, furnished aid that was a variant of the help provided by frames in art museums. Their edges set up areas that one could think of as being framed, and the imaginary limits were especially helpful before so large and frameless a scene with so many shifting sights to distract and allure.

Even before the postcards helped me concentrate on their contents, imposing their frames on reality was stimulating. The stimulus began in seeking the cameramen's exact spots. It meant the obligatory noticing of landmarks — like a certain high lamppost, the Canadian Club sign, the Father Duffy statue, the flag-pole in front of it, the Astor Hotel, the Pepsi-Cola waterfall, and so on. And not only did those landmarks come into clearer consciousness as I moved about to line them up in the relative positions they had in the cards; but landmarks not included in the cards struck me with renewed force when I realized they were excluded by the view I was seeking. The man blowing smoke rings from the Camel sign is a case in point. He was not in the yellowish card, so when I saw him, I knew, I did not have the imaginary frame of the card properly imposed on the scene. I had to shift my eyes till they looked more directly up into the X-shaped space ahead and only when I lost the giant smoker did I have the camera's exact view.

This brings me to perhaps the greatest source of the reciprocal stimulus. When you stand before a scene with a picture of it in your hand you have one of the most intense types of double-level perception. The secondary image is not a memory, nor an imagined fantasy, but something as concretely visual as the scene itself. And that secondary image, by being so tangible, not only loosens the grip that the primary image normally holds on the consciousness; but, by providing a counter visual magnet, it keeps consciousness mobile. The consciousness, in fact, in flitting from one magnet to the other, is kept in a state of far greater freedom and flexibility than usual.

The secondary image, too, is comfortably manageable. Not only is it small, but much is reduced into its limited size. Its objects, like those in paintings, stand still. No change of atmosphere alters their aspect. Having only two dimensions, it is easier to master visually than something three-dimensional. And being a particular kind of picture — a photograph — it has camera vision, which, as we have seen, is so different from normal sketchy seeing that it took human beings centuries to approximate it. What is more, this camera vision is so vividly frozen that it is removed from the flux of reality. Being a photograph, too, it has foveal sharpness of focus over its whole area.

Not only do these advantages operate individually, but they combine to banish what we have found is one of the great vision deadeners — fear. Confronted with a nicely framed set of pre-selected elements that have been taken out of space and flattened into two dimensions, and that have been assembled into a visual package of such convenient size, the mind feels a confidence that is hard to muster before what is overwhelming. Having a means of control, too, the mind is no longer at the mercy of the undisciplined nature of the eye. Thus, with fears of visual and mental inadequacies eliminated, one can go calmly about the process of questioning the scene, asking alternately, "How does this feature look in the card?" "How does it look in actuality?"

The advantage of smallness had come home to me particularly when I used the card with the bluish cast. Proust has a beautiful phrase: "that aggregate of impressions which we call vision." He was thinking, of course, of remembered impressions, too, but his description is true even of visions not augmented by memories. In one important respect, every vision we have of a big scene in life resembles an experience of a large canvas in a museum. It is an aggregate of small impressions. And in life we are even more at the mercy of our anatomical limitations. In James B. Fagan's amusing play about Pepys called *And so to bed* there is a line I have always remembered. The diarist had just brought his lady friend a pair of stockings. She was so delighted that she decided to put them on, but, of course, it would not be proper for Pepys to see her doing so. The solution arrived at was to make Pepys stand in a corner, with his back to her. "Oh, for a swivel eye!" he sighed.

Pepys' longing exclamation underlines one of our anatomical limitations. None of us has a swivel eye. We can only piece together 360-degree vision if we turn completely around. And because the neck is only moderately flexible, the 125-degree angle of vision up and down is even more limited than the 200-degree angle of vision from side to side. In consequence, every visual concept we have of the space around us is an aggregate of the impressions we have taken in after many movements of the head and a number of rotations of the body.

Where the visual concept of surrounding space is sharply detailed, the aggregate of impressions is even more manifold than in a concept put together from a few sweeping glances. This is because of the ocular limitation we encountered in earlier chapters: that the fovea centralis is the only part of the retina that picks up details in sharp focus. Thus every detailed awareness of a big scene must, of necessity, be a mosaic pieced together from thousands of foveal impressions.

The camera, however, does not need to assemble its pictures in such a painstaking, point-by-point way. It can take in every corner with the flick of its shutter, and because its retina, as it were, is all fovea, it can take in everything with almost equal clarity. Beyond that, a camera can outdo the eye in the size of the scene it can encompass. If you doubt this, try a simple experiment in the room you are now in: try to see its ceiling and floor simultaneously. If the room is small, you will find a good look at both at the same time almost impossible, yet simultaneous views of floors and ceilings, each pictured in detailed clarity, are commonplace in photography. Take the instance of the bluish card, which captured the way the dead panes of Times Squares' deserted offices reflect the signs that face them. Visually, this is a marvelous phenomenon. Why had I never noticed it before, even though I used to work at night just off the square? The explanation lies in the normal position of the head and the limited mobility of the neck. To see such a phenomenon you have to do something you don't usually do in the square: use your neck to aim your eyes higher than the tops of the visually magnetic signs.

The card, with its greater compass of single gulp vision, had the capacity to embrace both the Planters Peanuts sign and those fiery reflections in the windows high above it. It was also able to reduce the combined impressions to a card area that was easy for my eyes to grasp in a single glance.

When I looked up at the offices I saw the reflections were there. But the effort involved in that upward look — and in this case, it was made greater because my umbrella was serving as a visual dome as well as a sheltering one — was enough to underline for me how much of our noticing is restricted by our bodies' position in space, and the physical effort involved in overcoming the handicaps of a fixed position with an anatomy that in some respects is so cumbersome and restricted.

A major factor in the stimulus of postcards, then, is that a card can give your eye in a single look a much more all-embracing vision of a scene than the eye can get for itself.

Such a condensed yet broad vision is stimulating in many ways. It has the stimulus of the card in the museum in that it can both call attention to details that are widely separated and give an instantaneous awareness of relationships between those details. In a word, it can reveal the composition, which is perhaps its first step in inducing pictorial vision. The card can induce such vision in other ways, too, for insofar as a photograph is a picture it can make us see with artists' eyes, which is different from the sort of functional vision we have most of the time. For in ordinary vision we merely recognize known objects in their customary locations, whereas in pictorial vision, objects lose their isolation from each other and their detachment from their background as they fall into place like colored shapes on a canvas. Thus, when the eye shifts from card to scene and from scene to card it does more than oscillate between the real thing and a photograph; it also oscillates between two types of perception — standard recognition and pictorial.

And the story does not end here. Because in the condensed vision of the postcard everything is smaller than its counterpart in actuality, there is also oscillation between a world of large forms and a world of small ones. In each type of oscillation the eye is subject to the kind of intensified awareness the hand gets in going from hot to cold water. And for a similar reason: each thing dipped into is so different in degree. The world of physical reality is never a picture, and a picture is never the world, even when they share the same forms. And the same forms vary almost as much as hot and cold when they are on a large scale and when they are in miniature.

Tiny versions of objects we are accustomed to, especially if they are beautifully made and exact to the minutest detail, always seem adorable. Witness the charm of dolls' houses. And one reason many objects in postcards catch our eyes is that, being so small and yet so perfect, they win our affections. Being so small, too, some objects are unintelligible, which makes them doubly stimulating. For one thing, they are seen as pure forms and not as objects with a function. For another, they are puzzling, which leads us to lift our eyes to see if the life-size object will be intelligible. Generally it is, and we find that once more there has been give and take between the cards and the reality. Because each has given extra insight into the other, each has taken something from the other. The puzzling miniature has gained intelligibility; and the large object, generally only noticed as something with a definite use, has been given back its appearance as a pure form.

In the interchange, the affections as a source of visual stimulus come into play again, for we tend to cherish whatever we identify through our own cleverness. Thus life-sized objects, brought to our attention through their tiny counterparts tend to simultaneously jump into focus and leap out of the world of the commonplace into the realm of the visually significant. Thereafter we remember them fondly either because we have made them our own through recognition or because we have carried over to them the charm they had when they were Lilliputian.

That affections change perceptions points up a difference between humans and cameras. We may pride ourselves on being more loving than any machine. But the capacity for love also implies its opposite, and in distinguishing between one object and another, a camera is always less prejudiced than a human being. It has, as it were, an impartial eye; or, as some writers have defined as the aim of the Impressionists, an innocent eye. A camera does not discriminate between a reflection and a solid object any more than it eliminates the meshes of a screen. If an ugly iron grill stands before a beautiful scene, a camera will give as much emphasis to the bars of the grill as to the scene. And, as we have discovered, rather than focus on central objects, it captures everything on the same plane with equal clarity. Nothing is discounted, overlooked, or disesteemed.

This impartiality of the camera may have the defect of not, in our estimation, doing justice to what we most admire. But it carries the counter virtue of extending charity, as well as clarity, to objects we tend to think unworthy of notice. Its charity consists of reproducing them, regardless of their significance; and of reproducing them, not as we conceive them, but exactly as they appear. This includes making them large and prominent if they happen to be near. Often, too, it means revealing them from angles at which we don't ordinarily view them.

The camera's impartial judgment on what is visually interesting is, in case after case, sounder than our own. And this is another reason why objects in postcards often catch our attention unexpectedly. The cards, unable to discriminate or expunge, reveal the interest of things we tend to obliterate by seeing through or around them. Intrinsic interest, therefore, must be added to puzzling mystery and miniature charm as a source of stimulus. Once it, too, has set us off on the visual hunt for its counterpart in reality, the process is the same. And the hitherto scorned or unnoticed object is seized upon as a personal interest.

The fixed vividness of postcards is mainly valuable for being startling. It wakes you up, as it were, to the striking picture before you. Later, the fact that everything is arrested becomes, aesthetically, a disadvantage, but meanwhile its immobility is a great asset in aiding analysis. For, being uncomplicated by subsequent changes, static scenes are much easier to grasp than moving ones. An example is provided by the light trough framing the eight-story movie billboard. It was easier to grasp as the unmoving blur it was in the card than as the revolving belt of light it appeared to be in reality. And recognizing that I was not seeing a static blur was what helped me define the nature of the reality. Specifically, it showed that the camera reproduced glow so crudely that the bulbs were swallowed up; whereas in reality, the moving glow was so subtle that the bulbs retained their individual identity as they went on and off in orderly sequence.

This instance also illustrates one of the greatest sources of the reciprocal stimulus of card and scene: the negative prod that leads to the positive apprehension. Fundamentally, all still photographs are inadequate to the reality they picture. Lacking depth, distance, solidity, atmospheric changeability, and the movement of objects, photographs are necessarily only approximations, and one can be prodded negatively both by details and the over-all effect.

The major prod — that the card is *not* adequate — makes you aware of the importance of those subtle, hard-to-analyze elements that are missing — the life, the spirit, the atmosphere, the dimensions, the range of light and shade, the impact of human beings.

And as you feel increasing dissatisfaction with their absence in the card, you come to feel their preciousness and how essential they are to the reality before you. And you have a renewed sense of wonder, both of the fullness of that reality and of the fact that you, as a sentient being, can outdo the camera in all you can capture.

With details, the negative prods can come thick and fast. Take colors for example. That the Pepsi-Cola waterfall did *not* suggest a giant bar of barely colored margarine, and that the scene did *not* have a yellowish cast made me aware first of the whiteness of all the whites, and then of the unmixed individuality of all the colors that stood free of others. That one reflection was *not* the lilac of the bluish card led me to see it was really flamingo . . . and so on.

In the square, too, there were all sorts of negative prods concerned with shadows and highlights. The darkness in the sky was *not* like black enamel on a metal surface, it was — well, what was it like? More like the formless, bottomless, black at the entrance of a cave.

Postcards, then, by the very rebelliousness they stir, activate you into making your perceptions more precise.

The differences presented by old cards can have a very special stimulus. Here what is stirred is not rebelliousness, but imagination. With an old card, one does not get an object-for object correspondence. A blue sign, one is led to notice, has been replaced by a green one. Another sign brings the awareness that, after a brief Sheraton fling, the hotel that began commanding the square in 1904, regained its old, un-hyphenated identity in its final years. Similarly, Pepsi-Cola's shift to the waterfall reminds one how Bond Clothes, just after World War II, built the artificial Niagara on the roof of the new Criterion Theatre. And the thought of the clothing store recalls the fifty-foot Eve and her equally tall consort who used to guard the cataract before those giant nudes made way for the equally gigantic pop bottles.

As it happened, noting such changes the night I was in Times Square did not stir my imagination greatly. The grip of the present images, in fact, was too strong for me to even recall something I was old enough to remember: that the two-story building which supported the waterfall replaced the old Criterion, which had been a unit of Oscar Hammerstein's much taller pleasure palace, the Olympia. But that night it was too cold and rainy, and I was too absorbed with the present to remember that in the 1930's I had seen movies in that relic of the 1890's.

But if my imagination was relatively inert in Times Square, oh, the stirring of thoughts I had that sunny day on the top of Monte Alban when an old card set me contrasting greater extremes of past and present!

The year was 1948. Before my eyes, on the leveled top of the mountain was an enormous plaza. It seemed sunken because great flights of clean steps led down to it from structures on all sides. Yet in the card I could discern only one flight of steps, and the unkempt plaza was surrounded by mounds of no particular architectural interest. Nearly everything aesthetically impressive, then, was revealed as the result of excavation done since the card was taken.

The reconstruction was extensive enough to give me an idea of the great site in its heyday, long before the coming of the Spaniards. And the partially restored site is such that it is almost impossible not to conjure up its pageantry on great ceremonial occasions. Yet thanks to the vision of the more recent past provided by the card, I was able to match that vision of grandeur with a vision of how the ruins lay for more than four centuries — shapeless earth mounds hardly distinguishable from the contours of the windswept desolate hill on which they were eroding. Never on my own continent had I had such a sense of the sweep of time and the death of empires.

Among the cleaned-up ruins, my imagination would probably never have conjured up the vision of those mounds had it not been for that card. Perhaps not many cards can do as much for the viewer, but no matter. Even cards revealing minor changes can trigger the imagination. And once the imagination comes into play, not only is the vividness of a scene magically stepped up, but the perception of it gains a new vibrancy. For imagination is a type of engagement, and when one has discerned a story in a scene, or added something to it from one's own speculations, one has made it one's own by investing it with meaning. And because such meaning, caused by the fusion of outward reality and inner response, is so vital, ever after the experience of heightened vision dwells in the mind as a particularly marvelous memory.

A further lively agent in the stimulus of postcards clarified for me later, as I was reading a discussion as to whether retinal images are pictures, or patterns of light stimuli causing pictures. As evidence for the picture theory, one author said that if you kill an albino rabbit, cut out its eye and hold that eye up to a window, you find an inverted picture of the window on the rabbit's retina. I shuddered at such an experiment, but it heightened my consciousness of the retinal image. And suddenly I remembered those Times Square postcards. There I had been, standing, as it were, with my retinal images in my hands.

No wonder I saw so much better than usual. The vision printed somewhere in the dark interior of my head was also on glossy cards in front of me. And not only did I have my vision outside my head, but I also had the use of my eyes to study that vision. In other words, instead of the mind having to visualize chiefly by its own efforts, it had the eye as an ally, which was using all its apprehensive capacities to pore over the external replica of what lay buried in the brain. The eye was analyzing as well as transmitting. Together, the mind and the dual-acting eye worked as they had seldom been able to do in other collaborations. And I hadn't been obliged to pull my eyes out of my head to achieve it!

In describing my postcard exercise to friends, I have received varying reactions. Some have liked the idea, while others boggle at it, complaining that it is too mechanical, or that they prefer to use a camera and take their own pictures.

The mechanical objection is generally coupled with the complaint that the use of the postcards places too much stress on exactitude. I sympathize, for I am aware of the value of the subjective and poetic response to the world of visual reality. I concede, too, that the card exercise, especially in its first stages, is likely to inhibit the untrammeled, intuitive, emotional approach. But later — after the orientation has been found and the details placed — it starts providing a new kind of liberation. One might call it a new freedom to think from reality — and therefore truly about reality. Flights of thought of this kind may be less valuable than free-flowing fantasies touched off by a few impressionistic glimpses, but I'm inclined to doubt it. At all events, it is immaterial, for I do not claim scenes always have to be viewed postcard in hand any more than I say roses must always be examined through a magnifying glass.

But since the camera has now become part of our culture and advertising is continuously selling us on the benefits of canned vision, the camera complaint deserves a little discussion. For where observation is concerned, the camera is in the same class as words and books. It, too, is a two-edged weapon, with its visual service depending on its use. Used in certain ways, it can help open the eyes, but used as it so often is, it can close them.

If you are an advocate of the camera, the first argument you are likely to bring forward is that taking your own pictures, though it, too, is mechanical, does more to build feeling for pictorial composition than relying on the pictures of others.

For those who take photographs with artistic intent, this is true. And I agree that awareness of beautiful and interesting compositions is an important visual asset. I agree, too, that seeking a good composition makes a photographer size up the landmarks. And I think it is more creative to look for compositions of one's own than to merely try gaining the viewpoint that will give you the composition some one found before you. However, note the difference between a great painting and a diagram of its compositional lines. Books of art appreciation contain many such clarifying diagrams, but they also make plain that the triangle, the X, the circle, or whatever the basic structure might be, is not the picture itself. Looking for a composition, in fact, often involves dropping the psychological lids on everything else. So this particular advantage of picture-taking is relatively minor. And it scarcely operates at all with those who take pictures merely to have a record of where they've had a good time.

"But," I can hear the sputtering, "isn't the composition stimulus greater than you say? Doesn't having a camera one knows one is going to use, by making one alert to the good compositions that are available, also help one get into the looking gear?"

The answer is Yes. But note the distinction between knowing

you are going to take a picture and actually taking one. The former is likely to stimulate you to look, but the actual pressing of the button does not.

"But," you retort, "before you press the button you have to look through the viewfinder carefully. Doesn't the viewfinder act as well as the postcard?"

Here the answer is No. The viewfinder helps frame the composition, but otherwise it cannot come near a postcard in providing a good secondary image. It's too small and too awkward. With a finder you have to peek with one eye while both hands hold the camera and all you have is a tiny picture that is hard to keep steady. With a postcard you have a fair-sized picture that can be examined with both eyes; and besides being able to hold it comfortably with one hand, you can hold it so far from your head that your eyes can shift easily to the surrounding scene. The card, too, has the fixity that is a major source of both its stimulus and its helpfulness.

I hope by this time you will be weakening. But you may still have another argument up your sleeve. "Doesn't photography have the virtue of forcing you to take time?"

Yes, that's it. That's the one I was expecting. And it gives me the opening for what I want to say about the disadvantages of taking photographs — that is, from the point of view of fostering observation. The chief one, perhaps, lies in the temporal attitude of most people who take snapshots. They don't do it as a discipline to insure that they give viewing a decent amount of time. They do it to save time.

Earlier, I spoke of the eye's capacity to flash-glimpse and of how this magical power of seeing a visual field without any gaps lulls us into the belief that we see very well. Even the most ocularly complacent man, however, is not likely to argue that he can flash-glimpse as expertly as a camera. Whether or not we admit it, we all know the camera can take in more details, with nearly every one having remarkable clarity. We are even more keenly aware of the camera's superiority in another respect — its memory.

A camera may not have the intelligence to discriminate between the significant and the insignificant, but it can certainly remember. A negative will hold every detail of a scene for years, inevitably tempting us to rely on the camera's retentive power and thus into very bad visual habits.

The camera provides us with a device for obtaining records of what has been before our eyes without our needing to look deeply and fully. As a result, all too many of us take mechanical pictures to spare ourselves the trouble of taking living ones.

We even use cameras as an excuse for not looking. All the details, we tell ourselves, will come out in the developed photograph, so why bother even trying to take them in. As for the general spirit of the scene, well, the photograph will be enough to jog our memories. So we snap instead of gaze, then roll the scene away, practically unlooked at.

Even when the camera doesn't contribute to visual laziness, it often has other bad effects. For one thing, simply having it with us tends to make our primary objective photography, not observation. And this leads to visual rejection of anything we think would not make a good picture, with the drawback often lying merely in the lighting conditions. Having a camera, too, tends to keep us thinking too exclusively of the home audience. As we snap, instead of being absorbed in where we are, we are constantly aware of those to whom we will show the picture. And instead of looking for its own sake, we are looking for the picture that will win "ohs" and "ahs" when we are back home.

With a postcard, however, your whole being is where your eyes are. You are too busy trying to discern in the large scene before you the features shown in the card to give thought to anyone anywhere else. You even lose consciousness of yourself — that is, as anything more than a perceiving organism. And to become totally absorbed in what one gazes at is not only a happy experience, but one with a built-in memory device that tends to ensure its vivid persistence in the consciousness. Names, places, dates, even ideas, all tend to fade from the memory, but the visual image absorbed at such times of transport remains inexpungable. If you doubt this, look back on the high points of your life and see if you do not find that those that seem most marvelous, that return to you most readily and with the greatest degree of fullness, are those with a strong visual component that somehow preserves the whole experience as if in amber.

This brings up another advantage of the postcard. A card one has used in the manner I have described becomes a reëchoing memento of an exciting experience. No longer just a standard view of Rome or Florence, it is an exact record of what you saw. When you come upon it years later you will never do what many people do with their snapshots — that is, hold it up incredulously and ask "Where on earth was this taken?"

Postcards are particularly helpful in a strange town. For one thing, they show the place's chief prides, which are often the things most worth looking at. For another, they will help you find the "points of interest," by including landmarks that probably caught your eye on the way into town. Thus you will know, for example, that such and such a sight must be near the railroad station, or perhaps the bus station. And, if you are in a foreign country, the pictured landmark, speaking in the non-verbal language of physical appearance, can serve as a guide whose directions you understand.

In addition, the card will keep you alert for what you expect to see, as well as what you don't. You will find your card especially stimulating if your final approach is from a different angle. This is likely to happen, for photographs don't proclaim their orientation. When it happens, it will intensify your spatial awareness by showing you a recognized set of forms from an unexpected angle. And this type of double-level perception, besides strengthening your grasp of the space involved, fixes those forms in that space with especial solidity. The sensation is like the relief you feel at a trade show when a rotating exhibit you want to study comes to a halt in a frontal position.

In a strange country, the use of postcards can even win you friends. Passing natives who see you holding up a card and shifting around are almost sure to be curious about what you are up to. This gives you an opening. As they pause to look, you can show them how interesting the exercise is. They, too, will take delight in the cross stimulation of the detail in miniature and the detail in reality. And often, having become aware of your true interest in their hometown, they will either volunteer information about other interesting sights, or take you there personally.

But you don't have to be far from home to try the postcard trick. If you are in a restaurant, you can generally get a postcard of its dining room by merely asking the waiter. If you are in church, you are likely to find a postcard of it in the vestibule . . . and so it goes. Nowadays, postcards are omnipresent. And the trick works as well on Main Street — or Times Square — as it does on Monte Alban.

CHAPTER 16

Butterflies Move Their Eyes

In the plane going to Japan I read that the Japanese were not very religious. In place of church services and fixed creeds, the book said, the Japanese had such things as the tea ceremony and flower arranging. I remember thinking the equation unfair, for how could such incommensurables be placed in the same class? Had I been more of a churchman, I might even have thought the comparison blasphemous.

Nevertheless, I wanted to attend a tea ceremony. In Kyoto, which was Japan's capital long before Tokyo, I got my chance. The tea-master who would conduct it, I learned, was Jochi Yabunouchi. And the night before the appointment my anticipation was stepped up when the official guide of Japan assured me the Yabunouchi school was one of the three most popular tea ceremony schools. My two friends who had made the arrangements were reliable, so I knew the ceremony would not be a quick imitation dashed off for tourists, and I calculated from the coincidence of the Yabunouchi names that I would be experiencing something widely representative, administered by a man of ancient family.

The guidebook's account of the ceremony interested me greatly, though I found myself skeptical of the idea that drinking tea could be "disciplinary training for the promotion of enlightenment and mental composure."

The account gained interest from the fact that a day or two earlier I had visited Osaka Castle, a reconstruction of the original castle destroyed by American bombers in World War II. Because its exterior reproduces the five-storied structure as it was, and because it has its old moats and extensive grounds, the castle is still astonishingly impressive. White-walled, multi-gabled, with black roofs cuving upward and gray cyclopean masonry, the castle's air of romantic grandeur had made me curious about its history. So once inside, I was grateful for the legend under a portrait which said that its subject was the man chiefly responsible for the planning and building of the original castle: Toyotomi Hideyoshi, the peasant general who is often called the Napoleon of Japan.

Because I had been amazed by his castle, the name of the lean-faced general had sunk in. So what was my surprise to read in the guidebook that this conquering warrior was a force in consolidating something as sensitive as the tea ceremony. Zen Buddhists had developed the ceremony originally as a ritual, and in the fifteenth century the shogun, Yoshimasa Ashikaga, had transformed it into a secular institution. But it was not until a hundred years later, during Hideyoshi's period of dominance (1580 to 1598), that the ceremony took on the character of a national institution — largely because Hideyoshi loved the tea ceremony himself. His frequent retirement to enjoy it, plus his encouragement of various tea-masters, gave new status to the custom.

During the tea ceremony, I read, the conversation must be restricted to the objects involved. What one did, the book said, was look at everything carefully and confine one's talk to comment on what one saw. I made a mental note of this because I wanted to be sure not to make any faux pas. And the next day, on my way to the tea-master's house, I resolved that if any political questions occurred to me — or, for that matter, anything extraneous — I'd cut off my tongue rather than utter them.

My companions were Fumi Murayama, a young Japanese woman who had studied at an American college, and Yoshio Ushida, a Japanese newspaperman. On our arrival, we were greeted by the tea-master's twenty-six-year-old son. After leaving our shoes outside the front door, we were shown into a square room that opened to the south onto a garden. The three closed walls consisted of sliding panels, and there wasn't a stick of furniture, but on the floor were four square cushions, hardly thicker than mats. The floor itself, like those of most Japanese houses, was covered with wall-to-wall straw matting. Despite its plainness, however, the low-ceilinged room was attractive, and the purple of the cushions harmonized with the subdued gold of the walls. These last were subtly painted with scarcely discernible bamboo trunks, suggesting faintly that the house was set in a golden glade.

Needless to say there was a *tokonoma* — that is, a recessed area that housed the features customarily found in such alcoves — a scroll painting, a bit of sculpture, and a flower arrangement. As the guest of honor, I was motioned to the cushion nearest the *tokonoma*. Then we all knelt on our cushions and sat back on our heels.

A moment later our host came in. I am not sure what I expected a tea-master to be like, but I know I did not expect any one so unpretentious, so totally lacking in airs, as Mr. Yabunouchi. With his horn-rimmed glasses and white mitten-socks, he seemed like a mild high school teacher. His gunmetal kimono, contrasting with our Western clothes, suggested that before we came he had been down the corridor taking a bath.

He closed the panel through which he had come. Then he knelt, sat back on his heels and bent forward in the direction of the young woman. And not content with just bowing, he folded double till his forehead was touching the floor. His hands were in front of him, palms down on the matting. The young woman doubled forward till her forehead was on the matting too. It was her way of returning the obeisance.

When they straightened up, the tea-master shifted his position until he was directly facing me. Then forward he folded again in the same act of obeisance to me. Thank heavens I had seen the response of the young woman. I, too, folded forward, but I was not supple enough to get my forehead all the way to the floor.

It was a curious experience. Never before had anyone assumed such a position in front of me — a position commonly thought of as groveling; nor had I ever bowed so humbly to another human being. But by this time I had been in Japan long enough to enjoy bowing, and I felt a surge of reverent affection as my palms touched the matting.

After we had straightened up, the tea-master and the newspaperman folded up before each other as if they were postulants taking vows at an altar. And I remember feeling a thrill, which was part release and part realization. The release was from the notion that there was anything embarrassing or demeaning about such a salutation between humans; the realization was that it would be a much happier world if men and women could have in actuality the feeling for each other that was inherent in the reciprocal gesture. I realized, too, that repeatedly making the gesture, if one could do it without hypocrisy, would lead in time to having the attitude of which this act was the outward manifestation.

When the bows were over, a side panel slid open and a pretty, rosy-cheeked girl of about seventeen came in, wearing a white kimono covered with small pink flowers. From the kneeling position she bowed to us all; then, without saying a word, she set about preparing the tea.

"My daughter," said the tea-master, and though he did not say it in English I got the impression that he did, so simultaneous was the translation. And as I look back on the whole experience now, I find it hard to believe the tea-master never spoke a word of English. Nor do I remember which Japanese did the most interpreting. All I know is that communication seemed totally unaffected by difference of language.

By this time a certain problem was becoming acute. Unaccustomed to sitting on my heels in a kneeling position, the muscles down the front of my thighs were being pulled unendurably. Was it possible to sit tailor fashion, I asked. The tea-master chuckled and said of course. The important thing was to be relaxed. I have always felt comfortable sitting cross-legged, so once I shifted I felt at ease and I knew that from then on nothing was going to be an ordeal.

The tea preparer had to start from scratch, as it were, for the tea had not been brought in on a tray. The water, in fact, was not even ready; so before the tea could be made, the water in a metal urn laid on some charcoal had to come to a boil. The charcoal had to be inferred, for the urn almost filled a thick ceramic pot that suggested a bowl for a rubber plant or a big fern, but the inference was safe because I could see wisps of smoke and I had seen other charcoal fires set on sand beds in similar pots. As the water heated, the girl laid out various pieces of equipment, and I noticed how gracefully she moved her hands and how skillfully she managed to see that the hanging sleeves of her kimono never knocked anything over.

Different cultures often teach opposite manners. My own had taught me that it was the height of rudeness to express curiosity about any object a hostess used in serving a meal. You certainly never turned over a spoon and held it to a good light to see if it was sterling. Thus it was an effort to start what my reading had said was expected of me: to ask questions about and comment on my host's possessions. But I wanted to be sure I did the right thing, even if, to me, it seemed wrong, so I plunged in with the question: "What are all those toys in that alcove for?"

Apparently I had read aright. To my relief, this appalling piece of nosiness was welcomed and the tea-master happily began expatiating on the toys that were on display as if in a shop window. May 5th, which was coming up shortly, was Boy's Day in Japan, he explained, and it was customary to set out the family toys in honor of the boys of the family. The display, too, was to show how much the parents loved their children. He then lifted out a black lion mask that had white hair hanging over its eyes and a full set of gold teeth. The lion, he said, was meant to frighten away evil, and he demonstrated how the lower jaw was hinged so the mouth opened.

When it was returned, I asked about the small helmet with brass antlers. This, too, was lifted out for my inspection. I was told it was a replica of a sixteenth-century helmet. Boys were given such helmets to inspire them to be strong, like warriors.

As we talked about the toys, the daughter set something that looked like a roundish gray stone on a saucer before each of us. Apparently, it meant the tea was nearly ready, so we turned away from the toys and silently watched the young girl.

She took the lid off what looked to me like a round black ointment jar, ornamented with gold violets. But rather than ointment, it held something that looked like pumice powder, except that it was bright green. Then she picked up a bit of bamboo, curved at one end, which she used as a measuring spoon to dip out some of the green pumice, which she emptied into a round, handleless cup. Then, using a wood dipper, she scooped up some boiling water from the urn and ladled it over the green powder. Carefully laying the dipper down, she picked up what looked like a shaving brush. Then lifting the little mug she used the bamboo whisk to whip up the solution. It resembled foamy spinach soup by the time she handed it to her father.

Her father then placed it in front of the young woman and after he had done so, he doubled forward once more, head and palms to the floor. The young woman doubled to the floor in return. Before lifting the cup, she took a bite of her stone, which I saw must be some sort of cake.

"She does that so she will have one flavor in her mouth which will make her relish the contrasting flavor of the tea more sharply," the newspaperman explained. And sure enough, the young woman thereupon took her first sip of tea. We sat and watched as she finished her cake and tea in bites alternating with sips. She did not seem at all embarrassed that we were not having our tea too, nor did our watchfulness seem to trouble her.

After her cup was returned to the daughter, it was carefully washed. Now it was my turn. Again the green powder was scooped into the mug, the water ladled onto the powder, the solution whipped up, and the tea given to the master. Then the master placed the steaming cup in front of me and touched his brow to the floor. I returned the bow and picked up the cup.

"No, the cake first," said the watchful newspaperman.

Feeling a little foolish for having forgotten the right sequence, I took my bite of cake and found it mushy and overly sweet. But it did stimulate my taste buds and leave an aftereffect that made the green tea seem unforgettably bitter. Liking neither the cake nor the tea, I wondered how I was ever going to down them both with the other three watching me with such interest. But there was nothing but friendliness in their attitude and I managed. They laughed good-humoredly when I confessed that the tea tasted like medicine.

The whole ceremony was then repeated for the newspaperman. And I could not help smiling when it occurred to me that you might call that green powder "instant" tea, were it not for the fact that it took so long to serve.

After we had finished, I was asked if I would like to examine the jar that held the tea. As I did so I was struck by how beautifully the lid fitted; so exactly, in fact, that you could hardly see the seam cutting across the gold violets. The pose of the violets, I was told, was symbolic of the drooping reserve of the Japanese mother.

I was also given the bamboo spoon to examine, which seemed much like a little ski. Probably because he felt it would make the inspection more interesting, Mr. Yabunouchi went to fetch another spoon that he was still in the process of making. He set them side by side on the matting, showing how each was exactly the same length, and he explained the wire cradle that held the bent part of the incompleted spoon in its curved position. Making such a spoon was not as easy as the finished utensil suggested.

Because I was near the *tokonoma,* I could discern a swastika on the vessel that held the flower arrangement. It led me to express surprise that Japan, too, had the symbol that Hitler made so dreadful. The tea-master said of course Japan had it, but the arms of the Japanese swastika bent in the opposite way. And when he mentioned this I saw it was true: The swastika on the vase suggested counter-clockwise rotation, whereas Hitler's always seemed about to spin clockwise.

The swastika, the tea-master said, was the emblem of his family, and he held up the sleeve of his kimono to show that the symbol was there too, woven into the figured silk. His bathrobe, then, was not as humble a garment as I had taken it to be. I noticed, too, that he was wearing a gold wrist watch.

Knowing it was correct to be observant, I next commented on something that had been obscured by the daughter as she made tea, but which caught my eye now that she had withdrawn, taking the tea equipment with her. It was a rectangular screen showing a weeping willow on a field whose silver, with the passage of years, had turned leaden.

My question about the screen turned out to be particularly happy, for it was the family's greatest treasure. It was a gift to an earlier Yabunouchi, also a tea-master, by no less a personage than Hideyoshi. And the fact that, thanks to his castle, I knew who Hideyoshi was made his gift almost jump towards me. I really hadn't expected to find in a private house such a direct link with the Napoleon of Japan.

"This house is three hundred years old," said the young woman. Then she added with a hint of pride in her host: "The tea-master tradition has been handed down from father to son in Mr. Yabunouchi's family for twelve generations."

"Unbrokenly?" I asked incredulously.

Mr. Yabunouchi nodded, and it amazed me that this modest man should have a well-documented family that went back farther than that of most Mayflower descendants. In the United States he could look at a Daughter of the American Revolution as a parvenu.

When one goes to tea in an English-speaking country, there is a commonly accepted time for leaving. Since six o'clock was approaching, I was beginning to feel uneasy. On the one hand, I did not want to outstay my welcome; on the other, I did not want to suggest leaving if there was an important feature of the ceremony still to come. I thought there might be, since this gathering had been much less formal than I had expected (it had included smoking), and since nothing had yet come up that might be construed as being either "disciplinary" or sacramental. Surely, I felt, some climax lay ahead. To sound the matter out, I asked if there was anything religious about the tea ceremony.

"Oh, no," said the tea-master quickly. "It's like a party."

"Like a cocktail party," added the newspaperman. And I smiled at his half-knowledge of the West. He knew we had cocktail parties, but obviously he did not know much about their racket and gossip to think they were anything like this. A moment or two later he resumed: "Mr. Yabunouchi says the object of the party is to cause a right state of heart."

Shortly afterwards, when I realized that nothing essential to the ceremony remained, I suggested it was time to leave. We did not break up hurriedly, however, and before we left Mr. Yabunouchi had us crawl into a smaller tearoom. This one, he said, was for drinking tea in solitude, and he showed us a screen covered with letters from dear friends. One thought of them, he said, and remembered the blessing of their friendship, when one drank tea alone.

Walking back to the larger tearoom, we passed through the garden where the slanting gold light showed the sun was setting.

I felt extremely calm. Not recognizing the extent to which I had been disengaged from inner troubles, I did not know how the tea party had done its work. But there was little doubt that it had. Just outside the door, as we bowed our farewells to Mr. Yabunouchi, I was aware that I was indeed in a right state of heart.

In the midst of new experiences in a strange country, you often do not give due thought to each event. I know that while in Japan, I did not reflect enough about the tea ceremony. Thanks, however, to thinking I had done before going there I recognized that the ceremony, by insisting that the conversation be confined to what we saw, and by calling on the visual responses of each participant, was an especially effective exercise for getting into the looking gear. This comprehension worked both forwards and backwards. Retrospectively, it helped me coordinate a bit of prior Japanese knowledge with what I had observed up to the tea ceremony. Subsequently, it served as a sort of connecting cord on which I could string many observations in Japan that still lay ahead.

The prior knowledge was a Japanese visual exercise I had used quite often in the United States — that is, when I was sure there was no one around. I mention the need for privacy because of the ludicrousness of the physical position one must assume. The trick is to stand with your back to what you want to observe, legs apart. Then you bend over at the waist and, with your head upside down, look back between your legs at the scene you want to contemplate. It is an exercise that snaps you immediately into the looking gear. And nothing I know gets you so easily into a particular division of that gear. It is sharply opposed to the detail and simile subdivisions, and, though allied to the color and the aesthetic gears, it is nevertheless distinctive. It is . . . but let's experiment first. If you have never tested the trick and are alone, get up and try it.

If you had the good luck to be at home, weren't you amazed to see a finely composed picture rather than an assemblage of familiar objects? Probably at first, it resembled a brightly colored canvas by an abstract expressionist.

The most obvious factor in making the trick work is that the arch of the legs provides something we don't normally have in unconfined vision — a picture frame. But the subtler factors are really the more important ones, especially those that combine to create an impression of unfamiliarity. Not only are the eyes upside down, but the head, being only a foot and a half from the ground, obliges those eyes to look at everything from an unwonted angle. And with near objects, besides seeing their relatively unfamiliar lower parts, one sees them with their tops cut off.

In the first glimpse it is even hard to recognize what you are seeing. A highly fruitful state, for when one looks without recognition one is in the world of pure sensing. It is a world that is no longer the home of things, but the universe of appearances; or, as the painter Maurice Grosser has called it, "the world of the eye's sensations." Under normal circumstances, unless you are very shortsighted and take off your glasses, it is very difficult to achieve the shift of visual attitude that makes it possible to enter this world. Recognizing objects for what they are tends to keep us in the world of clear-cut identities, with everything having a known function. Appearances — if indeed they don't drop away — fall into second or third place. But, with the leg trick, appearances leap forward, because the selecting, perceiving, interpreting mind has momentarily been put out of action. Known things have lost their hold on the intelligence and we are confronted not by the world we recognize, but by the visual field. This temporary suppression of everything representational is what gives the impression of non-objective art.

The impression tends to be so vivid that, even after everything has become intelligible, the sense of a painting persists, for the forms and colors of the objects, and the composition they create, linger in the mind. For this reason, the gear might be called the painter's gear, or more particularly the Impressionist's gear. But since painters of other schools have worked themselves into it, too — and also some experimental photographers — it might be safer to call it the artistic gear. But there are objections here too. Artistic vision, such as one develops in studying paintings, tends to be a matter of responding to what is beautiful, whereas the gear we are considering includes, absorbs and transforms the mean and the ugly. Perhaps it is best just to call it the pictorial gear. And one can say that the scene glimpsed between the legs remains a picture because it has been seen with pictorial vision.

The suppression of identity, however, is not the only factor that makes the leg trick work so successfully. There are physiological as well as psychological factors. For, when one first looks back through the legs, three of the eye's greatest capacities are inhibited: seeing objects as distinct entities, distinguishing between objects and their backdrops, and placing isolated objects in space. Because these capacities are so useful we tend to employ them all the time. But the upside-down head cannot exercise them with its accustomed skill. As a result, everything gets reduced to a single picture plane, with foreground and background forms apparently side by side. And objects become merely picturesque shapes rather than detached units with specific uses.

Recalling the leg trick in the light of the tea ceremony, I realized it was not mere accident that the culture that evolved one should also evolve the other. Fundamentally, they sprang from similar motives, similar values, and people of similar character. One saw behind each the experimental type of intelligence that, once it has decided on certain goals, sets out to find ways and means to achieve them.

Both reflected a high regard for the value and pleasure of looking for looking's sake, and both were devices to heighten one's seeing powers to get the most out of looking. And the devices, I saw, were skillfully adapted for their different aims. The leg exercise works chiefly to induce pictorial vision, which is particularly useful in observing natural beauty. The tea ceremony works chiefly to induce what one might call connoisseur vision, which is especially helpful for the observation and appreciation of beautiful objects created by man.

Up to this point, I had merely noted Japanese aesthetic sensibility with the admiring wonder that seems to rise in all who visit Japan. But after correlating the two devices, I knew Japanese sensibility was not just an accident of genetic endowment, but the result of a conscious and highly developed cultivation of the art of seeing. And thereafter I began understanding why the Japanese insisted on making even such mundane objects as matchboxes and concert tickets so lovely to look at. Certainly, the Japanese literature I encountered focused sharply on visual appearances.

Needless to say, on such a trip I could not penetrate Japanese literature deeply, especially having to rely on translations. But as I left, a thoughtful friend gave me Harold G. Henderson's excellent little book, *An Introduction to Haiku*. It contained many examples of the little poems that, in the original Japanese, must have only seventeen syllables. I was charmed by the poemlets from the start. But not until my coordination of the leg trick and the tea ceremony did I understand why the poets were so often moved by mere glimpses of trivial objects; why such bald statements about things noticed were considered poetry, and why so many generations have revered citings that are really too brief to be descriptions.

Take, for instance, this haiku by Basho that Henderson quotes:

The mushroom;
from an unknown tree, a leaf
sticks to it.

This is more "poetic" in our sense than a lot of the haiku. But is it really a poem? And why should it have been treasured ever since "dear Basho" died at the end of the seventeenth century. The answers, surely, depend on how you feel about sharp vision. If, through looking, you have had many experiences of intense communion with small or commonplace things, you have a particular feeling about this kind of visual experience. And obviously the eye-minded Japanese have had many such communions: not only with leaves and mushrooms, but also with scarecrows, bullfrogs, sparrows, snow, bamboos, falling petals, butterflies, etc.

Thus to them, the mere mention of such things is enough to evoke the feeling of poetry. Then I realized I had a major key to haiku. The poets were moved both by their feeling for what they saw, and their feeling in having the experience of vision. And subsequent readers, because of their own past responses to the visual, have had comparable emotions ready to be triggered by such minor touches. Certainly, for a Westerner to be moved by haiku he must use his mind's eye to conjure up every visual appearance suggested in the lines.

But where my newly gained understanding of the Japanese concern with looking helped most was in comprehending that odd and multi-faceted creation, the Japanese garden. And I say "odd" because I had previously thought of a garden only as a place where one sat in summer. At first, even though they were enchanting, Japanese gardens seemed odd because they had no lawns, no flower beds, and no places to sit — that is, within the gardens themselves. But if they were very small — as many of them were — they did have sitting places along their sides.

What became clear to me after the tea ceremony was that Japanese gardens too were part of the cult of seeing. They were not meant to be sat in; they were meant to be looked at. Then I became aware how well planned they were so that their various features could be easily seen. If one tree was tall, say, there would be no other tall trees near it, with the result that its profile stood uniquely against the sky. Similarly, a small bush or a stunted tree would be isolated in the foreground so that its particular form could also be easily seen.

The "stroll" gardens fascinated me particularly. Though larger than the picture gardens, most of the gardens with paths were relatively small, too. But two features made a promenade in them seem like a long walk. One was the circuitousness of the paths, which wound their way through the small groves with a labyrinthine intricacy, so that, in fact, one actually did quite a lot of walking before one came to the end. The other factor was that there was so much to see, or perhaps I should say, so much worth looking at. Here it was a stone lantern, there a little pond. Or perhaps a bridge, or stepping stones, or a particularly attractive shrub, or an arrangement of plants whose colors offset each other. Whatever it was, one looked and looked, and at the end, it was impossible to believe the walk had been short. Anything during which one saw so much, surely, must have taken at least an hour . . . or so the illusion goes.

In *Meeting with Japan*, Fosco Maraini describes the rustic tea huts built in gardens. And I rejoiced when he defined their purpose as "the elevation of the mind by the contemplation of beauty." His definition, for one thing, enabled me to grasp a conclusion the inarticulate part of me had already reached: that during a period contemplating something beautiful, the mind, without any effort of our will, and often without our realizing it, passes to a finer plane. The Maraini definition also gave me the words I wanted for the role played by the garden in Japan. To the Japanese, a garden is not just a bit of nature around the house. It is an area he can integrate into his spiritual life; and to which, when his mind has become entrapped by mean concerns, he can retreat, and, once there, win liberation from those concerns by release into a world of beauty. And because so many of the gardens were so tiny as to be hardly more than plant arrangements, I realized that flower arrangements, on a still smaller scale, played a similar role in Japanese life.

Japan, then, presented a culture that, in contrast to our own, enlivened vision. And I kept hearing of further devices for stimulus and of deliberate social pressures to encourage looking for looking's sake. Besides the moon-viewing parties I knew about, there were gatherings for snow, cherry, and maple viewings. And I heard that the cultivation of the sensory perceptors extended even to parties devoted to the distinguishing of odors. I did not mind missing anything devoted to the aesthetic pleasures of smelling, but I keenly regretted never getting to a viewing. My visit to Japan was in late April and early May. The snow was gone and the cherry blossoms were nearly over, and it was too early for the moon of September or the autumnal maples. However, I saw enough that was beautiful and when I got back to New York I had a hard time getting un-Oriented.

The difficulty was partly because I wanted to cling to the Japanese experience. One of the devices I employed to make it last a little longer was to read about Japan. Naturally, the author for whom I made a beeline was Lafcadio Hearn, who assured me I had not been wrong in sizing up Japanese culture as particularly eye-minded. And he gave me further evidence of how much it fostered vision by telling me how each region had its *kembutsu* — that is, objects or places considered worth visiting to see. And if it be argued that all places have their "sights," one can point out that the Japanese *kembutsu* include — besides temples and gardens — such things as remarkable trees and curious rocks. Japan, then, holds many unexpected things in high visual esteem, and each region has its special beauty objects, which are commonly accepted as such and ranked as shrines to which pilgrimages should be made. And Hearn told me of still a further refinement. The sites from which these things of beauty can be seen to best advantage have been discovered, and since then, these vantage points, too, have become established in the popular mind as places of pilgrimage. Thus convention suggests both what one should see and where one should see it from.

Situations from which beautiful scenery may be looked at, Hearn says, are also called *kembutsu*. And I picked up the trail of an old friend when I learned there were particular *kembutsu* where the leg trick was still used to induce extra vision: wherever Mount Fuji can be seen reflected in water; and Amano-hashidate, a two-mile sand spit covered with fantastically contorted pines, which makes a lagoon of the bay it shelters from the Sea of Japan. When seen through the legs, the spit of land, they say, seems to be suspended in midair. No doubt this accounts for its name, "Bridge of Heaven."

Another way to prolong the Japanese experience was keeping up contacts with friends made in Japan. By good luck, one of them, Fumio Otsuka, came to New York and I was able to ask him many questions. Understandably, most of them were about what I had missed — the viewing parties.

Snow viewings, he said, were spur-of-the-moment affairs. They had to be, because it just wasn't any old snow that was looked at, but fresh-fallen snow. By tradition, the viewing party had to be organized before dirt or melting despoiled the snow's magical first beauty. Because such moments of perfection came without warning and lasted so briefly, they allowed scant time to round up guests. Snow-viewing parties, perforce, tended to be private, attended only by members of the family. What one would view would be the snow in the garden. Because of the cold, too, viewings would be indoors. When snow fell at night, such parties would have to take place very early in the morning to ensure against the ugliness of dissolution. In the morning, too, the snow was still likely to be resting, undisturbed, on the boughs of the trees. Sometimes, by luck, the snow would cease falling in the afternoon during a time of the full moon. Snow-viewings in the moonlight were especially treasured. And then Otsuka said something that went through me. On such occasions, the family would conduct the tea ceremony.

Knowing how that ceremony can shift one into the looking gear, and how it induces such quiet joy and such thoughtful affection for one's friends, I realized it would be the perfect activity for such an occasion. The ceremony and the loveliness of the snow would interact, with the ceremony intensifying one's awareness of the beauty of the world; and the pleasure of that moment of beauty deepening one's sense of the preciousness of all such incidents of heightened awareness.

The tea ceremony was also used in maple viewings, Otsuka said, but this was rarer. Unless one's garden was very large and planted with many trees, one generally had to go to the country to enjoy maples. And again one did not just look at any old maples. Maple-viewing parties were held in late October or November when the leaves turned scarlet. And another factor militating against the tea ceremony during such viewings was that in the late fall it was generally too cold to sit outdoors. The custom was to make an excursion with friends, the family, or office colleagues to a mountainous place famous for autumnal maples, preferably a place that also had waterfalls. Then one spent the day winding through the paths of the area, drinking in the colors and talking with companions about the beauty of the flaming maples.

Cherry-viewings, I judged, have tended to become rather rowdy. Generally they are excursions, too, and they are made to places famous for their great displays of foaming blossoms. Again because of insistence that the thing to be viewed must be looked at during a peak of beauty, and because cherry blossoms are short-lived, all cherry-viewings have to be crowded into the middle two weeks of April; and because the picnic excursions need time, Sundays, when people are not working, have become the conventional days for them. Thus large groups jam into trains and buses on the two or three Sundays in question. And such groups can hardly help but become excitable and gay since drinking saké is an accepted part of the ritual. Because there is singing and dancing, as well as rice wine, the viewings tend increasingly to resemble American office parties, since many groups are white-collar employees who work for the same company.

From Otsuka's tone, I could tell the "drinking parties" were not to his taste, that he considered them a vulgarization of an institution that was formerly far more poetic. Rich people, who have gardens with cherry trees, still maintain the more dignified approach. Because by this time it is warm, they set out red blankets in their gardens, and the girls wear kimonos. As at the snow-viewing, tea is served, so this visual adventure, too, is heightened by the observation-sharpening effects of the tea ceremony. And here, besides commenting on the objects used, as tea is served on the red blankets under the cherry trees, one is expected to comment on the beauty of the blossoms. In other words, one must verbalize for the benefit of others. And not just in prose. Guests are also expected to compose short poems about cherries, generally haiku.

Loveliest of trees, the cherry now. . . . How welcome a guest A. E. Housman would have been!

Of all the viewings Otsuka described, those that enchanted me most were the moon-viewings. Again I learned of discrimination as to when the viewing should be done, and insistence on a time of peak beauty. One views the moon only when it is perfectly round, and only in the month when its fullness has the greatest beauty. By common Japanese consent, that month is September, and September has the added advantage of bringing blessed coolness after the heat of summer.

Thus the moon-viewing party is a very special event, one which, like Christmas in our culture, comes but once a year. And I was delighted to learn that it resembles Christmas in being an event of particular excitement to children. Then Otsuka told me something that reminded me of my boyhood. Where I grew up, the ground was generally covered with snow by December 25th. Some years, however, were exceptional, and it seemed the snow would never come. On those years we would scan the sky each day looking for signs of the snow that would make Christmas complete. Sometimes it would be Christmas Eve before it started falling, and always, when we saw the white flakes, we would be so relieved.

What Otsuka told me was that Japanese children dread bad weather on the moon-viewing night just as we Canadian children used to dread uncovered greenness at Christmas. To ward off rain, or even cloudiness, the children make streamer-like dolls of white paper that they hang from the eaves. These are supposed to help ensure that the sky will be clear when the big night comes. Near moon-viewing time the children also go about singing, "Sun shine, sun shine," hoping their incantation will get the sun to cooperate in making the viewing a success.

Rain is dreaded even more than overcast. This is because of two conditions of moon-viewing. It must be done out-of-doors, and one must be able to remain outside comfortably, without moving around, for three or four hours. Also, rain would spoil the moon's rice cakes.

The sweet cakes of mashed rice were a feature that charmed me especially. It seems they are very special. Made in various colors — white, yellow, green, and red — they have a distinctive shape and are set out for the moon's delectation on a low table which is ornamented by an arrangement of *susuki,* a grass-like plant that grows in large plumes. At the end of the party, the human guests eat the cakes; but while the moon is the guest of honor, no one is allowed to touch them.

Besides preparing food for the moon, one dresses up for it. The viewing is always the cue for the girls to put on their *yukata* — their lightweight, flowered white cotton kimonos. The party is planned to begin just before the moon rises, and always, before the start, every artificial light is turned out. The idea is to make certain there is nothing but moonlight to flood one's heart.

If one lives near a lake and the water is utterly still, the moon-viewing party might be held in boats. A teahouse looking onto a garden is also a prized site for a moon-viewing. In general, a simple and even rustic site is desired so the splendor of the moon may be appreciated in contrast to something humble. Some people living in crowded quarters go to open places for their moon-viewing. Some city folk even go into the country where the air is clear and traffic noises are left behind. But most parties are held close to home, preferably just outside the front gate if there is a sloping spot that allows a direct view of the moon's path. Because the viewings are occasions of affectionate solidarity, the parties are generally small — just the family and one or two close friends.

The viewings last, Otsuka said, until the moon is almost directly overhead.

In my imagination, I had been following him step by step. And, having watched moons lift clear of horizons, I had understood how viewers at a party such as he described could watch the rising of a round harvest moon with absorption. But what happened once the moon was up? The question occurred to me because I always lose interest in the moon once it is so clear of ground objects that I can not gauge its climbing in relation to something fixed. And the moon, too, grows less interesting as it seems to shrink in rising higher. How, then, could such a group, particularly when perhaps half its members were children, remain absorbed and interested?

For the tiny children, Otsuka said, it was no problem. They seemed to love sitting quietly in the moonlight with their parents. But the active and energetic children of ten or twelve often had trouble sitting still so long. Those in their teens would often grow restless, too. They would start thinking of homework left undone and feel they should be indoors studying rather than wasting time sitting under the now stationary moon. But stillness and quietness were imposed on them by the Japanese tradition of unquestioning submission to parental authority. Children that began disturbing the mood by being naughty were reprimanded. Besides, there were aids to attention. For one thing, one sang songs about the moon drawn from old Noh dramas. The songs, however, were always unaccompanied, for it was felt such instruments as samisens and flutes would be too twangy or penetrating. They would jar on the moonlit calmness, whereas human voices, singing softly, tended to intensify it. Legends about the moon were recounted, and, as with the cherries, one was expected to verbalize one's impressions and share them with others. The children, too, would amuse themselves trying to see figures in the moon. They never looked for a human face, for the Japanese do not think there is a Man in the Moon. What they sought were the two rabbits pounding the rice cakes.

Then, of course, there was our old friend the tea ceremony. It was nearly always part of the party, and the conversation could turn on such matters as how the cups had new highlights and took on a different color when seen in the silvery light. And the composure induced by the ceremony helped get one past the restless period into a new phase of tranquil enjoyment when one no longer wanted to stir. And for the children, of course, there was the added enjoyment of being allowed to stay up so long past bedtime.

Generally, when it was time to break up, no one really wanted to end the spell, or at least not abruptly. The eating of the moon's rice cakes was always the friendly human function that allowed one to shift from the transport of the moon's beauty to the more mundane level of a delicious supper before going to bed.

When Otsuka finished his story I felt more regret than ever that I had missed a moon-viewing. The custom still haunts my imagination. Especially have I thought of its influence on children, for our culture has nothing like it. As I see it, Japanese children must be doubly impressed. The more sensitive would be especially impressed by the inevitable and extraordinary beauty of the experience itself, an experience intensified by its duration and by the enforced stillness as one's whole being is rapt in moonlit enchantment. And even the children less sensitive to natural beauty would be impressed by the attitude of the grownups: by the love of beauty that created such a friendly yet reverent ceremony; by the seriousness that insisted on patience and quietness in the presence of such beauty; and by the revelation of their parents' inner lives gained through observing them as they were animated by a poetic concern.

I have thought of the children in terms of habit, too. Their inclusion in the moon-viewings, besides transmitting to them such values as the need for time, calmness, and consecration in looking, and the worth of examining subtle effects and minute details, would also get the children into the habit of looking with thoughtful and discriminating care at a very tender age.

Shortly after Otsuka's visit, I received a letter from another friend I made in Japan, a young Shinto priest named Sadahiro Takayama. His letter came from his shrine, and he described how lovely it was at the moment of writing. It was early in the morning, the air was fresh and cool, birds were singing, and the sunlight was clear and lovely. Then the sentence he added made me smile: "Butterflies move my eyes."

What amused me was the charming quaintness of the English. Several hours later, however, when the sentence came back to me, I realized I had to wipe the smile off my face. Grammatically, there is not a thing wrong with that sentence. It has a subject, predicate and object, and I had been snobbish to feel superior. Then followed a realization that was truly humbling.

My understanding of the fovea centralis suddenly made me realize that it is perfectly true: Butterflies in flight *do* move your eyes. They do so because you can only see them clearly if you keep shifting your foveae in their direction. And shifting the foveae, of course, automatically moves the eyes.

Now I was admiring, not patronizing. To think that Takayama had analyzed what was happening to him so exactly that he had realized the butterflies were forcing him to keep his eyes in motion! For this implied that in the midst of a visual experience he was aware that his eyes were the mediator of the experience. And my amazement at this degree of self-awareness made me realize that most of us have such little consciousness of our eyes as we use them that we have no sense of their movement.

Even more remarkable was Takayama's underlying attitude — an attitude so different from anything we have in the West. If one of us should write a letter in a garden where butterflies were playing, we would say: "I am looking at butterflies." That is, we would mention ourselves first, the butterflies second. Ourselves would be the subject of the sentence. This is because it is characteristic of our observing that we tend to be more interested in ourselves than in the thing looked at. But many Japanese have come to look with such concentration and interest that often their first thought is of the object beheld. This seems particularly true when they withdraw deliberately, as they often do, to contemplate beauty.

Actually, their way of looking, as exemplified by Takayama's statement, is just as introspective as ours. It might even be considered more introspective. Yet the direction of the current is different. With us, the current flows from the self-cathode to the object-cathode. With them, the current originates in the cathode represented by the object and then flows towards the self. They are interested in how the object affects them; in contrast to our interest in what we think of the object.

Perhaps on the strength of Takayama's sentence I am generalizing too much about all Japanese. But it is safe to say that his visual approach is not uncommon in Japan. His people not only make a cult of seeing, but have ways of intensifying perception. And having been emotionally stirred by what they have seen, they have become interested in what happens to them while they look. Thus, as well as observing external objects with great care, they also observe their inner responses.

And this is what I mean by their introspectiveness: for it is certainly a weighing of inner feelings, and not just crude black and white feelings of indiscriminated pleasure or displeasure. Rather, it is a subtle weighing of the precise impact of the environment, an assaying that involves careful attention to every emotion felt, with especial focus on aesthetic responses. However, it is an introspection that is not self-based, but based on external factors that set up the particular reverberations they do.

I think it is this type of introspection that makes the Japanese so extraordinarily aware of the beauty of their surroundings, and so eager to make them beautiful, if they are not so by nature. Conversely, I think one of the reasons we are so tolerant of ugliness, so indifferent to the destruction of natural beauty, is because our self-centered introspection enables us to ignore our surroundings as we mull over our own desires, problems, motivations, characters, and anxieties.

I would like to make plain, though, that I do not think such contrary-facing introspections are due to differences in humanity. There are compelling external factors to account for what has developed in our case and what in theirs. We, for instance, have had the advantage of a big continent, which has bred in us the notion that it does not much matter what we destroy because there will always be new areas to move on to. The Japanese, however, are sharply aware that their country is small, and they know — and have known for generations — that, if life is to be tolerable in such crowded conditions, they must conserve and beautify what they have. Then, too, we tend to live in the future so the ugly present is easy for us to put up with because we are not so much living in it as passing through it. But the traditional Japanese live more in the present. With fewer hopes, fewer dreams, and perhaps fewer illusions about the possibilities of progress, they treasure their age-old knowledge of the pleasure of the moment, especially if it is poetically perceived. Finally, it might be said that, in a much briefer time, we have been as strongly conditioned by the inward-probing Freud as the Japanese have been by the outward-reaching Zen.

With its viewings, its poems based on observation, its insistence that impressions be put into words, its gardens, its widely useful tea ceremony, and its feeling for long-reverenced beauty spots, Japan has heightened my conviction of the importance of cultural factors as shapers of seeing.

My own continent had shown me how cultural factors can work to deaden vision. Japan showed me the opposite aspect of their force. Where they foster vision, they can work enormously to open people's eyes. Aesthetic alertness, of course, is not the be-all or the end-all of virtue — either national or individual. Indeed, there is evidence that such alertness can — and often does — co-exist with selfishness, driving will, and even cruelty. But the beauty of Japan, the graciousness of its living, the care the Japanese take of what they have, and the beauty of even the humble things they create showed me how much good can result when a whole people are observant. For inevitably, the ultimate consequence of being observant is to care about what you see.

Some Visual Games

It is interesting how many Western children's games depend on voluntary self-blinding. In "Blind Man's Buff" and "Pin the Tail on the Donkey" the child submits willingly to the blindfold. In "Hide-and-Go Seek" he agrees not to look until everyone is hidden. And in "Open Your Mouth and Shut Your Eyes" he willingly cuts off sight till the sweet surprise has been bestowed. In each case, too, an element of honor is involved. He is supposed to say honestly whether or not he can see as the blindfold is adjusted; and he crosses his heart and hopes to die rather than peek as the others scatter into hiding.

Consider, too, how many injunctions against interested looking there are in a child's life. Snooping and peeking are spoken of with scorn, and even punished. Children are told repeatedly not to stare. And when they use their forefingers to indicate objects they want identified, instead of being praised for intelligence in using the gesture to offset poverty of vocabulary, and instead of having such resourceful curiosity rewarded with a decent answer, they are sternly told not to point. Later, when they get to school and need an answer to an exam, they are rapped over the knuckles if they look for it in a book or a friend's paper. With the punishment comes the order not to cheat.

In each case, the element of morality enters. The child is asked to blind himself for moral reasons, either because the looking is sly, rude, indecent, embarrassing, or dishonest. And adults, largely to protect themselves, always insist on additional visual taboos. Certain closets and books are not to be looked in, and certain subjects — particularly those involving sex — are not to be investigated, visually or otherwise. And what adults consider immoral in life is bolstered, as in the games, with the attempted establishment of a non-looking honor system.

Small wonder there is so much psychological blindness in the world!

When one examines the games that foster observation, one finds precious few to offset the many that discourage it. I heard once of a mother who listed things in plain view in a living room (although some were deliberately placed high and some low). Then she gave each child who came to her daughter's party a copy of the list, and the game was to see how many of the things the children could find. But perhaps such a game invites more prying than most mothers want — certainly more paperwork. At all events, I never heard of anyone else trying it. In fact, I can think of only one children's game encouraging vision that is at all common: the one in which a number of objects are placed on a table, each child is allowed to look only so long and then he has to go into an adjoining room and list what he has seen. It's a good game and ought to be played often, but I rather suspect it isn't. I know in my own childhood it was too often abandoned when the hostess found some little girl bawling because she couldn't remember a thing.

Visual party games being so scarce, what is the score in more private games? How many parents have worked out games that they play with their children to make the youngsters more observant? I know of one father, a painter, who had a game he used to play with his little daughter. At odd moments he would tell her to shut her eyes and then ask her such questions as "What color is the sky?" or "What color is the earth?" If she found she could not remember exactly — for she knew he meant a particular sky and a particular earth — she would look with new sharpness when she opened her eyes. I heard of another father who loved lightning. Whenever there was a thunderstorm he would take his children where they could see it, and together they would study the color of the lightning, the colors the flashes revealed and the way the lightning forked.

A third father of my acquaintance, growing exasperated at how his children would sit in the back of the car reading on long motor trips, thought of a device to get them looking at the scenery. He offered them a nickel for every pheasant they saw. A fourth man got all the children in a summer resort looking for wildflowers in the area by offering a cash prize for the one who could bring in the most different species. And there are a number of parents who like to take their children on nature walks. On the whole, though, partly because they are products of an educational system that gave them little visual stimulus when they were children themselves, American parents do not encourage seeing habits in their children.

"My parents never gave a thought to making me more observant," said one young woman I questioned. And a man said ruefully: "My parents never played *any* games with me — much less visual ones."

The situation was almost as bleak with adults other than parents. Some former Boy Scouts had grateful memories of being told how to use their eyes to read trails, estimate the heights of distant objects, tell one tree from another, and test directions from the stars. A few who had been in plays remembered being encouraged to observe people's gestures in order to act given parts. Those I questioned who had been on farms remembered farmers making them notice things about animals, plants, and the weather. But with the majority I drew blanks. Evidently I hadn't been too uncharitable about the educational picture, for few could recall a teacher who had deliberately encouraged them to see more.

Parents and teachers failing, I will try to suggest a few visual games myself. And I don't call them exercises because, since they don't demand any monotonous, regulated repetition of given physical actions, they are not exercises in the ordinary sense. Indeed, they hardly call for any additional physical activity. Most of them boil down to something I first made explicit in discussing the Japanese leg trick: a shift in visual attitude. As you play, you don't use your eyes any differently; you merely look with what the pschologists call a different "purposeful set."

That your manner of seeing is influenced by the way you are "set" towards what lies before you, surely needs no arguing. For example, when I demonstrated how radically different the face cards looked when they were suddenly seen as portraits, I illustrated how a change in set led to a change in vision. Fundamentally, too, most of the gears I have spoken of have been entered by a shift of mental set. What I am going to recommend therefore are some devices that have eye-opening power because they change mental settings. They will not fundamentally alter those who are not eye-minded. But as an ear-minded person who was trained to depend too greatly on books, I can testify that the devices work. They do snap you out of unseeing into seeing.

The chapter will be less thoroughgoing than I planned, however, because I find I have already dealt with many of the games that were on my original list. With "Hunt the Simile" I have already supplied a name, and others become apparent as games when they are cited as "Pretend You Are a Reporter," "Write Descriptive Letters," "Keep a Visual Journal," "Let's Look It Up," "Make a Drawing," "Go to an Art Gallery," "Hold Post Cards up to Reality" and "Look Back Through Your Legs." None of these needs further elboration. And two others I have touched on — "Look Only at Colors" and "Take a Trip" — can be polished off with a few extra words.

The color game was introduced in combination with the trip game. For I showed how it could be played in a train, with the colors to be noted being determined by the objects that, in somewhat arbitrary fashion, flash on the eyes as the train overtakes them. It can also be played from a stationary position — the procedure there being the viewer's decision to note all the colors in a given area. It was this version I played when I looked for all the colors I could find in the sea as I looked down on a Caribbean beach. It can be played as the painter played it with his daughter, where one person asks unexpected color questions of the other, who has first closed his eyes so he cannot see. That this particular version is best with two players illustrates a fact about many visual games. Besides being playable alone, they can be played with one or two others, with the pleasure being still greater when more eyes are involved.

Using colored postcards in front of paintings is a specialized version of the color game. Still another version is to equip oneself in advance with a color chart. Such charts are distributed fairly readily by paint manufacturers, and, although they generally involve a measure of frustration, they can be stimulating. The frustration arises from the fact that invariably one finds colors in nature that are not on the chart; and even if one can match the hue, the color in nature will generally have something that is lacking in the paint sample. An autumn leaf, for instance, might be undeniably gamboge, yet it will have a glow not found in the flat yellow rectangle on the chart. Or the full moon might very well be Chinese white; though the phrase "Chinese white" falls far short of conveying the radiance implied in the less exact word "silver."

Even when inexact, a chart can be helpful in establishing a shade by showing those it approximates. Thus you can sometimes describe a sky fairly well by placing its hue midway between cerulean and cobalt. And a puzzling brown might lie somewhere between raw sienna and burnt umber. Playing the game with the chart has the added advantage of building up your color vocabulary. As you fix the standard colors ever more firmly in your mind, you can spot and name their relative shades more easily. Which means you can feast your eyes on the colors without the diminution of attention involved if you have to drop your psychological lids as your mind rummages about for hard-to-find color labels.

That "Take a Trip," in addition to other things, is an excellent visual game has been inherent in the number of illustrations drawn from journeys while on vacation. I was on a vacation when I watched the fire in the courtyard. That ride in the old car over the Continental Divide to Grants was made during a summer holiday. The exasperating reading of the sign boards in the spring countryside took place while going away for the weekend. And the simile hunt during the flight from Ottawa to New York was made at Christmas time.

When you travel on vacation you observe more as a matter of course. And it is not just because seeing is one of your purposes. It also happens because when you are on a trip you see things freshly because you are outside the taken-for-granted orbit in which you spend most of your life. Then, too, you are more relaxed and less preoccupied, and these inward conditions, that are both conducive to seeing, coincide with having more time to spend in looking. A trip, too, is always a great investment for the visual future, for the new impressions brought into the consciousness enrich the reservoir of visual images. Thereafter the new images lurk in the mind, eager to reach out to attract kindred material, and ready to serve as metaphors, similes, and keys to understanding.

The vacation relaxation of "Take a Trip" dramatizes, through contrast, the greatest stumbling block to playing what I call "Spend a Third of a Day Watching." That obstacle is the old visual enemy we found so potent among the elements in our culture that deaden vision: the factor that I said did most to make our society hostile to observation for its own sake — the premium placed on activity.

Because I was fairly harsh on the consequence of this attitude — the horror of idleness — I would not need to say more on the subject were it not that this particularly wretched segment of our Puritan heritage has remained so strong. In fact, it has proved even stronger than our puritanical feelings about sex, for nowadays there is a good deal of sexual leeway. Yet, in this other area of moral obligations we are still haunted by the whispering insistence that always we must be occupied constructively. We hear its echo on every hand: as much in Isaac Watts' "For Satan finds some mischief still for idle hands to do," as in the parent's exasperated "Don't just sit there twiddling your thumbs — do something." And it has influenced those brought up in the Anglo-Saxon tradition so powerfully that most of us feel guilty if we are not active every moment.

Unfortunately, this energetic tradition has never admitted looking just for the enjoyment of looking into the canon of justifiable activities. Such exercises as struggling with others to kick a football up and down a field all afternoon are considered morally worthy. But woe betide the boy who just wants to sit in a field and watch the clouds. That's wasting time.

Similarly, calling on neighbors, to be bored by a lot of repetitious conversation, is considered a proper way to pass an evening, whereas sitting alone on a park bench or a curb, without even reading, is considered to be that most shocking of vacuums — doing nothing. It's bad enough in the evening, but if done in the morning or the afternoon — well, it's hardly better than vagrancy.

Our society, however, does relent in one circumstance. Doing nothing but look is permissible on vacation. This, in fact, explains why vacations are almost the only times when most of us do any non-utilitarian looking.

More vacations, then, would seem one way of offsetting the eye-deadening effects of our Puritanism. Yet one cannot be sure even of this, for Puritanism has started its deadly work on vacations, too. More and more resorts boast of their "organized activities," and travel becomes more purposeful as the automobile and the plane make us increasingly able to go to places where we "do" the sights at breakneck speed, keeping even more active than at home.

It seems to me a surer way of offsetting that Puritanism is to emulate the Japanese by incorporating idle looking into the canon. If it can be established and recognized as a laudable occupation rather than a waste of time, it will win acceptance as an activity to be fostered. The battle for this recognition will perhaps be a long one, but you, as an individual, can help by starting with yourself.

Begin, please, by accepting the idea that one activity open to you is sitting still and looking at something. On a winter night, for instance, you might decide to make watching the fire your entertainment for the evening. On a summer night, if near a waterfront, you might decide to visit a pier just to watch what passes on the water. There are any number of opportunities. One important thing to consider, though, is that there is enough movement at your chosen site. And one must be prepared to give oneself wholly to the looking. One must also allot a given time span for it, preferably a whole morning, a whole afternoon, or a whole evening.

So generous a time allotment is particularly important in a non-vacation period. And not just because the sights to be absorbed require it; the span of time is also needed for the necessary preliminary relaxation. Making the shift from our normal condition of preoccupation — a condition of not-looking — to the condition of looking just for the interest of what is to be seen, is not easy. So time should be allowed for one to grow relaxed enough to pass from one stage to the other.

There is another reason why the extended time needs to be decided in advance. Remember, I am advocating looking just for pleasure — idle looking, in fact. For even though I think there should be purpose behind the resolve to do some watching, what is to be watched should not be predetermined. And for this type of unplanned looking the requisite relaxation is particularly hard to achieve. What you have to do is to outsit your impatience — perhaps your own disapproval — by staying in one place until the desire to do anything purposeful leaves you. And often the only thing that can keep you still that long is the resolve not to budge for at least an hour, but if you stick to it, the non-budging nearly always does the trick. Time without action ceases to be hard to endure; something loses its grip on you, and the impetus to act is stilled. And it is then that you pass into a new capacity to observe, to respond to what you observe and to think about both your responses and what has stirred them.

Often to reach this stage, you pass through a condition close to stupor. But once the stupor lifts, as it did before that fire in the courtyard, all sorts of unexpected things begin happening. You find your attention caught by something that never caught it previously. Often the item will stir your curiosity or your imagination, and first thing you know you will be off on a tack you never sailed before.

For instance, I recall that in a garden in Connecticut, where I had been looking idly for some time, my attention began to be increasingly claimed by a two-tone arborvitae. My first response was that the cedar-like evergreen looked somehow incongruous, but I hardly thought of the tree until a little later when the explanation of its two colors came to me. The outer edges, I realized, were lighter than the parts nearer the trunk because the fringes were new growth. Next I noticed that the boughs of nearby pines also had paler tips. But these tips of new growth were merely a paler green, whereas the pale tips of the arborvitae differed in hue. They were golden — the sort of gold that edges pines as the sun rises. And suddenly the source of the incongruity became plain. I was seeing the tree in full afternoon light yet it had the look of a tree touched with the gold of dawn.

The pleasure of that realization has remained with me. And I remember a similar instance in Washington. One Sunday morning I had plopped on a bench in Lafayette Square with no intention of looking at anything in particular. For a long time nothing aroused my special interest. Fate had taken me to a bench just behind Clark Mills' statue of Andrew Jackson on a pint-sized horse. All I did when I first noticed it was smile at its naïveté. But as my eyes wandered from children feeding pigeons, to distant fountains in front of the White House and various strollers passing by, I gradually became a little more conscious of that absurd statue. What was wrong with it? Then I realized the general would not be lifting his bicorn so nonchalantly if the horse under him was really rearing. My attention wandered away, but as the general's back and the rump of the horse were very close, I couldn't help looking further at the monument. And then I noticed that it wasn't just because the horse was too small for its rider that the ensemble was wrong: Jackson was sitting bolt upright, whereas a man on a horse that was on its hind legs would be leaning forward to counteract the rearing of the animal. I was willing to let the observation go at that. But the statue remained before my eyes, and suddenly something deeper occurred to me. The bronze statue, I realized, aimed to capture a transient moment in an enduring medium. And I saw the statue did justice to neither. The enduring bronze was mocked by the transience of the lift of the horse; and the movement was deprived of the transience that was part of its essence. And this led to insight into why there seems to be something wrong in nearly all over-active statues. Enduring mediums, surely, should be reserved for the celebration of enduring attitudes.

When I took my leave of the general, I knew my morning had not been wasted, that these unexpected thoughts arising from unplanned noticing had been more creative and rewarding than many sessions of deliberate study. I knew, too, that it was through the extended exposure of the equestrian statue that its retinal image had grown vivid enough to engage my thoughts.

So one advantage of allotting a third of a day for idle looking is that retinal images we might ordinarily resist are given time to win their way into the consciousness. Simultaneously, it allows us to come into readiness to receive what we have not previously considered. Either way we benefit, not only in unexpected pleasure, but because objects that catch our attention involuntarily extend our minds for the very reason that they are things we have tended to shun or ignore.

Going for a stroll can be a good version of "Spend a Third of a Day Watching," especially among static scenes where the necessary movement has to be provided by one's own locomotion. But, in actuality, there are very few scenes that really are static, and there are two reasons to choose seated watching over watching while walking. While sitting, one can detect and appreciate the movement in a scene that one ordinarily misses by going through it too fast. And walking consumes energy, thereby encroaching on the store of energy that, when seated, is wholly free for observing.

Sitting has an incidental advantage deriving from the fact that one's eyes are nearer the ground. Thus they are more likely to be caught by puddles, insects, foraging sparrows, and lost or discarded objects — things, that is, against which in ordinary living the eyes are generally doubly shuttered. There is not only their physical distance as we stand above them — a distance that makes some of them all but invisible; but there is their social distance. For our culture, as I have said, has a lamentable visual snobbishness about objects close to the feet.

If you argue that spending two or three hours watching is too solitary a diversion, you can combine it with another excellent visual game: "Borrow Your Friend's Eyes." I have demonstrated how it works by telling of several occasions when I profited from such loans: with the face cards; with the birds when my friend lent me his eyes for the Egyptian hieroglyphs; with my bits of ancient Mexican pottery when I took advantage of the eyes of the archaeologist; and with the radiating spokes of the basket's shadow in the La Tour painting when I borrowed my friend's eyes at the Frick.

Generally, those loans were not consciously sought. Indeed, the instance of the birds was an accident that would have been avoided had it not been for Ed's interest in Egypt. But eye-borrowing, as the tea-drinking Japanese know, can be deliberate. And you needn't do it surreptitiously, for everyone, whether consciously or unconsciously, has had the experience of lending his eyes to others. So you can ask friends to do voluntarily, and with full awareness, what they have often done. Nor need you feel you are imposing, for the request automatically implies that you are willing to lend your eyes in return.

Stated in terms of specific action, you ask your friends to look at something with you and to report not only what they see but how they are struck by it. You, in turn, tell your impressions. Friends will vary in their willingness to play the game, depending largely on their interest in the visual world. But the game can be played superficially even with people of the most glancing vision.

Stephan Nalbantian played it with us in bringing up power lines, and I remember getting two fellow newspapermen to play it during dinner at Toffenetti's just off Times Square. I didn't expect them to be willing to concentrate, so I only suggested that each of us contribute his first impression to a specific appearance. I picked the upward flaring corner of the partition housing the restaurant's kitchen.

"It's like the prow of a ship," volunteered Edward Downes. John Briggs then played Alphonse to my Gaston and insisted that I speak next. "I see gold-like sheathing whose colors vary according to the reflections, some being almost white, some almost red, with the reds and the whites being tempered by the basic orange-gold."

"What I was wondering," said John, "was whether the sheathing was made of real copper or of copperized paper."

So each of us had seen the corner differently! Because of his particular set, one was struck most by its form, another by its variegated color, and the third by its material. By pooling our responses, not only had we come to sharper awareness of the corner, but we had received amusing evidence of how each perceiver's perceptions are influenced by his particular makeup.

Note that one of the responses came in the form of a simile, indicating that "Hunt the Simile" is a game that can be played in company, as well as alone.

A word of warning, though, about borrowing your friend's eyes. Most Westerners, remember, have not had the visual disciplining of the Japanese, who have been attending viewing parties since childhood. So if you want to spend an afternoon or evening watching with a friend you must be sure the friend is not only willing, but able, to play the game. For where vision is concerned, friends — like words, books, and cameras — can operate both ways. And this is largely because they use words. Thus they can sharpen your vision by their articulateness about what they observe, by the quality of their responses, and by the knowledge, the background, and particular interests they bring to what you are observing. Also, because they are set differently, often their comment will simultaneously alter your own set and make something seem to change before your eyes as you shift to their set. And because discerning a story behind visual appearances tends to make scenes and objects more vividly memorable, some friends can often bring something into focus by supplying a story element, either from imagination or knowledge. But friends can also deaden your vision by claiming your undivided attention as they talk about non-visual matters. So if you want to organize a successful viewing party, be careful that you don't invite an unobservant chatterbox.

There is something else you can borrow as an aid to viewing — your own hands. Actually, little urging is needed, for it is something we all do spontaneously. The number of times a mother says "Mustn't touch" to a child suggests, in fact, that we tend to touch before we look. As adults, we have the same impulse. And the proof that when we reach out with our eyes we also tend to reach out with our hands is provided by the signs one sees so often in stores and museums. "Please do not handle," "Do not touch the paintings," etc. With many the instinct to use the hands as an aid to vision is so strong that it is compulsive. And often we use our hands without awareness that what we are doing is supplementing the findings of one sense with the reports of another.

We use our hands to test the surmises of our eyes. Our hands bring us the "feel" of things — their weight, shape, and surface texture. And besides giving us information as to an object's hardness or softness, its brittleness or its density, our hands increase our sense of its reality, its three-dimensional existence. Our hands help in less obvious ways, too. They enable us to aid our visibility by carrying illumination to objects too big to move. With small objects, our hands lift them closer to our eyes, and take them to advantageous lighting. Our hands can turn objects around to be examined from many different angles, or take things apart for us to examine interiors.

Not so generally recognized, though, is that, with objects that are movable, our hands also considerably extend the time spans that we are able to devote to observing. They do this by allowing leeway to the eye's natural restlessness — a restlessness that makes it difficult to concentrate for long on anything of limited size that is stationary. But when an object can be turned about and held away at different distances, prolonged concentration is relatively easy. And the hands can facilitate such examination even more by bringing a second object close to the first. The archaeologist did this with the Mexican sherds, and my eyes, free to shift from one to another, dwelt untiringly on those bits of broken pottery for a span that would have been almost torture to sustain had the sherds been under glass in a museum.

Using the hands to bring additional objects into the visual field, besides allowing still further play for the eye's mobility, also, of course, allows for a particularly stimulating type of double-level perception. For not only can they bring the objects close together, they can manipulate them into such a variety of juxtapositions that you achieve a multiple set of contrasts and parallels. And if you doubt the stimulus of this, remember that it was my hands that kept arranging, selecting, and realigning the face cards, which yielded so much when they were examined side-by-side in various combinations.

The hands, too, can play an important role in vision by manipulating optical aids. Already I have discussed the camera as such an aid. And while I conceded that as long as it keeps its carrier on the alert for beautiful compositions it is an aid to vision, I also pointed out its dangers. And it should be added that the camera is not as useful as other less self-operative optical aids, such as microscopes, telescopes, binoculars, and magnifying glasses. Like the view-finder of the camera, all of these provide a frame that isolates the field to be observed. And they make it possible to play on a smaller scale a game that can also be played in a larger way with doors, arches, arcades, porches, and windows.

One might call it "Framing." And optical aids sharpen vision in the same way as architectural frames. For at the same time as they assist concentration by isolating a segment of reality, they eliminate distractions by excluding features outside the frame. And optical aids, of course, have the advantage of sharpening the focus within the framed area. But unlike the camera, such aids won't take the selected picture for you. With them you have to take your own. But the aids, by means of magnification, make personal picture-taking easier.

If I were writing for specialists, such aids would have a chapter to themselves. But aided vision — other than the standard correction provided by glasses — is not my theme; so I feel no need to stress the obvious help of the telescope in seeing the greatly distant or of field glasses for the moderately far. The same is true for the microscope in seeing the infinitesimal. These marvelous aids deserve mention, however, and it is worth noting that, besides enabling you to enter worlds the naked eye can not see, magnifying lenses help with the world you can see. Not the least of their gifts is their power to startle. Indeed, a first glimpse of a friend's eyeball under a magnifying glass can be terrifying.

What startles us is that an amplified object looks unfamiliar; and its strangeness is heightened by the fact that the glass, with its limited area of clear focus, has taken the object out of context. The unfamiliarity and our unwonted emotional response are both eye-opening, and it is hard to tell which provides the greater visual stimulus: the newness of aspect or the fact that we no longer feel it is something too ordinary to be considered.

In discussing art books, I suggested swinging a magnifying glass in systematic arcs over the plates. The trick is worth recalling because the experience with art reproductions is representative of all lens-aided study. For when each new vignette appears as the glass moves from segment to segment, you are repeatedly startled by the combined effects of framing, amplification, and the creation of new gestalten at the expense of old. For in these vignettes, things you missed before leap out at you, particularly if you are studying reproductions of paintings by Italian primitives, Netherlandish painters, or other artists who crammed their pictures with story details or interesting bits of still life. Then, when you take the glass away, you will note that many of the details, which previously seemed invisible, are readily observable, and will remain so. The same principle is at work with details in the landscape around you that are brought into framed focus by field glasses.

Besides the power of the gestalt — the larger entity that swallows up its embedded details — there is the fact that smallness sets up psychological barriers. Often we do not discern small things because of a fixed idea that they are too tiny to be taken in. Yet the persisting visibility of small details brought into our awareness through magnification proves they were clearly observable all along.

In many cases the previous invisibility of minutiae is as simple as I have suggested. That is, we never saw the details either because we failed to look in their direction, they were overwhelmed, or we were convinced they weren't visible. Yet sometimes the situation is a little more complicated. Here we come once more to that old aid to vision — knowledge. Often what happens in magnification is that the object is revealed clearly enough to be identified. In a landscape, it might be the top of a steeple beyond a distant tree; or in a painting of The Last Judgment, a triton in the hands of one of the devils herding the damned into Hell. Whatever the object, its subsequent visibility is always due in part to the fact that, once we know what it is, intelligibility allows it to pass easily into the mind.

Many of the games I have suggested, such as "Hunt the Simile," "Pretend You Are a Reporter," and "Keep a Visual Journal," are word games. "Look Only at Colors" involves finding words to describe the colors, and verbalizing is a part of the Japanese-style viewings. The subject of intelligibility brings me to still another word game. It involves extending to appearances of many kinds the sort of analyzing writers of art books do so well with works of art. A name for it might be, "Account for Puzzling Impressions."

The lengths to which it can go, and its extraordinary potentialities, can be found in the pages of Proust, who searched for the significance of his impressions with a sensitivity hitherto unmatched. You need not try to rival him, nor will I attempt to explain the game as fully as he does. But I would like to echo his suggestion that the best time to play is when your emotions are stirred by an impression that puzzles you. This, after all, is a common experience, for we often encounter objects of a familiar type which, for some reason or other, seem different than usual.

Pausing to account for the difference is nearly always illuminating. The first stage in the unraveling is to recognize that, although there is undoubtedly much that is subjective in the puzzling response, it has also been influenced by objective factors. What, one asks, are they? This initiates the visual hunt, as one shifts the eye from part to part of the chosen object, always carrying in the back of the mind the question: "What is unusual in the part or in the total arrangement?" Recently, for instance, I saw an elderly man for whom my first feeling was one of revulsion. He looks like something you'd turn up under a stone, I said to myself. Yet when I looked again I saw this was unjust. His unhealthy appearance was due largely to the fact that he looked tired and sick. There was really nothing unpleasant about his features — or his expression. What, then, had caused my first impression? I set about searching, and by the time I got to the top of his head, I had my answer. His bald pate had none of the normal pink of healthy old men but was the white of slightly dusty paper. And I saw this pasty dome — the effect of all blood drained away — had caused my first impression.

In another instance, a young woman explained the odd look we were both aware of in the eyes of a mutual friend. "Haven't you noticed," she asked, "that he hardly ever blinks?"

A satisfactory explanation for an impression generally fixes it in the memory, so that what was merely a fleeting glimpse becomes a permanent acquisition. And if the mind is sluggish before the puzzling appearance one can draw up a set of questions as an aid to analysis. Is the oddness in the form or the color? Is it because the appearance is supernaturally clear or not clear enough? Is it because of some incongruity with the surroundings? What memory does it stir? Is there some disproportion of the parts? Such questions, self-directed, can start new chains of reaction, for words can be used to find other words, and one's own questions, no less than the questions of others, can both direct the eyes and enforce a shift in the set of one's attention.

Yet even though practice makes one increasingly adept at accounting for curious impressions, the objective explanation is not always immediately forthcoming. But this does not matter. Indeed, the delay can even heighten the pleasure of the solution. Finding a needed answer can certainly bring one of the greatest pleasures of reading. I know that in my case I long had the impression that a lot of buildings of the thirties had a look of blankness, an impression that remained subjective and inexplicable until I came upon a chance remark in a book. Most modern windows, said the author, do not have sills.

I snapped my fingers in delight. And I have often had this experience of delight when a book — or sometimes a friend — pops out with a phrase that makes a puzzling impression explicable. So this game of centering on what strikes you as strange often helps certain periods of enforced or voluntary idleness pass more pleasantly. Even if the explanation continues to elude you, the search plants in your mind a filament of eager mental life, which, like a sea anemone's tentacle, keeps reaching out for the descriptive tidbit that will give it a sense of happy fulfillment.

There is a fable sometimes utilized to demonstrate different kinds of perceptions. It tells of a lump of gold ore lying in a path. A gorilla happened to step on it, so he picked it up, saw it was a piece of rock and threw it down again. Then a native came along. He was a member of a primitive tribe that knew nothing of working metal, but the gold glinting in the rock caught his attention. He picked it up to admire it. Then, when he grew tired of the pretty yellow veins, he, too, threw the rock down. Finally, a modern mining engineer came by. He saw the chunk of rich ore and instantly recognized it for what it was. As he knew it meant there must be more gold in the area, he set about finding where the ore came from, acquiring the land, and organizing a mining syndicate.

The fable certainly illustrates the role of knowledge in seeing, but I introduce it here to show how the same thing can appear differently to different people, according to what they bring to it. It also serves to introduce the next game: "How Would It Appear to a . . . ?" (The dots are to be filled with whatever imaginary viewer the player wants to select.)

Two more stories will make the game clearer. One is about a mouse who was being nursed by its mother. The mouselet happened to look up to a corner of the ceiling where it saw a bat. "Look, Mummy," said the baby mouse, "an angel!"

The other is about a city boy, born long after electric refrigerators had become standard in all the homes he knew. One summer, however, he stayed overnight at a friend's cottage on a lake where there was no electricity. When he came home he reported to his parents: "They have the craziest fridge. Nothing but a wooden box with one big ice cube in it."

In each story something familiar is revealed in a fresh way by being seen through eyes different than our own. And this is the secret of the game — to look at something and imagine how it would appear to a different sort of creature. The bat's appearance to the mouse suggests what you might get if you decided to imagine you were an animal. The way the ice appeared to the city boy is an example of what you might get if you pretended to be a child seeing something new and yet related to his own experience.

The ore story shows that a stone age primitive is a stimulating possible viewer. An earlier instance of his potentialities was given when I imagined him picking up a face card and being so mystified by its orientation as to conclude it was one of the white man's gods. And I am grateful to the imagined primitive who gave me stimulus with a button. For he made me realize how that commonplace object would strike a stone-age man who had previously been obliged to knot all his clothing in order to keep it about him. A fastening disk that could be turned on its edge to go through a slot — a truly marvelous invention!

There are many other imaginary viewers who can be selected. As I have suggested, at a party you can pretend that instead of being a guest you are a visiting sociologist. As Kipling suggests in *Kim*, you can pretend you are a spy and look about for the sort of information that might be useful to your side. Conan Doyle revealed the possibilities of looking with a detective's eye. And I especially recommend looking at objects as if you were an archaeologist digging up your civilization a thousand years hence.

This particular choice once enabled me to have a wonderfully stimulating dinner hour with a salt-shaker. I was reading about some archaeological excavations in Mexico and the author's speculation about the uses of certain things he dug up set me off. What,

I asked myself, would an archaeologist be able to tell about our civilization if in 2151 he came upon this salt-shaker buried in the rubble?

The shaker was a hollow, octagonal glass pyramid, with a silvery cap. As I rotated it in my hands, I realized it would tell the archaeologist that we knew how to work metal, that we had the secret of glass, and that we knew how to make glass vessels of fairly odd shape. What condiment or powder was stored in the vessel might be hard to determine, but it would be fairly easy to see it was a shaker of some sort. Knowing that the cap unscrewed, I saw that the vessel would reveal that we also knew the principle of the screw. Then came my greatest illumination. The shaker would also reveal that, thanks to the screw principle, we had learned how to do something very difficult: to combine two such dissimilar materials as glass and metal so that at one moment they could be very strongly joined, and at another, taken apart without damage to either. Obviously, there was a lot more to a common restaurant salt-shaker than I had ever imagined.

My pleasure in buttons and salt-shakers underlines that most of my emphasis has been on the observation of objects, and in the final game of this chapter I will return to objects in isolation. But meanwhile, I would like to take an exactly opposite course: to recommend an exercise that tends to obliterate the "thingness" of objects. With the Japanese leg trick, I suggested one such exercise; another is a game that grew out of my experience in Times Square. "Study Reflections" is the easiest name for it; though many of its advantages can be reaped as well in the study of shadows.

The great secret of the Japanese leg trick, I said, was that by reducing our powers of recognition it brings us into the world of pure sensing. Reflections, provided they are not mirror reflections, do the same thing. For reflected objects being reversed, are generally even harder to identify than those seen through the legs. Obviously, too, the observing is more comfortable when the inversion is in the thing beheld, rather than ourselves; but there are also other advantages. One is that with most reflections, the period of non-recognition is considerably longer than in the leg trick. Another is that one gains benefits comparable to those arising from the inhibition of certain visual faculties — such as placing objects in space — without paying the price of bodily disorientation leading to temporary loss of visual acuity.

In other words, when appearances leap out at you — and they leap from reflections just as they do from under your legs — they leap out at unfuddled eyes. And they have this power for similar reasons. For in non-mirror reflections you can not distinguish between objects and their backdrops. Consequently, not only do you see both with equal vividness, but you see them as part of an ensemble because you can neither isolate the objects as disparate entities nor place them in space. Put still another way, you see reflections, of necessity, with pictorial vision.

Studying reflections, then, becomes a means of inducing the sort of painter's vision which we have conceded is difficult. And one reason reflections can do this is because nearly always the objects reflected are close at hand. Thus, once reflected objects have been identified, you can stimulate your seeing by shifting your eyes back and forth between the object and its appearance in the reflection.

Part of the stimulation is general, for the oscillation demonstrates how different pictorial seeing is from customary seeing. It does this because almost inevitably, as you shift from object to reflection, you shift from one type of seeing to the other. Looking at the object itself you see a thing of known function set in space; looking at the reflection you see a picture. The reflection-picture, of course, contains objects, but in it they are seen more as part of the picture than as themselves. Or put in terms of psychological response, looking at an object your uppermost preception is of its identity; looking at its reflection your chief consciousness is of its appearance.

Say the scene is a corner of your living room. Looking at it directly, you see the telephone (something on which you make calls) standing beside the lamp (something that gives you light); and the color of the wall behind them tends to disappear. But in a reflection, the telephone becomes a curious black dumbbell on a black stand that contrasts vividly with the Indian-red cylinder that supports the white bell, and with the apple-green wall that provides a unifying field for the composition.

With an effort of will, of course, one can achieve these effects without reflecting aids. The trick is to look at an ensemble of objects with the resolution to see only appearances: in looking towards some girls at a table, for instance, to give the girls no more importance — no more identification as objects of interest — than, say, the plates in front of them or the parallel counters and walls of the cafeteria in the rear.

Generally, though, to see things only as colored forms, one has to half-close one's eyes. This is because the mind nearly always has the upper hand in vision, and the mind is more interested in functions and identities than in appearances. In fact, it so loves to be confronted with intelligible objects of understood function that it tends to make us sacrifice the appearance of things so that our grasp of their function will be paramount. Thus, time and again, too easy an identification of an object drops a veil of invisibility over it. And after the quick recognition we see the identity and not the thing itself. The half-closing of the lids is necessary, therefore, to foil the mind's identifying power.

But with reflections you need neither effort of will nor half-closed eyes. Mirrors excluded, reflecting surfaces automatically reduce everything to a single picture plane, making foreground and background objects appear side-by-side, and presenting objects primarily as picturesque appearances. And, curiously enough, even though reflections at first tend to transform objects into mere picture components, they ultimately give us a deeper awareness of objects as things.

Note, however, that I have thrice ruled out mirrors, for their perfect reflection spoils this game. To be successful, the reflecting surface should have some curvature, or some imperfection to distort what it reflects. In Times Square, it will be remembered, I found the glistening rain-soaked pavements, the high office windows, and the plate glass of the Chinese restaurant stimulating surfaces to study. And once I was home, I found the spherical teapot and the Aladdin's lamp creamer were also fascinating reflectors. Recall too, how startled I was when I peered into a teaspoon and saw my face upside down.

Actually, that was just the beginning of my exploration of the teaspoon, for I have found this humble utensil provides a particularly good reflecting surface to explore.

The bowl of a teaspoon is almost always full of lovely shapes and colors, and as you look into it you will find that at first they are hard to identify. This combination of loveliness and puzzlement is what makes the spoon so stimulating. What, you wonder, is that gold disk in the center? You look around and see no gold disk. But then it dawns on you. Why, of course; the spoon is facing upwards and that disk reflected in it is the ceiling plate that holds the sockets for your bulbs. And you look at that gold disk with a fresh respect for its appearance. Then you ask what are those lovely green shapes that impinge on the trapezoid of light that must be the window. A lift of the eyes shows they are the leaves of your straggly poinsettia. And again, you have fresh respect for the beauty of those leaves as they stand against the window with the transfixing light giving their greenness uncanny luminosity.

And so it goes. The coral of your tablecloth looks lovely reflected on the silver cylinder of your coffee pot. A cup that you thought chiefly pink and white is seen to have a decisive gold line. A red postage stamp on the white expanse of an envelope becomes a Mondrian touch. And besides seeing these things with fresh eyes because their distorted shapes make you aware of their appearance rather than their function, you see them as part of an ensemble because they are all framed on the same reflecting surface.

Reflecting surfaces, too, can show you objects from unlikely angles. A curved surface can reach around corners, reflecting things your eyes could only take in by sweeping more than two hundred degrees in all directions. It stands to reason, too, that every shiny surface you look into will automatically reveal different angles of objects than those you see. This is because you are looking towards the surface, whereas the surface is looking towards you.

Reflected images are influenced by the texture of the surfaces on which they appear. And besides the degree of glossiness, there is the influence of whether the surface is smooth or bumpy. And because surfaces have so much distorting power they contribute greatly to the game. They allow us to decide on whether we want to play easy or difficult versions. For several reasons I particularly recommend the latter.

One is the practice they give in studying the unintelligible.

And the visual advantage of such study becomes apparent the moment one thinks of experience in acquiring other skills. Progress is made not by doing over again what one can already do easily, but by trying to do what one can't do yet. Observing nothing but the intelligible is like only playing games that are easy. To really extend your visual skills you need to practice on things that are hard. And reflections on irregular surfaces provide wonderfully good exercise in discernment, partly because of their difficulty, and partly because you can find aid in the things reflected.

In this game your hands help in a new way. Often a reflection will be so distorted that the object causing it is unidentifiable. If you move your hand in front of the reflecting surface, its movement will betray which distorted image is that of your hand. That identified, you can move your hand from object to object, and when, in the reflecting surface, you see your hand coming close to the puzzling appearance you get an inkling of what you were looking at. Then you can confirm it by touching the suspected object, which, if you are right, will be evident when the reflected hand and object meet.

Generally, the distorted version of the object suddenly becomes miraculously intelligible. And now knowing what it is helps you analyze just how it is changed in reflection. Then, as you follow the ins and outs of its contour in the reflection you get one of the best kinds of visual practice — practice in absorbing irregular shapes.

For with irregular shapes, especially those that are hard to identify, you really have to see what is under your eyes. This is in sharp contrast to symmetrical shapes, which are all too easy to dismiss as mere circles, triangles, ovals, squares, or rectangles. With them, you often come away with only a concept of the geometrical form suggested — that is the pre-existing pattern you have imposed on them. But with the irregular, the asymmetrical, you absorb an exact percept, and in doing so, have a much more vital experience of the thing perceived. For what you have taken in is the object's retinal appearance, rather than an idea of it. And in the process of absorption the object imposes its own life on you; thus, at the same time as you take in something new, a shape that was not in your consciousness before becomes planted there.

And the reflected shape is not the only new percept you acquire. In discussing drawing I spoke of how our minds resist the distortions imposed on objects by distance and angle of placement. As a result, we can see a cube in perspective and still think of it as a square box and not as a diamond. But the distortions in most reflecting surfaces are stronger than our eyes' power to reassemble objects in frontal aspects. We have to see the distortions. And, in seeing things pulled out of shape, our shape-obsessed eyes are invariably opened to new realities of their appearances. The cycle in fact, is completed, for the reflections that begin by robbing objects of their thingness, end up by returning it in still fuller measure.

Color is certainly one of the properties returned in heightened degree. Some shadows, too, will heighten the color sense — especially the light-penetrated shadow of a glass of red wine on a white tablecloth. But generally shadows give you only gray or black forms. However, shadows, too, are forms reduced to a single surface with the relative position of their parts, either behind or in front, eliminated. And they are stimulating in the same way as reflections, for you know they represent some reality, but because of the distortion you often cannot recognize it. If you keep your eyes on the shadow, trying to figure out what causes it, you search the shadow's form. Then, when you raise your eyes to check, the shadow a thing has cast generally makes you see the original thing with new vividness and insight.

Both shadows and reflections provide the stimulus of double-level perception, for you are always able to turn your eyes from one to the other. And just as the distorted image gives you a fresh awareness of the appearance of the original, so does it, in turn, enable you to search the reflection or the shadow with the increased visual skill supplied by greater knowledge.

Reflections are most beautiful, and most spectacular, on lakes or calm bays. Yet they can also be beautiful in such humdrum places as puddles, spoons, mudguards, store windows, teapots and polished table tops. Indeed, reflections are perhaps most useful with the overly familiar, for they have a way of restoring to taken-for-granted objects their lost visibility.

The study of reflections is likely to bring us many instances of pictorial vision, and this fosters an appetite that increases by what it feeds on. Because the more we consciously look for pictures in the world, the more the pleasure derived from them leads us to develop our pictorial vision. For once we learn to see pictures in life — to be aware of the richness of the visual field, that is — we increasingly look for beautiful pictures, or at least pictures that will be tellingly expressive. Not only do we look for more Braques in the objects on our tables, but for more Seurats when we go to the shore. And in time, unaided, we begin to discover the pictures in life that give us the greatest aesthetic satisfaction.

Now for the final game which returns us to objects isolated from pictorial context. It might be called "An Object a Day," for it consists of examining one thing each day that you have never looked at closely before.

It might be a flower in a vase, a spray of mountain laurel, the catch of a window, the scoring of a nail file, a salad fork, the bell-ringing system of a bus, the way skin bunches up at the knuckle of a finger, the core of an apple, the paw of a dog, the net-like roughness of a cantaloupe rind, a weather vane seen in a hardware store, the circle of struts that opens an umbrella, the printing of a distinctive trademark, a crane hoisting girders to build a sky-scraper, a bit of weaving, or the way a man's shirt is made. The object really does not matter, as long as it is something you have not studied deliberately before. Neither does it have to be inhuman, for you can take a tired old woman sitting alone at a table in a cafeteria, a couple in animated conversation across the aisle of a subway, a group of picketers, a guard in a bank, or a woman in church. And you do not even need to consider a whole individual: You can decide, say, just to look at noses, or lower lips, or the movement of the hands of the people in the row beside you as you wait for a play to begin. Any occasion, any locale can be used; and every new activity furnishes new visual opportunities.

But there should be no waiting for new activities, for the game is often most eye-opening when played in the midst of old activities. Sometimes, too, the greatest surprise comes when the article selected is one that has been glanced at many times. Wherever possible, one should be emancipated from eye-closing snobberies. Above all, there should be no disdain of the commonplace. The chances are that the commonplace will turn out to be the most interesting for the very reason that has made it so: that it belongs to a class that has been interwoven into human living for so many generations. For the type of studying I advocate also involves a little speculating, especially about history.

Two things are particularly helpful for such speculation. One is consulting the dictionary. If, for instance, you chose to study a cantaloupe, the dictionary will tell you that it was first grown in Italy and that it took its name from its place of origin, the Castle of Cantalupo. You will also find that it is related to the cucumber and the watermelon — a fact that should whet your curiosity to examine them too, in order to see how they resemble and how they differ from the cantaloupe, which you now have clearly in mind.

Or, if you have examined a drinking glass and wondered why anything so stable should have been called a tumbler, you will find the name was once a remarkably precise description of a certain type of glass that actually tumbled. Having a pointed bottom, it could not be set down safely until it was empty.

If your dictionary is a large one, it will give stimulation, too, by providing drawings which, as likely as not, will give the correct names for the different parts of an object you have chosen to observe. An example is the way a dictionary illustration, in Army days, confirmed that sepals was the right word for the green shields protecting the rose petals. And the unexpected names for subsidiary parts will often lead to other entries that still further expand your comprehension of what you are studying.

The other great aid for speculation is our old friend, double-level perception in the guise of comparative looking. By this I mean looking at other objects of the same class to determine just how the chosen object compares with its counterparts. If one has chosen a toothbrush, for instance, it is useful to stop and think what other brushes might be around to look at. Getting out an old watercolor brush, one finds it has only a single clump of filaments embedded in a circular holder, which makes one more aware that toothbrush bristles are planted in a number of circular pits. Then perhaps one wonders why the pits are set in parallel rows. Is it because the bristle clumps clean more efficiently by being set out in such an orderly fashion? Or is the brush easier to manufacture when the clumps are in straight lines? Then one takes down a whisk, which is seen to be much more primitive, not needing machinery for its manufacture. And then under the word "brush"

in the dictionary, one finds the word "brushwood." This leads one
to wonder if it got the name because it made good brushes; or if a
word like underbrush suggested that the cleansing scrapers made
from it should be called brushes. And one looks with delight down
the long road of invention from a bundle of sticks used by a peasant
woman to sweep the ground outside her hovel to a hygienic little
brush that is used to polish one's teeth inside one's mouth.

Or say one's eye has been caught by an unusual chain and one
has decided to pick it as the visual object for the day. A chain that
caught my eye at Isabel Whipple's, for instance, seemed to consist
of a sequence of little tuning forks. Because of this, I examined
it more closely and found that the tuning fork effect of the frontal
view derived from the fact that each link had two eyes: an oval
one, that looked as if it had been steam-rollered; and, below it, a
smaller, circular one set at right angles. Each long eye was threaded
through the circular eye of the preceding link, and the smallness of
the circles enabled the chain to lie very flat. Comparing it to another of Isabel's chains, a crude affair attached to a sixteenth-
century alms box, I realized that ordinary interlinking circles or
ovals of uniform size can not help but be un-flat because each has
to swing at right angles from the other. Then my eye lit on the
chain of one of Isabel's dog leashes. When I picked it up I saw that,
even though its links were single-eyed and uniform, this chain,
too, was relatively flat, because each oval was twisted at the point
where it interlinked with the next. Later, when I saw how many
other chains utilize this twisting device, I felt ashamed for having
handled chains so often and observed them so little. The chains
led me back to the road of invention, and I realized that the chain
was the result of man's quest for something that would fulfill the
function of cord in tasks where cord would be neither strong nor
durable enough.

If one gets bored with plain daily looking, interest can be
added by combining it with "On and Off Looking," a game that
makes looking an especially delightful pastime, and which is so
good for the eyes that Huxley recommends it as an exercise in *The
Art of Seeing*. What it does is exploit the eye's capacity for flash
glimpsing. A version of the game the painter used to play with his
daughter, its first stage is to look at an object briefly. Next, one

closes one's eyes. Then one tries to remember as many details as possible of what one has just looked at. When the memory can furnish nothing further, one looks again. In that second look one is always especially struck by the features that failed to return in the interlude of attempted recall. Often they are what might be called "bridge" features, for they connect the details that were successfully recalled. And it is specially satisfying to catch them the second time round, for in addition to adding logic to the ensemble, they are often more interesting than the more conspicuous elements that caught the eye the first time.

During the second look, too, it is much easier to think about what is before the eyes. This is because ocular absorption and mental reflection are different processes. What the game has done has been to enable you to pursue them both simultaneously. And it has done this by first letting you do them separately. For the first looking, of course, is ocular absorption, whereas the recalling is reflecting. And what made the reflecting possible was that closing of the eyes broke the force of that old bugaboo: the grip of the present image.

If the chosen object is particularly complex, you can shield your eyes once again and then in a new period of recall try to put together first and second impressions. Often on the third look still other details will become apparent. If you have lots of time and are in a secluded spot you can even vary the game by taking a siesta between looks. I well remember such an experience in the cloister of a deserted monastery in Mexico. I had been studying the cloister for some time and after a while I began to feel drowsy. It was a lovely summer day, and no one was around, so I acted on my impulse. I stretched out on a stone banquette and fell asleep. When I awoke, my eyes were aimed towards the vaulting of the ambulatory. How lovely it looked, and when I swung my feet to the ground I was amazed to find that the whole cloister had taken on the same sort of heightened beauty as the vaulting. My refreshed eyes, too, were able to take in all sorts of new details.

Still another variant of "On and Off Looking" can be played with a pencil and paper. In this version you try to draw the object that you flash-glimpsed. The difficulties you encounter will be doubly salutary: on the one hand, they will renew your conviction of the sketchiness of preliminary seeing; on the other, they will make the overlooked features strike you with especial force because you will be so glad to get them in order to fill in the blank spaces and at the same time to improve your drawing. Drawing, of course, aids daily looking much as it aids plant looking. That is, it enables you to fix in your mind aspects which for want of words to describe them, or the necessary defining knowledge, you would probably not take in normally.

Visual experiences always tend to have sequels, as I have already illustrated. In the courtyard they came in quick succession, as vision swung from fire to candle, from candle to electric bulb and from bulb to neon sign. At the Ottawa airport when I was hunting for a simile for the checkerboard hoarding, the sequel came so long after the original experience that at first the cereal package manifested itself only as a stimulus stirring a sense of recognition. When my archaeologist friend tutored me about my Mexican scraper stone, after only a short interval I saw those stone chisels at the Museum of the American Indian for what they were. A further example of a well-planted image leading to later vision of something else of the same class was the way my drawing an iris led first to the vision of the wild iris, and then to my response to the iris of the Japanese artist. And the sequel to the Seurat show was the experience at Stamford Bay.

This tendency of one observation to prepare for another accounts for perhaps the most exciting aspect of "An Object a Day." For our chosen objects pay us unexpected dividends by the way they are always bringing their kin into the house. An observation of yesterday or the day before, or perhaps even a week back, will make us pull something vivid out of our environment that we never expected to notice. The surprises may come either from what catches the attention, or from the unanticipated correlations that suddenly click together in the mind.

With chosen objects no less than with those noticed by accident, subsidiary aspects come to our attention if we observe carefully. And they, in turn lead to other observations, as the following dramatized chain of sequels will illustrate.

Act One occurred one evening in New York just after I had turned out the lights to go to bed. Glancing out the window, my eye was caught by a silvery raggedness in the sky. Once I realized the strange effect was caused by clouds partially obscuring the moon, I decided I would view the moon until it rose clear of the jagged clump of stratified clouds. As it lifted above the cloud cliff, I saw the moon's top right corner had been nibbled away. Its incompleteness at this particular corner reawakened a curiosity that had stirred in me several years earlier when on a significant evening I had watched the moon rise in Mexico. There, too, the upper right hand corner had been missing, and I had wondered whether this was because the waxing moon had not yet fully plumped out, or because the moon, having reached the full, was beginning to wane. Out of reach of books at the time, I was unable to satisfy my curiosity. But this evening in my apartment I could — or thought I could. So I turned on the lights again and got down the *Columbia Encyclopedia*.

Although I did not find the answer to my particular question, what I discovered was so interesting that I felt the moon had proved a particularly good object-of-the-day. As by this time man-made Sputniks and Explorers were orbiting around the earth, I was very conscious of satellites. Consequently, two facts in the *Encyclopedia* struck me especially. One was the moon's enormous size in comparison to the little balls and darts that man had set in orbit; and I had a greater sense of awe and wonder that our planet could have a satellite a quarter of its own size.

The second exciting fact was the discovery of earthlight. That is, that just as the moon, in reflecting the sun, gives light to the earth, so the earth, reflecting the same sun, gives light to the moon. Further, the encyclopedia said we could sometimes see the glow of earthlight on the moon, it being visible when the outer curve of the moon was discernible at the opposite pole from the bright crescent. Since I had frequently seen this phenomenon I was delighted to have the explanation that it was earthlight that outlined the ghostly orb.

This prompted a question: Which way did the horns point when they seemed to clasp the orb? I could not recall if the crescent was a C or a reversed C. And this made me more curious than ever to find in which direction the moon filled out, from left to right, or from right to left.

Act Two had a number of scenes. The first was in a Second Avenue bus late at night. After having seen a young woman to her apartment, I was on my way home. The day had been a happy one and I had not thought of examining anything special. But in the bus I remembered I hadn't done my looking for the day. What shall I pick? I asked myself. The answer that came unexpectedly was the coins in my pocket.

I got them out. The first one I looked at was a nickel, headed with a strange looking gentleman with a pigtail. Who on earth was he? Turning the nickel over, I saw a house that had printed under it, in tiny letters, Monticello. Oh, he must be Jefferson, I exclaimed. And I realized I hadn't looked closely at a nickel since the passing of the one with the Indian head — last issued, I learned later, in 1938.

Finding Washington on the quarter and Lincoln on the penny, I wondered who was on the fifty-cent piece. I did not have one with me so I could not check. But I liked the idea of trying to see if I could picture a half-dollar in my mind and read it from the mental picture. When I tried it, however, my mind was blanker than I had expected. Finally, the coin flashed before me, and I breathed a sigh of relief. Of course. It was Liberty, a big head of Liberty in profile.

When I got home my complacency received a blow. Because I save them, I had a lot of half-dollars on hand — not one of which had a big Liberty head. What I had recalled was the silver dollar. Instead, some of the fifty-cent pieces had Benjamin Franklin, while others showed a full-length Liberty, apparently sowing wheat as she strode along. By segregating the two types of half-dollars, I judged that Franklin must have replaced the sowing Liberty sometime after 1947. (The Kennedy half-dollar had not yet been issued.)

The reader who remembers the girl in the airplane who resembled a goddess on a Greek coin will recall that at that time I had no interest in coins. Well, it grew by leaps and bounds as I studied those of the United States. And the bulkhead between two compartments of my memory suddenly gave way. Coins and medals — why hadn't I seen their relationship before? Clearly a coin was a medal used as a medium of exchange.

I began querying friends about coins and found that coins proved, as conclusively as playing cards, that people can have fascinating objects under their eyes day in and day out — and never notice them.

One friend, Elizabeth Riley, did not know that Franklin had come on the half-dollar, nor that Jefferson had replaced the Indian on the nickel, but she knew all about quarters. She knew that those issued between 1892 and 1916 were designed by Charles E. Barber, that the quarters from 1916 to 1930 had an eagle in flight, and that Washington began appearing on the quarter in 1932. When I asked how she knew these things, she revealed she was a small-scale capitalist. She owned the washing machine in the basement of her apartment building. Her interest in quarters developed from her forays to empty the machine.

Elizabeth had not only lots of quarters, but a most ingenious and interesting way of saving them. She had a series of green books, each equipped with quarter-sized depressions in which the coins could be snugly placed. These blind windows were equipped with transparent plastic strips that could be slipped into the thick pages to cover the holes, thereby forming panes to keep the coins from falling out. Moreover, there was a window for each quarter of each year, and the fact that nearly every year had more than one quarter was news to me. And here Elizabeth introduced me to still another mystery about coins. Taking a magnifying glass, she showed me a tiny D embossed on a new quarter in the arched space just under the crown of laurels. Some had a little S in the same spot. The letters, she explained, were mint marks. The quarters with an S were minted in San Francisco, those with a D in Denver, and those without mint marks in Philadelphia.

"Could I get similar books for fifty-cent pieces?" I asked. "Probably," she said. And a day or two later, when I passed a coin store just off Times Square, I went in, asked if such books were available, found they were and promptly bought three: one with windows for the standing Liberties issued between 1916 and 1938, one with windows for the standing Liberties of 1939-1947, and the third for the Franklin half-dollars that began appearing in 1948.

Having ventured into a coin shop for the first time, and having made friends with the owner by buying something, I took a further plunge in numismatics. In Mexico I had found coin imprints in a plaster wall that had interested me. The imprints had been made by Maximilian's soldiers, who did it to while away their boredom when garrisoned there during the French occupation. I had made rubbings of the imprints. Could the coin expert identify the coins from the rubbings? I asked. He said he could.

This led to a study of Mexican coins, which proved every bit as interesting as the U.S. ones, and of course, before long I had bought several books on coins. Reinfeld's showed that my gum-chewing lady of the air journey was a dead ringer for a goddess on a Syracuse silver decadrachm of about four hundred B.C. Scholars, said Reinfeld, disagreed as to whether the goddess of the coin was Artemis, Arethusa, or Persephone.

The final scene of Act Two, the coin act, was back in my apartment. Nina Davenport, my niece, then sixteen years old, was visiting me. One of the numerous objects of apparel she had left strewn around was a copper bracelet, whose dangling charms consisted of coins. With my new interest in coins, it naturally caught my attention. Eagerly I seized on it as my object for the day. Three countries were represented: Canada, the Union of South Africa, and Pakistan.

When I had studied the coins for as much as I could glean unaided, I turned for help to one of my coin books. It explained that the star and crescent I had seen on one side of the Pakistan coins represented a Moslem state. Pakistan, said the text, was given dominion status in the same year as India — 1947.

On one side of the Canadian coppers I had noticed that King George VI's head was circled by the words "Georgivs VI D: G: Rex et Imp." I looked at it again to ascertain its date. Sure enough, it was 1946 when the British King was still Emperor of India. Would later Canadian coinage, I wondered, reflect the change of the king's status after the freeing of India. Excitedly I fingered the bracelet to see if there was a later Canadian coin. To my delight there was — dated 1952. And what words did I find circling the selfsame profile of the selfsame king? "Georgivs VI Dei Gratia Rex." Now he was merely king. And I realized with what sensitivity coins reflected the histories of nations when I saw that the liberation of India had led to an alteration in the coinage of Canada.

Act Three occurred a week or so after my niece had gone and life was calm again. I was walking homeward along Forty-Second Street. It was almost midnight and I remembered I had not done my looking for the day. As I wondered what to choose, I approached the same *Daily News* building that had towered over the poor news dealer who had gone after his flying comics. The building, I knew, had interesting exhibits in its lobby, and this gave me an idea.

The reader who has been in that lobby can perhaps guess what caught my attention: the charts showing the phases of the moon — not only for the current month, but for the next three as well. The charts meant I had the day-by-day appearance of the moon through four complete cycles. And what did I find? The new moon was always a C in reverse, plumping out from right to left. Once it was past the full, the seeming erosion began at the upper right corner. In other words, those two moons I had watched with such interest — the one in Mexico and the one from my apartment — were both moons on the wane. Further, I found that when the reversed C holds an orb made visible by the glow of earthlight it is a new moon that so reveals its total burden.

Something else in that lobby caught my attention: the colored layout of the flags of the United Nations. Moon quarterings being so fresh in my eyes, I noted with preternatural sharpness that six of the flags bore moons. They were the flags of Egypt, Turkey, Tunisia, Lybia, Malaya and Pakistan. And the moons were accompanied by stars. What I had learned from Nina's coins let me know instantly why these particular countries displayed the star and crescent. They were Moslem nations. The crescents formed regular "C's," which meant that, thanks to the enlightening charts I had just studied, I could tell what sort of moons they were. They were not, as I had always thought, new moons — but old ones. And I left the lobby with a sense of delighted surprise. Who would have thought that looking at the moon and studying a few coins would lead to such an understanding of flags?

EPILOGUE

CHAPTER 18

The Advantages of Seeing

WHEN you read the title above, I hope you wondered if this chapter was necessary. Perhaps you felt the advantages of seeing had been stated with sufficient clarity to eliminate the need for recapitulation or further stress. If there was no new ground to be turned, probably they would have been. But a whole field exists that I have hardly touched. Up to now I have spoken almost entirely of the effects of looking on the mind. I have shown seeing as a source of knowledge and interest, of amusement and entertainment, as a means to insight, as a stimulus to the imagination, and as a road to aesthetic awareness. But using one's eyes also affects the soul — or if you prefer a more modern word, the psyche. It is the advantages in this area that I want to end with.

Dissociation is a word that psychologists have made familiar in recent years. This separation of mind and body in its most acute stage is recognized as a psychosis. I am not qualified to discuss it in its extreme form, or even when it is caused by internal, possibly neurotic factors. But I have seen enough of twentieth-century city living — a type of living that is becoming ever more widespread — to know something about the sort of dissociation that tends to become habitual with normal people who live in the modern way.

Increasingly, it seems to me, our minds and our bodies are in different places. Their periods of separation, too, seem to be growing longer. If this seems a little abstract and even illogical, let me point to one of the far-reaching inventions of our times — the movies. When sitting in a darkened movie theatre, eyes glued to the screen, your mind is apt to be in such a different place from your body that, when the lights come on at the end of the film, you are often surprised to realize where you are. Such dissociation is not necessarily bad; in fact, if the movie is a good one, it can be very salutary. It is dissociation nevertheless; and a type made even more common by a somewhat later invention — television. Children start looking at television at a younger age than they go to the movies, and they spend more time in front of it than their parents ever spent in motion picture theatres as youngsters. Adults, too, spend longer hours before TV sets than they ever spent in movies. Witness the fact that watching old movies is only a part of their total television absorption.

The development of fast transport has also increased the dissociation in our lives. Swift automobiles and trains already were carrying our bodies through landscape so rapidly as to make it hard for our minds to feel at all part of the scenery flashing past. And this tendency has been accelerated by the airplane, as any passenger can tell you who has gone to sleep just outside New York and awakened near London. Even when you sit up a whole day in a plane and so have a wakeful awareness of distance, you still find when you land that your mind has not been transported as swiftly as your body, and it normally takes another twelve to fifteen hours before your mind catches up with the rest of you.

There is increased dissociation in all factory work where tasks are so mechanically repetitious that one can go about them like an automaton, one's mind a million miles away. Dissociation exists in much of today's white-collar work. Typists and file clerks can be so taken up with paperwork that they go through a day hardly knowing what the weather is like. And executives, besides being absorbed with planning and attending to details while they are at their desks, can walk through the streets so preoccupied with their problems as to see nothing but curbs and stoplights. The busier people are, in fact, the more likely they are to be dissociated from their surroundings. And modern life, as most people will attest, seems to get busier and busier.

Machines, too, are playing their role in increasing dissociation by taking over more and more of the jobs relying principally on either brawn or mechanical repetition. And one of the effects of automation is confining man's working activities increasingly to brain work. This is by no means altogether bad, and much brain work is absorbingly interesting. But its very absorbingness tends to increase dissociation. The man caught up in reasoning, theorizing, or jockeying ideas can be even more detached from his body than an executive worrying about business problems. The philosopher engaged in abstract thinking can perhaps be the most dissociated of all.

A certain amount of dissociation is inevitable in life, and often, especially in times of nervous tension, it is a godsend. Too much of it for too long, however, is undoubtedly harmful. I do not understand all the mechanisms involved, but I know the deserted body begins setting up its own claims that lead to conflicts. And the active mind, operating apart from the body, grows desiccated for want of nourishing contact with physical living. The symptoms are clear: a feeling of isolation; of being cut off from life and from one's fellows; a sense of suffering from what the mystics call "spiritual dryness"; and in general a feeling of reduced vitality. Often, too, one has periods of depression or irritability out of proportion to the small setbacks and minor irritants that touch them off.

How does one bring one's mind and body back together? The best means is a vacation. And I am convinced that one of the chief reasons we return from vacations feeling so restored is not because we have rested — because sometimes we haven't; not because we've relaxed — for often we've been terribly active; not because we've been playing instead of working, but because our minds and bodies have been rejoined. Every moment our minds have been in the same place as our bodies.

Vacations, however, come only once a year. Isn't there some easier interim cure for dissociation? There are several, and one of the very best is looking at things.

Again, I can hear a murmur. Didn't I cite looking at movies as a prime example of dissociation? I did, and that apparent contradiction helps prove my point. Let me explain: Our absorption in movies, which can be so great as to virtually obliterate our sense of surroundings, is proof of how intimately our eyes and our beings are joined. Where our eyes are, there will our beings be also. The exception is when we drop the psychological lids to ensure that ocular perception does not interfere with the pursuit of our plans, troubles or preoccupations. And this exception also proves the closeness of eyes and beings, for it shows we can not pursue those mental preoccupations uninterruptedly *unless* we drop the psychological lids.

Where our open eyes are taking their own pictures, our whole natures — minds as well as bodies — will be present. And notice the stress on the direction of the initiative. At the movies and before our television sets we are not taking our own pictures; we are absorbing those of the cameras. When we are reading, we are not taking our own pictures either, for then we drop the psychological lids on everything except the printed page, using our eyes only to interpret letters. Reading, it is true, can stir the imagination and in the course of reading many pictures flash on the mind. But these are not pictures taken by the eye. They are pictures concocted by the imagination. They foster dissociation, whereas sights that the eyes take in, without any intervening agents, grapple one's nature to them. To reach out to an object with one's eyes is to come very close to it. And repeated efforts of this sort are among the best cures for the general malaise that enters, often unrecognized, the life of those whose minds and bodies are dissociated too much. It is not for nothing that a doctor will counsel a patient convalescing from a nervous breakdown to see new sights.

The eyes are one of the links that help preserve the wholeness of body and soul. They perform this function partly by bringing the psyche into a living connection with the world of bodily reality. And that intercourse with reality also aids that part of the psyche we know as the intelligence. I owe the insight I am about to pass on to Rudolf Steiner, the Austrian philosopher, who founded the anthroposophical movement. He was the first to make me aware of the differences between two types of thinking. In advocating his own type of thinking — the only type he classed as genuine — he pointed out that much of our so-called thinking is just a following in the rut of traditional ideas. Much of what we accept as thought, he implied, is merely the act of grasping and then repeating the thought of others. Moreover, much of our thinking is based on concepts of objects that have been evolved by our predecessors. In other words, our ideas tend to grow out of concepts other people have constructed rather than from direct observation. We tend, he said, to think *about* things, rather than *from* things.

Steiner died before Dr. Alfred C. Kinsey brought in his famous report. But that Kinsey's approach to sex seemed so radical is a striking instance of the force of Steiner's point. Sex, heaven knows, had been on people's minds for centuries. There had certainly been lots of thinking *about* it. But Kinsey decided it was time to learn the truth of sex by observing sex itself: to let thinking about sex arise from the observable and collectable facts.

Fundamentally, this method of thinking is the one logicians call inductive. Since it involves reasoning from parts to wholes, it is necessarily slower and more painstaking than great exciting leaps to thrillingly simple generalizations. It also requires much more suspension of judgment, which, in turn, requires patience, for the human mind seems to hate holding concepts in incomplete form.

Using our eyes in exact observing helps us have the necessary patience, for objects observed in and for themselves prove to be so inherently interesting that generally we do not fuss about our incomplete knowledge. Rather, we rejoice in it for its promise of fields which will be a pleasure to explore. Looking, then, helps us to endure the insecurity of suspended judgment at the same time as it keeps us collecting evidence that will lead to sound conclusions.

The struggle to organize and correlate impressions can be lessened if, instead of trying to force artifical relationships on things, one continues patiently to collect observations, letting them reveal their true relationships in the course of time. Often, too, the relationships that, after many observations, will suggest themselves to you — many times effortlessly and frequently with a sense of surprise — will be sounder than the hypothetical relationships you might construct through deliberate mental effort.

In such moments of surprise, you will become aware that even though all you thought you were doing was observing — in fact, when you thought that in suspending judgment you were deliberately not thinking — you were actually thinking all along. You will realize, too, that you were misled about your lack of cogitation by your old ideas as to what thinking was. There is a perfectly good word for this type of unstrained, almost unconscious thinking. Nowadays, it has an old-fashioned ring, but it has living meaning when it is understood. The word, of course, is contemplation.

Contemplation is the thinking that emerges after, and because of, observation. And this type of thinking, besides being often more fruitful than theorizing from abstractions, has the great advantage of being unmarred by dissociation as you are engaged in it. Not only will the relationships you discover from contemplation be fruitful and soundly based on reality, but some, if you are fortunate, might be things no one has noticed before.

Even if you do not achieve genuine originality of thought, at least your thinking will all be first-hand. D. H. Lawrence once exclaimed in exasperation at having his ears stuffed with "wads of chewed newspaper." And anyone who has suffered from bores whose opinions all come from the newspapers can appreciate the force of his statement. If you do your thinking from things — that is, from the accumulated findings of what you have noted with your own eyes — you can be sure you will not be a bore of this type. In fact, you will quickly find that so many people are so unobservant that they will listen to you with surprised delight at the way you can call their attention to things they never noticed.

Looking, by leading to sound, first-hand thinking, can strengthen intelligence. But the good effects of communing with reality through the medium of the eyes do not stop here. And this brings me to another matter whose operation I cannot satisfactorily explain. But that it exists is certain, and mankind reveals that it has recognized the phenomenon by the number of expressions that correlate bodily nourishment with seeing. "Feast your eyes on this," "food for the soul," "drink your fill of the scene," "starved for beauty," "hungry for the sea" — these are five that come readily to mind.

It was drawing, I think, that first made me consciously aware of this mysterious phenomenon. On a certain day, at the end of a drawing session, I realized I had a feeling that I could isolate as being the same feeling that had filled me at the end of other drawing sessions. It was a combination of serenity, elation, enrichment, and satisfaction. Looking back over such experiences, I saw the last-named — the satisfaction — was explicable in terms of pride in handiwork. But what about the other ingredients?

Another day, after having looked long and lovingly at a maple tree, I had the multiple sensation again — proof that it was not dependent on drawing, for on this occasion I had not sketched a line. Perhaps, I said to myself, it came about because I looked at the tree *as if* I had drawn it.

Then I laughed as I saw I had matters the wrong way around. In the earlier instances the act of drawing in itself did not cause the communion; rather it came as a by-product of the drawing. In other words, almost against my will, and certainly without intent, I had communed with my subject simply by staying before it so long — a longevity enforced by the fact that, because I am poor at visualizing what I can not see, I had to stay a long time to complete the drawing.

However, this understanding did not solve the essential mystery for me. I still do not know why this sort of psychical nourishment passes into us when we spend a quiet, unbroken period with a work of art, some aspect of nature, or a man-made scene. But I know it does, just as surely as the Japanese know it. A tentative explanation is that there is such a thing as reality — that is, the truth or essence of things — and that we become enriched when we absorb it. And, though the eyes may be the chief route of entry, I do not think this reality of things lies in appearances alone. For you do not receive this enrichment when you merely study a photograph of a tree; nor do you get it in reading about trees. For this reality you absorb from the outside world is a different thing than information. Reading facts, in comparison, is a barren experience.

Of one thing I am certain. Color is especially rich in psychical vitamins. Taking in color, somehow, does to the gray and desolate soul what taking in warmth does when one reaches out towards a fire after long hours in the cold. And at the same time as they nourish and warm, colors — especially the bright ones — seem to illuminate one's inner being. When one comes away from an art gallery with a sense of being irradiated, often it is as much from the colors one has absorbed as from the visions of the artists. Much of the thrill of spring, I think, is because of the return of color.

And one of the reasons people who know the tropics keep longing to return to them is to be immersed once more in that world of vivid, exalting color. Having fed on such colors, the soul feels starved in an environment that is visually drab.

A visual experience, then, besides being influenced by factors I have called extra-visual, is also more than ocular. In addition to the visual impressions absorbed, it includes what results in the psyche because of the absorption of those impressions. Because of these changes in the human electrode in the visual circuit, although the optical experience has both objective and subjective elements, it cannot be said to be wholly one or the other. And although the being expands because more of the world has been taken into it, it is hard to tell which part of the being has benefited most. Is the gaining of a vibrant and enduring experience, for instance, more a contribution to the mind or the soul? Insofar as it establishes a lively interest that is sure to be self-increasing, it can be classed chiefly as a benefit to the mind. But perhaps what it does to heighten one's appreciation of life is chiefly a blessing to the soul.

Visual experiences tend towards two main types — the spontaneous and the induced. With the former, it seems there is a sudden effortless opening, with hundreds of impressions rushing in. With the latter, new emotional comprehension comes slowly, after a bit-by-bit accumulation of visual details. Either way, there is enrichment for both the mind and the soul. For one result is an increased feeling of aliveness. Another is a much greater sense of total awareness, for the faculties are somehow interconnected and, when one faculty is brought to the state of highest attention, it often lifts the others to the same fullness of participation. Thus, with the visual opening, one generally also gets a sharper awareness of how things sound, how they feel, how they smell — how, in fact, they are. This awareness, of course, may be the cause of the feeling of greater aliveness; or it may be the other way around. Whichever is the generative cause, the combination brings happiness.

Boredom certainly vanishes. And it may be that nowadays this is an even greater blessing than coming to the road of awareness through the pathway of observing. I say this because boredom is one of the great evils of our time. It tends to destroy both the mind and the soul.

Loneliness is another particularly sharp problem in modern life. Against this, too, seeing is a major help. For there is a wealth of companionship, as St. Francis well knew, in our sister the moon, our brother fire, and all the hierarchy of creatures. And if affectionate gratitude to the companionable world increases your appreciation of it, you encounter one of the happy interactions of vision. Witness the obvious fact that we have most power of appreciation with what we can see well; least, with what we see dimly. Thus learning to see clearly heightens our capacities in the dimension of appreciation; and greater appreciation — which leads to greater enjoyment and love — makes for still clearer visibility.

Because so many psychological factors enter into seeing, and because our powers of observation are also influenced by such physiological factors as our health and how well rested we are, our seeing powers vary considerably. Sometimes we see very poorly, sometimes well. And it is safe to say that we see best when two conditions coincide: that is, when our minds are clear and our spirits are calm.

That those two parts of our being are seldom in either state in our modern industrial civilization may account for a lot of not seeing. It might be argued that we are prisoned in a vicious circle: that we haven't time to see much because we are too rushed and too disturbed, and the more rushed and disturbed we are the less power we have to see. There is much truth in this. But thanks to the beneficent influences of seeing it is within our powers to reverse the direction of the circle.

More seeing can help calm us down; greater calm can lead to a clearing of the mind; the conditions in unison can lead to richer observing; which, in turn, brings us full circle by inducing still greater calmness.

The cycle was suggested in broad outline when I told how the looking I did in Mexico healed me of my wartime bitterness by turning me outward once again. And the operation of the cycle was detailed in the story of the fire in the courtyard. But because the one account was too general and the other emphasized the seeing that accumulated, I would like to give an example that will illustrate the process more fully by dwelling more on the inner changes.

It happened one very hot summer in Manhattan. It was a hard time for me emotionally, for I was struggling with a deep sense of failure, and the feeling that perhaps I had taken a wrong turn in life. One Saturday afternoon I could sit at my typewriter no longer. The heat as well as the work was oppressive, and I decided to make my way to a spot that at least would be a little cooler — a pier off Forty-ninth Street, jutting into the East River.

I took my troubled spirit with me and for a while I sat inertly on the big gray timber fronting the wharf. I felt lonely, yet I was too depressed to want to seek out friends. In those days I did not look about me as consciously as I do now and I was too sunk in my own troubles to be interested in my surroundings. But there were gulls hovering near the pier and a magnetic interest in these birds had been planted in my mind by a previous experience. I had written about gulls in the manuscript whose many rejections had done so much to shake my confidence in myself and my chosen path. In explaining my return to Times Square with the postcards, I said that having written a description you want to see published gives you a specially keen desire to re-observe what you have described. And as the gulls played about in the air over the pier and occasionally landed in the water, this particular desire stirred in me. For I realized that if I watched them closely I might get some details of their behavior that could help me improve the gull sequence.

I was able to use the visual aid of self-questioning because writing the sequence had established a specific question in my mind: How do gulls brake their flight when they want to slow down? I remembered as a boy at summer camp how we were taught to bring a sailboat into a pier. The trick was to find the direction of the wind and then, at the last moment, to veer directly into it so that its impact on the spread canvas would bring the boat to a dead stop. This gave me a clue. Did the gulls also use the wind to help them slow down?

Up to that time, I had made no note as to which way the wind was blowing. But the desire to answer my question led me to see that it was blowing up the river from the south. Then I noticed that a gull made a landing facing south. Was that accidental? I asked, or will I see all the gulls land in that direction? Eagerly, I watched for descents. Gull after gull landed facing south. Even those who had been winging north would veer either towards the pier or out over the river as they turned south to drop to the surface. So the gulls all landed into the wind!

I began to be excited. And seeing how the gulls used the wind in landing opened my eyes to the fact that they also used it in other ways too. When they wanted to rest they would curve northward and take advantage of the wind behind them to carry them along with less winging. I noticed, too, that by altering the angles of their bodies they could take more advantage of the wind. Those about to land, I saw, would suddenly tilt themselves upward. In doing so their wings, which before had been cutting the wind edgewise, would suddenly present the wind with a wide, outspread surface. These broad white wings acted like our sails at camp. The birds were brought almost to a dead stop, and it was then that they dropped effortlessly to the heaving water.

How happy the rest of the afternoon was as I watched the birds use their knowledge of the winds to aid them in their play. And as I became increasingly skillful in detecting the wind motivation of their movements I came to feel almost as if I were flying with them. By dinner time I left the pier singing.

What had happened was this: The gulls had caught my eyes; my eyes had begun to follow their winging; my being was linked so closely to my eyes that it, too, began to follow the birds; as I became absorbed in the birds, I forgot my troubles; those troubles, shaken free, lost their hold on my mind; my freed mind gained new power to understand the birds' veering, tilting, stroking, and soaring; this understanding made observation easier; the easier it became the more my eyes fastened on each sweep of the gulls and the higher my spirit lifted. I grew calm and patient because both my mind and spirit had been released from the grip of the elements making them agitated and impatient.

In effect, then, my eyes were responsible for my burdens slipping away. And please note that, as well as forgetting my troubles, I forgot myself. And freed from specific problems, I was freed

— at least for the time being — from wanting to be a success, from wanting literary recognition, even from wanting friendship and understanding. Because my attention had been shifted from myself to the birds, I had been turned outward once more, and all the good effects of outward-turning had followed.

In the intervening years, I have been blessed with a number of experiences similar to the one on the pier. And these specific occasions have enabled me to understand the experience in more general terms. Grief, pain, anxiety, and preoccupation with problems, as I said in discussing the personal vision deadeners, tend to cut us off from the visual world. And they hold in common the fact that they are all subjective. That, visually, the majority of us live most of the time in a subjective world was illustrated in the chapter on reporting. That escape from subjectivity is difficult was brought out in the chapter on knowledge and time. Now what needs to be added is what was implied through my wartime depths: subjectivity can be, and, indeed, generally is, exceedingly painful. And one of the great things contemplation can do is to lift us off the torturing wheel of subjectivity onto the saner ground of objectivity.

Fundamentally, I think self-involvement is the chief source of human misery. And surely self-pity is a reflection of that misery. Many people who recognize the destructiveness of self-pity — and its boringness to others — increase their unhappiness by feeling guilty about their self-commiserations. Yet this guilt complicates rather than cures. The more effective means of escape is to turn the attention outward. The visual world cannot banish our troubles, but at least it can drive them out for a while, and, in so doing, help hold them at bay. And the periods of release it provides have effects that tend towards more permanent liberation. One of those effects is to stock the reservoir with the sort of impressions that Wordsworth called "food and life for future years." Another is the increasing of visual skill combined with strengthening of the visual habit. A third might be called the leavening of patience. For the saying that patience is a virtue is not an idle one. Patience is far more than a device for enduring suspense. Unmistakably, having true patience is good for us. And insofar as the joys of the objective world lead us into periods of prolonged patience, they improve our souls. They do likewise insofar as they bring us into the happier world of self-loss.

Self-forgetfulness in a fantasy world — if this can really be called self-forgetfulness — can be isolating and perhaps dangerous. But self-forgetfulness in the world of reality is so profoundly beneficial that, even if the effects of seeing were not marvelous counterforces to the elements in our civilization that make tranquility so difficult, I would still urge seeing upon people as a means of self-loss. For Jesus spoke truly when he spoke of loss leading to finding. He was speaking of loss of life for His sake, but less drastic losses can have the same effect. For when one has lost oneself in contemplation of the visible world one often discovers one has found oneself.

Because detachment from self is brought about by engagement with something bigger than the self, it is not a form of dissociation. So in this kind of self-loss one does not just float away. Rather one's compassion for others increases. For heightened vision embraces people, too, and as they become more visible their sorrows become more apparent. Then one comes to a better understanding of a peril cited in the Litany — "blindness of heart."

For there is a relationship between psychological blindness — eyes that look and see not — and blindness of heart. And the ending of one often leads to the ending of the other. And surely the framers of the Litany understood this, for look at the perils attending the heart's blindness from which we should cry for deliverance: "Pride, vainglory, and hypocrisy, envy, hatred and malice, and all uncharitableness." Such a list profitably extends the roster of vision deadeners.

In discussing transfigured vision, I said that although it often came suddenly and unexpectedly, on analysis it was nearly always seen to be the result of long preparation. The chief reason the element of preparation is not more generally recognized is because most of it is subterranean. As well as being hidden in the processes of inner development, it is so piecemeal that small accumulating details are hardly noticed. Certainly, the relationships between them are not detected.

Generally, we experience transfigured vision in a startled flash: that is, it happens, apparently spontaneously, at moments when we don't expect it. But it also can happen, like induced vision of a lesser kind, at the end of a long session of careful observation. Then, it is as if invisible curtains we have been probing suddenly part; or as if the walls of the hall surrounding us magically lift up into the flies like a transformation scene in a pantomime. The heightened vision that has succeeded from the earlier sharpened vision is itself succeeded by this new sort of awareness, in which depth on depth of significance is revealed and the heart, marvelously at peace, knows the true beauty of the world.

Now I cannot promise that, if sufficiently prolonged, careful observing will always lead to transfigured vision. On the contrary, I am sure it won't. But sometimes it can, and this is an advantage of seeing I would like to stress: that it can be part, and sometimes the catalytic part, of the spirit's preparation for a moment of illumination.

By contributing to the falling away of anxieties, by easing tension, by changing one's living rhythm from hectic to calm, by filling the mind with a sense of wonder at what has been observed, by renewing the wellsprings of love and by filling one with a sense of gratitude, it can make illumination more likely. And transfigured moments are in themselves so precious that even what merely paves the way for them is to be cherished.

I will return to transfigured moments shortly, but meanwhile let me develop a few intervening ideas. One came to me in Mexico in the Church of the Virgin of Solitude, or La Soledad, as she is known in Oaxaca, where she is venerated. Year after year I found myself drawn to her church. I used to go there and sit so I could be among the people of Oaxaca who came to pray to her. I especially loved going there on late Saturday afternoons. Saturday is Oaxaca's market day, when Indians from the surrounding villages bring their goods to market. Many take advantage of being in the city to come to pray to Soledad.

The same year I went to the pier to watch the gulls, I also went to Soledad. The gull cure had been only temporary and fits of depression had recurred. On this particular Saturday afternoon I was in an easy frame of mind, but, as I was to discover, I had been living on the surface for a long time. This came to me as I saw the earnestness of the Indians. The sight of a mother coming up a side aisle on her knees, holding a baby in one arm and a candle in the other hand, is common in this church. Sometimes one sees whole families approaching the altar on their knees. And they do this so unselfconsciously, with such open sweetness of countenance, and with such loving devotion, that inevitably one finds one's own inner feelings altered by the ambient they create.

La Soledad consists of only a white, rather waxy, tranquil face and a pair of praying hands. The rest of her is a gold crown with four large arches, and a conical black velvet cape which, like the black dress it partially covers, is richly embroidered in gold and silver. I cannot say I believe in her. Yet on this particular Saturday, as I found myself growing gentle and more serious as I sat among her worshippers and petitioners, it occurred to me that what was so spiritually good for these people — and for me indirectly — was not *what* they believed, but *how* they believed. Their spirits were blessed, I felt, by their own devotion: by their loving something, by their trusting something, by their approaching that something with love and humility.

This led me to an intellectually shocking conclusion: that it does not much matter what you revere so long as you feel reverence because of it. In other words, the intellectual content of belief is not particularly important. What is good for your soul and brings you to a state of grace, I realized, is an attitude of outgoing love and trusting devotion to something you value so much that you feel reverent before it.

I was reminded of how people working at the Metropolitan Opera spoke of Bruno Walter's approach to Mozart, and I realized these villagers had the same sort of feeling for their Virgin as Walter had for "The Magic Flute." And the contrast between the two objects of adoration strengthened my feeling that intellectual content hardly mattered. Those Indians worshipping that doll in whom I did not believe were obviously more truly religious than I was. This was not merely a conclusion brought about by watching them. It came about by the atmosphere their reverence helped create and by the influence of their devotion on my own spirit. I found myself moved to pray to my particular God in whom I did believe. And as I left the church, I knew that much of the encrusted hardness that had grown over my unworshipping soul through the year of bitterness had been dissolved.

The feeling that in individual lives the intellectual content of belief hardly mattered — that is, providing reverence was dominant — was strengthened for me when I read a very interesting essay by a doctor who had made an extensive study of alcoholics. The writer, Dr. Henry M. Tiebout, largely through working with Alcoholics Anonymous, had been able to observe a number of people who were converted to different religious beliefs. Despite the varying creeds they turned to, he found something remarkably uniform about them. There was a similarity in their new happiness, in their new enthusiasm for what they now believed, and in their new approach to life. How, he asked himself, could adopting different beliefs lead to such similar manifestations? His question led him to realize there must be an element common to all conversions, an element independent of specific faiths that were accepted by the intelligence. Finally, that element came clear to him. It was a yea-saying to life. Negative attitudes lost their hold on these people and they came into a new enthusiasm for living, a new desire to go forward.

Jung was another elucidating thinker. In *Modern Man in Search of a Soul,* he stated that fully a third of his patients had no clinically definable neuroses. What they suffered from was "the senselessness and emptiness of their lives." And Jung made me further aware that only the convictions that life had purpose, significance, and value could overcome the despair arising from the feeling of senselessness. His words not only deepened my belief in the relative unimportance of intellectual content, they isolated what was important in what religion had to give. If it gave the sense that there was purpose, it did not have to define that purpose; nor did it have to give a watertight explanation of the significance of life as long as it conveyed the conviction that significance existed. And it did not have to come forward with absolute concepts, as long as it inspired the heart to feel that the value of life was something you could not possibly doubt.

I come now to the advantage which provided the fundamental impulse to write this book. Having lived through a number of shattered faiths of my own, having seen how important it is for human beings to have something to believe in, having learned how hard it is to have faith in any of the old beliefs, and having come to the conclusion that all new faiths are likely, in the end, to prove as fallible as the old ones, I would like to propose the practice of observing as a substitute for faith.

But I do not urge it as a philosophy. For we do not find happiness through the philosophies we hold. Besides, it is not a philosophy. It has no systematic structure and it does not seek to explain the relationships of man, God, and the universe. It is something one can have faith in nevertheless. Perhaps one might say it provides the necessary certainty for the very fact that its ultimate worth does not depend upon it proving true.

If this seems irresponsible, let me review some of the faiths that have broken down. And let me say at the start that the existence of those faiths shows how absolutely essential it is for humans to have a basic certainty. Ultimately, the cynic, no matter how cultured and intelligent, goes to pieces if he does not find some foothold of belief. And the mass enthusiasms for new panaceas show how whole societies lunge after new certainties when old ones falter.

In the nineteenth century it was the old Biblical certainties that faltered. Darwinism and the findings of geology, in destroying the credibility of the Adam and Eve story, not only weakened the whole authority of the Bible, but in doing so swept away many of the explanations that had been so acceptable for so many generations: such explanations as that Adam and Eve's disobedience accounted for the labor and hardship in the world and that their fall led the Ruler of the Universe to be a harsh God. The old questions as to why evil and injustice exist in the world had to be faced again.

Then, the old explanations that they were largely to prepare us for our heavenly rewards, and that those rewards would compensate for all the sufferings of the good and the just on earth, broke down as astronomy, by revealing the magnitude of the interstellar spaces, made the existence of heaven seem unlikely since it was obviously many millions of light years farther out in space than had been thought previously.

As religious beliefs that had sustained their parents seemed increasingly shaky, new generations began constructing new faiths of their own. Most of them were social faiths — universal literacy, education, democracy, industrialization, socialism, and communism ushered in by proletarian revolutions. Not all of these have broken down — just as not all the religious certainties have gone — but what a beating those social faiths have taken in the twentieth century. And now we are less sure of them. Literacy, which promised so much, has had the unexpected and appalling concomitant of making people more easily victimized by written propaganda. The high educational level of the Germans did not prevent them from flocking to Hitler. Democracies, in struggling for national survival have joined hands with dictatorships and dropped atomic bombs on Hiroshima and Nagasaki. Industrialization, though providing many material comforts, has clamped humans into living patterns that are not the heaven-on-earth that was hoped. Socialists, voted into political power, have not set up the ideal states their followers dreamed of. And Communists, having seized power, have signed pacts with Nazis and created authoritarian instruments of oppression.

Nowadays, in fact, it is hard to be a crusader for anything. That God is ultimately just, that man can remake the earth into a new Eden, that an adequate philosophy can be found — fundamental beliefs like these are now practically impossible to hold; that is, to hold without a measure of doubt so great as to weaken the dynamic force of the faith.

But is this such a terrible impasse? I have suggested that a religion's intellectual content is not its best part. More precious, I have contended, are the value of an open, loving, humble attitude of reverence, and the value of yea-saying — the desire to go forward with enthusiasm for living. What I want to state now is that seeing is perhaps the best road to those particular values — religious values that might be called non-credal, if one can define negatively those values which do not depend on articles of belief.

Certainly there is one thing I am sure of. The man who has learned to use his eyes will never ask himself: "Is life worth living?" It is a question that does not even arise for him. He knows from the evidence of his eyes that the natural world is so wonderful, intricate, beautiful, and strange that he is never going to exhaust its interest. He knows, too, that those who have preceded him have left such a legacy of beauty in their art works and such a fascinating body of gadgets in their inventions that he is never going to exhaust the interest of man's creations either. Having this knowledge, he has a faith that makes yea-saying easy, and that carries an open, reverently humble attitude as one of its inevitable consequences.

He knows, too, that he will never be let down in his faith, for it does not depend on the correctness of his explanations, but on the fact that there will always be further things that need explaining. Nor does his faith depend on matters turning out either happily for himself or beneficially for society. Divine purposes do not have to be "good." He is not weighing the world for its kindness, its social justice, its moral laws, or its conforming to an expected pattern. He is weighing it for its appearances, and those, he knows, will be endlessly interesting, inexhaustibly rewarding.

The use of the eyes in the study of appearances, then, can help us to wholeness of being by reknitting the mind and the body. It can lead to accurate thought by being based on the reality of things rather than on ideas about them. It can nourish us by currents that pass between us and what we contemplate. It can clear our minds and calm our spirits. It can shake the grip of our troubles and lessen the weight of our burdens. It can enable us to lose ourselves. It can give us the conviction of significance and the certainty of faith. It can bring us into spiritual grace by inducing the non-credal attitudes that are the uncontestable aspects of religion. And it can do all these things when it leads to nothing more than heightened vision.

When it leads also to transfigured vision, ah! then it lifts the totally associated being into a certainty of a still greater association, a still greater wholeness. It leads to an apprehension of an ultimate reality greater than the sum total of accurate conceptions. It fills the being with a nourishment it can draw on a whole life long. It does more than clear the mind and calm the spirit; it fills the former with light and exalts the latter. And it brings a certainty that is not merely the sureness that what one believes cannot be proved wrong, but the conviction that the insight one has gained — more than being a revelation of what is unchallengeably right — is truth itself.

BIBLIOGRAPHICAL INDEX

Bibliographical Index

(The numbers following the titles indicate the pages of this book based on, or citing, the works listed below.)

Ansley, Clarke F., ed. *The Columbia Encyclopedia in One Volume* (Columbia University Press, New York, 1947). 12, 320.

Arnheim, Rudolf. *Art and Visual Perception* (University of California Press, Berkeley and Los Angeles, 1954). 237.

Beardslee, David, and Wertheimer, Michael, eds. *Readings in Perception* (Van Nostrand, Princeton, Toronto, London, New York, 1958). 153.

Benham, W. Gurney. *Playing Cards: The History and Secrets of the Pack* (London, n.d.). 20-22, 61, 236.

Bennett, Arnold. *Riceyman Steps* (George H. Doran, New York, 1923). 119.

Berenson, Bernard. *The Italian Painters of the Renaissance* (Phaidon, London, 1952). 68, 77, 234.

Blake, Robert R., and Ramsey, Glenn V., eds. *Perception: An Approach to Personality* (Ronald Press, New York, 1951). 82.

Carmichael, Leonard; Hogan, H. P.; and Walter, A. A. "An Experimental Study of the Effect of Language on the Reproduction of Visually Perceived Form." *Journal of Experimental Psychology*, 15 (Washington, 1932). 176-177.

Cary, Joyce. *Art and Reality: Ways of the Creative Process* (Harper, New York, 1958). 177.

Chesterton, G. K. *What I Saw in America* (Hodder and Stoughton, London, 1922). 67.

Church of England. *The Book of Common Prayer* (Innumerable editions since 1549). 339.

Colette. *Creatures Great and Small* (Farrar, Straus and Cudahy, New York, 1951). 179.

Columbia University Study Program in Rapid Reading. *Prospectus* (Book-of-the-Month Club, New York, n.d.). 74.

Columbia University Study Program in Rapid Reading. *Some Simple Tests of your Present Reading Habits* (Book-of-the-Month Club, New York, n.d.). 74.

Doyle, Arthur Conan. *The Complete Sherlock Holmes* (Doubleday, Garden City, New York, 1960). 307.

Encyclopædia Britannica (14th Edition), Vol. 2. "Architecture" (Chicago, London, Toronto, 1938). 176.

Fagan, James B. *And so to bed* (G. P. Putnam, London, 1927). 254.

Francis of Assisi, St. "The Canticle of Brother Sun," *Writings of St. Francis* (Franciscan Herald Press, Chicago, 1964). 335.

Friedländer, Max J. *Early Netherlandish Painting from Van Eyck to Bruegel* (Phaidon-Garden City, New York, 1956). 227-228.

Fry, Roger. *Transformations* (Doubleday Anchor Books, New York, 1956). 77, 237-238.

Fuller, Henry J. *The Plant World: A Text in College Botany* (Henry Holt, New York, 1941). 200, 202-203, 231.

Gibson, James J. *The Perception of the Visual World* (Houghton Mifflin, Boston, 1950). 70, 261.

Grosser, Maurice. *The Painter's Eye* (Rinehart, New York, 1951). 256, 276.

Hargrave, Catherine Perry. *History of Playing Cards* (Houghton Mifflin, Boston and New York, 1930). 14-16, 19, 61.

Hearn, Lafcadio. *Glimpses of Unfamiliar Japan* (Houghton, Mifflin, Boston & New York, 1894). 280-281.

Henderson, Harold G. *An Introduction to Haiku* (Doubleday Anchor Books, New York, 1958). 278.

Huxley, Aldous. *The Art of Seeing* (Harper, New York and London, 1942). 70, 77, 317.

Huxley, Aldous. *Eyeless in Gaza* (Harper, New York and London, 1936). 46-47.

James, Henry. *The American* (New York Edition of the Novels and Tales of Henry James, Vol. II, Scribner's, New York, 1907). 82.

Jung, C. G. *Modern Man in Search of a Soul* (Harvest-Harcourt, Brace, 1933). 342.

Kelemen, Pal. *Medieval American Art* (Macmillan, New York, 1956). 236-237.

Kinsey, Alfred C. *Sexual Behavior in the Human Male* (W. B. Saunders, Philadelphia and London, 1948). 331.

Saint-Exupéry, Antoine de. *Flight to Arras* (Reynal & Hitchcock, New York, 1942). 46.

Smith, Nila Banton. *Read Faster and Get More from Your Reading* (Prentice-Hall, Englewood Cliffs, N.J., 1958). 74.

Soria, Martin. *The Paintings of Zurbaran* (Phaidon-Garden City, N.Y., 1953). 227, 239.

Steiner, Rudolf. *Practical Training in Thought* (Anthroposophic Press, New York, 1949). 330-331.

Tatsui, Matsunosuke. *Japanese Gardens* (Japan Travel Bureau, Tokyo, 1956). 278-279.

Tiebout, Henry M. "The Act of Surrender in the Therapeutic Process" (mimeographed paper read to the New York Psychiatric Society, Oct. 3, 1945). 342.

Tourist Industry Bureau, Ministry of Transportation. *Japan: The Official Guide* (Japan Travel Bureau, Tokyo, 1959). 267-268, 271.

Waetzoldt, Wilhelm. *Dürer and his Times* (Phaidon-Garden City, New York, 1955). 228-229.

Webster's New International Dictionary, Second Edition (G. & C. Merriam Co., Springfield, Mass., 1934). 187, 199, 315-316.

Wordsworth, William. "Lines Composed a Few Miles Above Tintern Abbey," *The Complete Poetical Works of William Wordsworth* (Houghton, Mifflin, Boston and New York, 1932). 338.